21世纪高等学校专业英语系列规划教材

人力资源管理

专业英语教程（修订本）

李 严　李浚帆　主　编
　　　孔晓春　副主编

清华大学出版社
北京交通大学出版社
·北京·

内容简介

本书包括6个部分,分别为人员管理、薪酬与福利、绩效管理、培训管理、个人发展和组织发展。每个部分含2~4个单元,每个单元的课文都与本部分的主题密切相关。每篇课文后面附有本单元的生词表、注释和练习。全书后附有总词汇表和课文参考译文。

本书既可作为人力资源管理及相关专业的专业英语教材,也可作为相关专业教师进行双语教学的参考工具书,同时还适合人力资源管理行业的从业者阅读参考。

本书封面贴有清华大学出版社防伪标签,无标签者不得销售。
版权所有,侵权必究。侵权举报电话:010-62782989 13501256678 13801310933

图书在版编目(CIP)数据

人力资源管理专业英语教程/李严,李浚帆主编. —修订本. —北京:清华大学出版社;北京交通大学出版社,2011.12(2021.2修订)
ISBN 978-7-5121-0786-1

Ⅰ.①人… Ⅱ.①李…②李… Ⅲ.①人力资源管理-英语-教材 Ⅳ.①H31

中国版本图书馆CIP数据核字(2011)第229963号

人力资源管理专业英语教程
RENLI ZIYUAN GUANLI ZHUANYE YINGYU JIAOCHENG

责任编辑:张利军 特邀编辑:易 娜	
出版发行:清华大学出版社 邮编:100084 电话:010-62776969 http://www.tup.com.cn	
北京交通大学出版社 邮编:100044 电话:010-51686414 http://press.bjtu.edu.cn	
印 刷 者:北京鑫海金澳胶印有限公司	
经　　销:全国新华书店	
开　　本:185 mm×243 mm 印张:14.75 字数:480千字	
版 印 次:2021年2月第1版第1次修订 2021年2月第6次印刷	
印　　数:10 001~11 000册 定价:39.00元	

本书如有质量问题,请向北京交通大学出版社质监组反映。对您的意见和批评,我们表示欢迎和感谢。
投诉电话:010-51686043,51686008;传真:010-62225406;E-mail:press@bjtu.edu.cn。

前言

　　进入 21 世纪以来，人力资源管理日益成为企业管理中非常重要的领域。与之相适应，企业对人力资源管理专业人才的需求也迅速增加。同时，随着全球化的不断加深，越来越多的跨国公司进入中国，它们既给我国带来了最先进的人力资源管理知识，也带来了对掌握人力资源管理专业英语的人才的需求。为了帮助人力资源管理及相关专业的学生提高英语水平，掌握专业英语词汇，熟练阅读相关的英语文献资料，我们特此编写了这本《人力资源管理专业英语教程》。

　　本书按照"21 世纪高等学校专业英语系列规划教材"的体例进行编写。全书由 6 个部分组成，每个部分分为若干个单元。每个单元由课文、生词表、注释、练习组成，并穿插相关的案例、背景知识等内容模块。本书既可作为人力资源管理及相关专业的专业英语教材，也可作为相关专业教师进行双语教学的参考工具书，同时还适合人力资源管理行业的从业者阅读参考。

　　本书包括 6 个部分，分别为人员管理、薪酬与福利、绩效管理、培训管理、个人发展和组织发展。每个部分含 2～4 个单元，每个单元的课文都与本部分的主题密切相关。每篇课文后面附有本单元的生词表、注释和练习。全书后附有总词汇表和课文参考译文。

　　本书每个单元都根据课文内容穿插了一些补充阅读材料，对相关的知识点、案例或背景进行介绍，在拓宽读者知识面的同时，也增加了课文的可读性和趣味性。每个单元的练习题型主要包括问答题、名词解释、判断题、翻译题和讨论题。

　　本书的编者之一在知名跨国公司从事了多年的人力资源管理工作，在本书中结合其丰富的实践经验，从工作实践及当代国际流行理论出发，探讨人力资源领域最值得关注的话题，介绍跨国公司常用的人力资源管理方法和工具，并通过自身体会启发读者以发展的眼光开展人力资源管理工作及进行自身能力的培养。

　　本教材具有以下特点。
　　(1) 内容全面丰富，涵盖人力资源领域的各个重要模块。
　　(2) 课文可读性强，理论联系实际，并穿插丰富的相关案例及背景知识介绍，以期让读者在轻松的阅读中掌握知识。

（3）介绍人力资源管理从业者必须掌握的专业英语词汇，以及当今国际流行的人力资源管理理论。

本书得以面世，有赖于北京交通大学出版社的大力支持，在此深表谢意！

由于作者水平有限，书中难免错误与遗漏之处，敬请广大读者批评指正！

编　者
2021 年 2 月

目 录

PART Ⅰ Staffing
人员管理

Unit 1 Help Your People Look for a New Job—Are You Ready? .... (2)

Unit 2 New Way to Spot the Candidates .... (11)

Unit 3 How to Make an Interview Effective? .... (17)

Unit 4 Retention from the First Day .... (28)

PART Ⅱ Compensation & Benefits
薪酬与福利

Unit 5 A General Compensation Structure .... (38)

Unit 6 Intangible Reward .... (47)

PART Ⅲ Performance Management
绩效管理

Unit 7 Implement a Successful Performance Management Process .... (56)

Unit 8 What Should We Appraise? .... (66)

Unit 9 Make 360-degree Feedback More Effective .... (74)

PART IV　Training Management
培训管理

Unit 10　To Start with Competency Modeling ················(84)

Unit 11　Implementing the Four Levels Training Evaluation ············(94)

PART V　Personal Development
个人发展

Unit 12　Three Steps to Personal Career Development ············(104)

Unit 13　Lucky George—A Typical Talent Development Program ············(113)

Unit 14　Leadership Development Approaches ············(120)

Unit 15　Identify the Right Leadership ············(129)

PART VI　Organizational Development
组织发展

Unit 16　OD Basis ············(140)

Unit 17　Employee Engagement ············(150)

Unit 18　Succession Planning ············(159)

Appendix 1　Glossary ············(167)
　　　　　　词汇表

Appendix 2　Reference Translation for Texts ············(188)
　　　　　　课文参考译文

References ············(230)
参考文献

PART I

Staffing

人员管理

Unit 1

Help Your People Look for a New Job—Are You Ready?

The economic crisis since 2008 has made life changed for many people. There are advices from the financial experts about reducing expenses and reserving 6 months living cost as emergency cost. Finding a part time job on top of current full time job is also one of the solutions. However the crisis has deprived many employees the full time job itself. Therefore not only the financial advices are needed, the solution on searching for a new job is sometimes helpful especially for those people who never think of leaving the employers which have to take layoff[1] as the only remedy to get through the economic crisis.

At the end of 2009, there was a Hollywood movie *Up in the Air* in which George Clooney acted as an HR professional whose main job was to fire people. In the real world, to fire people is indeed one of the responsibilities of an HR manager. However, if you want to be more professional, you should not only fire people, but also help your people look for a new job.

Anny, a software engineer in a mid-sized technology company, just experienced that a few months ago. At that time she has been working in a famous IT company for 9 years. She joined the company when she graduated as a B. S.[2] in a first-class university. She loved the culture of the company and the job itself. She got promotions as expected. The company was just her second home.

She felt her heart broken when the layoff was announced. Anger and doubt made her cry into tears. She couldn't believe that in the first days. The IT company organized training courses to guide the leaving employees on how to control their emotion and their career transition. Anny benefited from those courses and stepped out of the frustration gradually till she found her current job. When talking about her first employer, she still appreciates the working experience she gained during the 9 years and the career assistance before layoff.

Helping the leaving colleagues in time to look for a new job is as important as calculating accurately the compensation package[3] to them. The company as a corporate citizen, must take the responsibility of minimize the negative impact from layoff for both employees and the society. There are many more to do for HR professionals than just a sheet of notice.

Box 1-1

Unemployment Compensation

In many US states, workers who are laid off can file an unemployment claim and receive compensation. Depending on local or state laws, workers who leave voluntarily are generally ineligible to collect unemployment benefits, as are those who are fired for gross misconduct. Also, lay-offs due to a firm's moving production overseas may entitle one to increased re-training benefits.

Certain countries (e. g. France and Germany), distinguish between leaving the company of one's own free will, in which case the person isn't entitled to unemployment benefits and leaving a company voluntarily as part of a reduction in labor force size, in which case the person is entitled to them. An RIF (reduction in force) reduces the number of positions, rather than laying off specific people, and is usually accompanied by internal redeployment. A person might leave even if their job isn't reduced, unless the employer has strong objections. In this situation, it's more beneficial for the state to facilitate the departure of the more professionally active people, since they are less likely to remain jobless. Often they find new jobs while still being paid by their old companies, costing nothing to the social security system in the end.

There are two sides to be taken care of at the same time. One is the mental side, and the other is the process side.

Layoff is a dramatic organizational change in a company, while losing job is even more serious in the personal life of employees. During this period, employees have different emotions through different stages.

First reaction upon the layoff announcement is generally shock and denial. "Are you kidding?" "I can't believe it." Then after they start to accept the news, many people are angry and frustrated by the hit. They will challenge the company why there is the decision, and how about their future. They feel the betrayal and regard themselves not part of the organization but the opposite side of the company. With the implementation of the layoff, some people are very depressed because they find nothing good in this process. They haven't secured any new job. The old colleagues leave one by one. They think they become some useless people.

In this difficult time, from the company side, or as a leader, what is most helpful to those employees, is to provide sufficient information. The reasons behind the decision, the arrangement of the layoff, the compensation to the staff, and extra support from the company are to be explained and clarified repetitively in order to be really sufficient. The managers should be real good listeners to allow staff express their anger and concerns, and should give immediate feedback to them. Sometimes managers have to say they don't know about some very trivial items or something not decided yet. Just say that honestly, but make sure you will come back to staff with the answers soon. Don't be afraid of the challenging questions, because they are part of the understanding.

Generally when there is mutual understanding, the positive dialogue begins and employees would be willing to work with the company for the following procedures. Now the necessary trainings can start to help the employees to know more and deeper what the company can do for them and what they should change for themselves as well. When the confidence is restored, not necessarily with a new job in hand, many employees finally accept the reality. Time needed to achieve this final stage varies among different people. Give some time for them to deal with it. And the target of this process is the same anyway. When employees have to leave the company, they should leave with the good connection and appreciation. That's the end stage.

Bearing this mental side in our mind, the process side is then easier to be designed to match the mental stages.

Before the big announcement, a briefing meeting to the managers is proved to be a common and useful approach. If it's possible, do that one or two days earlier than the town hall meeting[4]. Managers then have longer time digest the message and prepare for answers to possible questions.

During the town hall meeting, a clear presentation helps employees to understand why and how. Managers should be prepared to be interrupted from time to time, but the time should be controlled within one or two hours. Don't abuse the presentation time to be an endless Q&A[5] time. Bringing the basic and standard information officially to all is the purpose of this step. Questions regarding specific cases could be collected and answered later after the town hall meeting.

Unit 1   Help Your People Look for a New Job—Are You Ready?

The information including the standard presentation and the accumulating Q&A should be published by either bulletin board or company web site or both. Since it always relates to the legal issues, the same standards must be applied and answers must be consistent for same cases in order to be in line with the laws and regulations.

A career assistance program is also popular in many companies that have to start layoff. Generally an external consulting company can take that role to help employees realize their emotion change, to support them in the process of finding a new job.

Many companies have the rehire policy saying that when there are new vacancies, they will consider first the employees who are laid off due to organizational change. And we all know these true stories in reality. So don't just lose interest in those leaving employees. This is just a small world.

Box 1-2

Rehiring Former Employees: The Case for Rehiring

Anne Berkowitch, CEO of SelectMinds—an HR consulting company, says there are several crucial reasons why businesses should consider rehiring. The first is that the cost-per-hire is typically decreased. You already know the candidate, so you don't have to worry about hiring a third party recruiter.

"It's a much more informed decision on both parts," she says. "The alumnus knows the company. The company knows the alumnus, so the hiring decision is made with a lot more information than what is captured on a resume."

Because the returning recruit already knows what she or he is signing up for, Berkowitch says the retention rate is also significantly higher. Former employees who have left the company and want to come back have likely seen that the grass isn't always greener on the other side. Even if their departure from the company wasn't voluntary, they're already familiar with both the corporate culture and the job description. In fact they are less likely to leave once they've been brought back.

Another key factor in considering bringing back a former employee is that the on-boarding process is much quicker. In fact, Berkowitch says her clients have reported that "time to contribution" for rehires is half of that of external recruits.

"They hit productivity a lot faster," she says, meaning the company itself will save time and money that would have gone into training.

On average, Berkowitch reports that companies can save around MYM15,000 to MYM20,000 per rehire. "What that captures is lower cost-per-hire, faster productivity and retention rate," she says.

Not only can it save money, but it may also help you with business development, as former employees who have spent time away from your company have typically acquired new skill sets and contacts over that time. Dr. John Sullivan, a professor of management at San Francisco State University, says: "Having worked for a competitor can be worth a lot."

Vocabulary

professional	n.	职业人士，专业人士，行家
emergency	n.	紧急情况，非常时期
deprive	v.	使失去，剥夺
layoff	n.	裁员
remedy	n.	补救措施，救治手段
responsibility	n.	责任，职责
announce	v.	宣布，通告
emotion	n.	情绪，情感
transition	n.	转变，过渡期
frustration	n.	失败，挫折
gradually	ad.	逐渐地，逐步地
appreciate	v.	感激，感谢
assistance	n.	援助，帮助
calculate	v.	计算
corporate	a.	公司的，法人的
minimize	v.	使最小化
negative	a.	负面的，消极的

Unit 1 Help Your People Look for a New Job—Are You Ready?

sheet	n.	一张，纸张
mental	a.	精神的，心理的
dramatic	a.	戏剧性的，剧烈的，引人关注的
reaction	n.	反应
announcement	n.	宣布，通告
denial	n.	否认，拒绝接受
frustrated	a.	有挫败感的，失意的
challenge	v.	质疑，质问
betrayal	n.	背叛，背信弃义
opposite	a.	相反的，对立的
implementation	n.	执行，履行，贯彻，落实
depressed	a.	沮丧的，消沉的，忧郁的
sufficient	a.	充分的，足够的
arrangement	n.	安排，筹备，布置
explain	v.	解释，说明
clarify	v.	澄清，阐明
immediate	a.	立刻，即时
feedback	n.	反馈
trivial	a.	琐碎的，细小的
honestly	ad.	诚实地，坦诚地
understand	v.	理解，谅解
mutual	a.	彼此的，相互的
positive	a.	积极的，正面的
dialogue	n.	对话
confidence	n.	信任，自信
restore	v.	恢复，重建
necessarily	ad.	必需地，必要地，必定地
achieve	v.	实现，达到
connection	n.	关系
appreciation	n.	感激，欣赏
match	v.	匹配，适合
briefing	n.	简报，简单告知

common	a.	通常的，常见的
approach	n.	方法，手段
hall	n.	会堂，会议厅
digest	v.	消化，领会，整理
presentation	n.	陈述，发言
interrupt	v.	打断，妨碍
abuse	v.	滥用
officially	ad.	正式地
purpose	n.	目的，作用
accumulate	v.	积累
bulletin	n.	告示，公告
consistent	a.	一致的，协调的
regulation	n.	规章，制度
unemployment	n.	失业
voluntarily	ad.	自愿地
ineligible	a.	无资格的
misconduct	n.	行为不当，渎职
distinguish	v.	区别，区分
accompany	v.	陪伴，陪随
redeployment	n.	转移，重新布置
objection	n.	反对
facilitate	v.	使顺利，使方便，促进
professionally	ad.	职业化地，专业化地
jobless	a.	没有工作的，失业的
popular	a.	普遍的，流行的，受欢迎的
rehire	v.	重新雇佣，再次雇佣
vacancy	n.	（职位）空缺
crucial	a.	非常重要的，关键性的
recruiter	n.	招募人，招聘者
alumnus	n.	校友，以前的伙伴
capture	v.	捕获，获得
retention	n.	保持，保留，留住
acquire	v.	取得，获得，学到

Unit 1 Help Your People Look for a New Job—Are You Ready?

1 layoff   名词，含义为：裁员、解雇，与动词短语 lay off 的含义相同。
2 B.S. （Bachelor of Science） 理学学士
3 compensation package   补偿方案
4 town hall meeting   指一种非正式的公开会议、市民会议、座谈会等。一般而言，其规模不会太大，话题宽泛自由，气氛也比较轻松。
5 Q&A（questions and answers）   提问与回答

I Please answer the following questions according to the text.

1. What did the financial expert advise people to do during the economic crisis?
2. Is firing people one of the responsibilities of an HR manager?
3. Is helping the leaving people look for a new job one of the responsibilities of an HR professional?
4. What is the first reaction of employees upon the layoff announcement?
5. What is most helpful to those employees being laid off?

II Please explain the following terms and phrases in English.

part time job   full time job   training course
career transition   working experience   career assistance
compensation package   corporate citizen   layoff announcement

III Please read the following statements carefully and give your choice: True or False.

1. The financial crisis since 2008 has made life changed for many people.
2. The financial expert advised people to reserve 5 months living cost as emergency cost.
3. At the end of 2008, there was a Hollywood movie named *Up in the Air*.

4. Anny couldn't accept that she was laid off by her first employer until she found a new job.
5. There are many more to do for HR professionals than just a sheet of notice when announcing layoff.
6. Layoff will change a company little.
7. Some people are very depressed because they find nothing good in the process of layoff.
8. A career assistance program is also popular in many companies.

IV Please translate the following paragraphs into Chinese.

1. Layoff, also called redundancy in the UK, is the temporary suspension or permanent termination of employment of an employee or (more commonly) a group of employees for business reasons, such as when certain positions are no longer necessary or when a business slow-down occurs.
2. Originally the term layoff referred exclusively to a temporary interruption in work, as when factory work cyclically falls off. The term however nowadays usually means the permanent elimination of a position, requiring the addition of "temporary" to specify the original meaning.
3. When a company is struggling financially its employees could face a layoff. Preparing for a layoff may shorten the period of time you will be unemployed. Here are steps you can take to help keep a layoff from hitting you too hard.
4. Employers took 1,651 mass layoff actions in October that resulted in the separation of 148,059 workers, seasonally adjusted, as measured by new filings for unemployment insurance benefits during the month, the US Bureau of Labor Statistics reported on Nov. 23, 2010.
5. It's no secret that the past few years have been rampant with cutbacks and layoffs. As businesses are slowly beginning to rebound, however, it might be time to consider re-staffing. There's no recruitment method more cost-efficient or time-efficient than rehiring reliable former employees.

V Please do the following oral exercises with your partner.

1. Discuss your views on the title of text.
2. Play the parts of an HR manager and a leaving employer when the former announced the layoff to the latter.

Unit 2

New Way to Spot the Candidates

It's always time consuming and somehow frustrating for someone to find a new job. And actually it is almost the same for a recruiter to find a suitable candidate.

Most companies post their job advertisements on the newspapers and Internet and expect the potential candidates may find the advertisements and send their resumes to the appointed address. Then after the screening and interviews, the recruitment job is done, and hiring managers get their fingers crossed[1] to hope they really find someone they want.

Besides the most common ways, companies will turn to head hunters[2] to search for people to fill some senior positions or positions with very limited talent supply. Those head hunters are regarded as more professional in searching and selecting. Generally those job agencies[3] possess huge talent data base which the in house HR[4] can not afford to create and maintain.

Box 2-1

Head Hunting in HR

Originally, head hunting is the cruel practice of taking a person's head after killing them. It was practiced in historic times in many parts of the world.

For head hunting in HR, there is a more formal term "executive search". Correspondingly, a head hunter refers to an executive search firm which is essentially an employment agent for upper management.

An executive search firm is a type of employment agency that specializes in recruiting executive personnel for companies in various industries. Executive search agents/professionals typically have a wide range of personal contacts in

> their industry or field of specialty; detailed, specific knowledge of the area; and typically operate at the most senior level of executive positions.
>
> Executive search professionals are also involved throughout more of the hiring process, conducting detailed interviews and presenting candidates to clients selectively, when they feel the candidate meets all stated requirements and would fit into the culture of the hiring firm, as well. Executive search agencies typically have long-lasting relationships with clients spanning many years, and in such cases the suitability of candidates is paramount.
>
> It is also important that such agencies operate with a high level of professionalism. Executive search agencies often also provide clients with (legal) inside rumors gleaned from contacts within their clients' competitors.

Internal referral is also quite often adopted by companies. Colleagues know better than external head hunters or even internal HR people whether their friends will like the company and the job they are currently doing. Considering higher passing ratio than other channels, the internal referral is deemed as a very effective and cost-saving way, although there are usually bonuses to be granted to those who successfully recommend suitable candidates.

Recruitment managers like to share information about vacancies and job seekers through their networks by posting job advertisement on Internet, sending e-mails or just short messages via mobile phones. The latest trend however is the network on Facebook, LinkedIn, Twitter[5] and other social networking sites.

The most amazing side of this new approach is that so many people are connected as long as you find just one entry. Compared with the traditional ways, it is definitely a very productive recruitment channel.

On these social media, there are not only formal resumes showing the education background and working experience, but also the topics, the suggestions and the competencies or values behind the words. "I once was looking for a production manager," says Celia Pickus, recruiting manager of a medium size manufacturing company. "It was hard for me to select a better one between the two candidates. Then I managed to search some discussions they put on the web. I chose the one who speaks like our managers do. And it is proved to be a right decision."

Would this become the most popular recruitment channel in the near future? According to Ms. Halverson, senior vice president for learning and talent development at the recruiting firm MRINetwork, job searching and head hunting through social media is almost like "has replaced the white pages[6]". Recruiters sometimes don't know how to find someone who does't have a presence online. "It's non-negotiable—you have to have a profile on a social networking site."

Of course it can't be the only way at current stage. Many people looking for work have never had reason to set up a presence online and have no idea how to do with it. These people worked in industries like manufacturing, where Facebook and Twitter weren't a part of daily life. Or they had plugged away at the same company for decades and never felt the need to make a resume, let alone a LinkedIn page describing their job history. These people have all the skills necessary for new jobs, but few of the skills required for the job-search process.

How to use these new tools is not only a technical issue. More often it's about how to promoting oneself in a right and consistent way.

Jacob Schmid, an IT consultant based in Los Angeles, lost his job with a German technology company in 2008. Jumping into the job market for the first time in 20 years, Mr. Schmid did what job seekers have always done—he sent out his resume and waited for companies to call him back. He didn't get any takers.

Scouring the Web for tips on job hunting, Mr. Schmid found several sites and forums with advice on how to set up his "personal brand" online. He began to blog about his work and then to use Twitter to reach out to others in his profession.

"I was very uncoordinated at first, really stumbling a lot. I didn't know what I was doing or what to talk about," he said. But over a few months, Mr. Schmid got the hand of it—he got better at writing short posts about his work, at pointing out his posts to the right people on Twitter and being consistent, but not overbearing, in advertising himself.

A former colleague noticed the posts by Mr. Schmid and recommended him a freelance position with a Norwegian technology company.

All of this took a lot of energy. Many job seekers are not aware of the importance of expanding their sphere of influence through Internet. That's why teaching people on how to use the social networks is becoming one of the main things that the consultants do in career counseling offices, according to Nancy Richmond, assistant director of career counseling and exploration at the Massachusetts Institute of Technology[7]. "We're showing them that using social media is a great way to show employers that they're on the forefront of cutting-edge trends. It can be extremely helpful for their careers."

If you're looking for new job opportunities, have you ever thought of this?

English
人力资源管理专业英语教程

Vocabulary

spot	v.	认出，找到，发现
consume	v.	消耗，花费，浪费
frustrate	v.	使挫败，使落空
potential	a.	潜在的，可能的
advertisement	n.	广告
appointed	a.	指定的，约定的
screen	v.	筛选，甄别
interview	n.	面试，面谈
recruitment	n.	招聘，招募
executive	n.	执行官，总经理
correspondingly	ad.	相应地
selectively	ad.	选择地
span	v.	跨越
professionalism	n.	专家气质，职业特质，职业水准
rumor	n.	传闻，流言
glean	v.	搜集，拾遗，发现，查明
competitor	n.	竞争者，竞争对手
referral	n.	介绍，引荐
bonus	n.	奖金，红利，额外津贴
profile	n.	形象，轮廓，人物简介
scour	v.	搜寻
uncoordinated	a.	不协调的
stumble	v.	绊倒，蹒跚行走
overbearing	a.	傲慢的，自大的
freelance	n.	自由职业，独立职位
sphere	n.	范围
forefront	n.	前沿，最前面

Unit 2 New Way to Spot the Candidates

1. get their fingers crossed 信奉基督教的人进行祷告时通常会双手十指交叉，因此这个短语可以译为：祈求上帝保佑自己好运。
2. head hunter 猎头公司
3. job agency 招聘中介，人力资源代理机构
4. in house HR 公司自己内部的人力资源部门
5. Facebook, LinkedIn, Twitter 国外几家新兴的社交网络服务网站
6. the white pages 指传统的纸质简历。
7. Massachusetts Institute of Technology 麻省理工学院（MIT）

I Please answer the following questions according to the text.

1. How is it for a recruiter to find a suitable candidate?
2. What is the most common way for companies to do recruitments?
3. What is a head hunter?
4. What is an internal referral?
5. What is the latest trend of recruitment channels?

II Please explain the following terms and phrases in English.

time consuming   job advertisement   potential candidate
senior position   talent data base   recruitment manager
job seeker   education background   job searching

III Please read the following statements carefully and give your choice: True or False.

1. It's always time consuming and somehow frustrating for someone to find a new job.
2. Few companies post their job advertisement on the newspapers and internet.
3. Head hunters are regarded as more professional in searching and interviewing.

4. Internal referral is also quite often adopted by companies.
5. External referral is deemed as a very effective and cost saving way.
6. Recruitment managers like to share information about vacancies and job seekers through their networks.
7. Searching through internet is the only way to find a job at current stage.
8. Many job seekers are not aware of the importance of expanding their sphere of influence through internet.

IV Please translate the following paragraphs into Chinese.

1. A recruiter is someone engaging in recruitment, or the solicitation of individuals to fill jobs or positions within a corporation, non-for-profit organization, sports team, etc. Recruiters may work within an organization's Human Resources department (typically) or on an outsourced basis.
2. Outsourced recruiters typically work for multiple clients at once, on a third-party broker basis, and are variously called headhunters, search firms/agents, agency recruiters, or recruitment consultants.
3. An internal recruiter (alternatively in-house recruiter or corporate recruiter) is member of a company or organization and typically works in the human resources (HR) department, which in the past was known as the Personnel Office (or just Personnel). Internal recruiters may be multi-functional, serving in an HR generalist role—negotiating, hiring, firing, conducting exit interviews; as well as managing employee disputes, contracts, benefits, recruitment, etc.—or in a specific role focusing all their time on recruiting.
4. The Internet is a place where you can find thousands of job opportunities all over the world in every imaginable field; a convenient way to apply for jobs; an excellent place to research potential employers. However, the Internet is not an employment service and you should think twice before sharing your personal information.
5. We frequently hear from job seekers who are frustrated with job hunting on the Internet. They have posted their resume on the major job boards or searched for and responded to job postings—but have heard nothing back from employers.

V Please do the following oral exercises with your partner.

1. Discuss the ways of job searching mentioned in the text.
2. If you are a recruiter, how will you spot a suitable candidate?

Unit 3

How to Make an Interview Effective?

No matter how different the recruitment processes are in companies specialized in various industries, an interview is definitely a must-have link, comparing with some nice-to-have steps like personality assessment, logical test, and group discussions.

Box 3-1

Job Interview

A job interview is a process in which a potential employee is evaluated by an employer for prospective employment in their company, organization, or firm. During this process, the employer hopes to determine whether or not the applicant is suitable for the job.

A job interview typically precedes the hiring decision, and is used to evaluate the candidate. The interview is usually preceded by the evaluation of submitted resume from interested candidates, then selecting a small number of candidates for interviews. Potential job interview opportunities also include networking events and career fairs.

The job interview is considered one of the most useful tools for evaluating potential employees. It also demands significant resources from the employer, yet has been demonstrated to be notoriously unreliable in identifying the optimal person for the job. An interview also allows the candidate to assess the corporate culture and demands of the job.

Multiple rounds of job interviews may be used where there are many candidates or the job is particularly challenging or desirable. Earlier rounds may involve fewer staff from the employers and will typically be much shorter and less in-depth. A common initial interview form is the phone interview, a job interview conducted over the telephone. This is especially common when the candidates do not live near the employer and has the advantage of keeping costs low for both sides.

Once all candidates have been interviewed, the employer typically selects the most desirable candidate and begins the negotiation of a job offer.

That's why job seekers look forward to get the phone call requiring the interview, and that's why plenty of advises are given to them about how to dress, how to talk, and how to behave like a confident professional in order to attract the attention of the interviewer.

It sometimes does work. Some surveys show that a glance within 3 seconds determines the first impression. Most interviews last for one hour, but many interviewers make their decision in 3 minutes. There are many reasons behind that such as stereotype, or mirror-hiring[1] etc.

Box 3-2

Don't Hire People Just Like You

"Mirror-hiring" has its positives, but a diverse work force can enhance innovation and productivity.

When you recruit and hire new employees, do you often find that you're searching for people just like you? Similar in mannerisms, appearance, intelligence and culture? Perhaps also possessing the same educational background, experiences and maybe even gender, race and religion?

If you do hire employees this way, then rest assured that you're not alone. At the same time, however, you're also just like many bosses who are selling themselves and their companies short.

You are doing what I call "hiring by looking in the mirror."

By hiring a clone, you may be missing out on a number of opportunities that may prove difficult and problematic. That's because for the sake of conformity, you might be rejecting people with skills both complementary and supplemental to your company that would permit its culture to grow and expand with outcomes that could create a more productive, innovative, challenging and rewarding environment.

When you adhere strictly to a narrow hiring profile, too much "likeness" can lead to corporate "in-breeding". The inevitable result is that the new hires look like, think like and act like you, the boss. This "group think" situation results in employees not challenging each other, not asking enough "why" questions, settling for agreement where disagreement would conceivably produce more options, perspectives, opinions and viewpoints. Often, people reject good but "different" ideas, or worse, they never voice divergent opinions because they would appear "dissimilar" and therefore unacceptable.

Though "mirror hiring" may help you resolve an issue or take action more quickly, with all this uniformity, what happens to innovation and creativity? And what happens to risk-taking? Who becomes the "devil's advocate" who can propose alternate lines of reasoning or different goals?

This is a crucial suggestion that you, the successful entrepreneur, might use to avoid too much in-breeding and conformity that can hinder productivity, innovation and profitability.

Consider being open to diversity, not just in terms of race, gender or sexual orientation, but also in terms of skills, attitudes, interests, backgrounds and experiences. Appreciate that each person can bring a unique—yes, sometimes individually different—approach to the workplace.

Employees with differences can appropriately challenge each other more often and quite effectively. Differences can cause people to think, act and feel in new and different ways. Innovation, productivity, morale and satisfaction can increase when diversity exists in a collaborative atmosphere. The key words here are "collaboration" and "innovation".

Differing opinions can spark new thoughts and ideas for processes, procedures, products and services, but everyone still needs to work toward a common goal. And, if you, the entrepreneurial boss, are willing to take the chance to try something new in your hiring, many competitive bottom-line opportunities can unfold.

As Apple's motto used to say, "Think Different."

As a skillful interviewer or as the HR professional, we should try to avoid such interviews. We aim to put right person in the right position with the help of effective interviews.

First, what are we trying to find or verify during the interview?

It's easy to accept that we want to check if the person can take the job and deliver satisfactory performance. Then naturally we think about the job requirement, which recruiters always have in hand with the name of JD[2]. The tricky part is what kind of information we get from the candidate can be the proof that she is the right person for that position.

Education background, working experience, professional certificates are something jump to our heads quickly. However they are not sufficient to draw a conclusion. They are evidences for the technical or knowledge side, which alone can't guarantee the job performance. Many companies write in their job advertisement that they need people to be "result oriented", "able to face pressure", "creative in problem solving". These competencies or behaviors are actually the focus of the effective interviews.

How could we know that the candidate possess the competencies we need? The behavioral interviewing[3] is the answer.

Box 3-3

Traditional Interview vs. Behavioral Interview

In a traditional interview, you will be asked a series of questions which typically have straight forward answers like "What are your strengths and weaknesses?" or "What major challenges and problems did you face? How did you handle them?" or "Describe a typical work week."

In a behavioral interview, an employer has decided what skills are needed in the person they hire and will ask questions to find out if the candidate has those skills. Instead of asking how you would behave, they will ask how you did behave. The interviewer will want to know how you handled a situation, instead of what you might do in the future.

Remember what you hear from the candidates when you ask them to describe themselves? "I'm a responsible person." "I'm diligent." "I'm a quick learner[4]." "I work hard." "I'm a team player[5]." Sound great, right? According to the behavioral interviewing philosophy, these are only statements, which do not provide any real behaviors. What interviewers should do in an effective interview is to collect examples or evidences of what the candidates said and did in the past, because past behaviors predict future behaviors.

The way to quickly find the matched behaviors is asking for STAR[6]. S stands for the situation, and T for Task. Situation and task describe the background of certain behavior. A indicates the actions taken including what the actions are and how they are implemented. R means the result brought by this behavior.

When the candidate is talking about his hard working, he may tell you that they were working for a very important bidding proposal when someone in the team felt sick and had to leave for hospital (Situation). They must have all the materials ready within 4 hours (Task). He then volunteered to replace the sick member and continued working for 3 more hours (Action). At last the proposal was completed in time, and finally they won the bid (Result).

If instead the candidate says "I think I will volunteer to work over time in order to complete the task with tight schedule." This is opinion but not real behavior. "I plan to read more books so that I can teach better." "If someone doesn't complete the task, I will work with him to find the root cause[7]." Remarks like these are not behaviors either, they are just theoretical or future oriented statements.

Besides those vague statements, plans, theories, or opinions, what we also meet frequently is the partial STAR. "I feel with the fast changes in technology, our software package was going to be obsolete in about six months, so I started to look for a replacement. I read up on all the available programs and tested most of them." The interviewers may feel that this guy was really doing something proactively, but the example is not effective if there is no result clarified next.

An experienced recruiter will ask, "Did you at last find the replacement?" If the answer is "Well, the global IT department launched a good replacement in 3 months before I could find my solution", there is a question mark on whether his study is really meaningful.

If he says "I couldn't continue that because later there were too many priorities in need of my efforts", the STAR itself doesn't look like a persuasive one.

If the story goes like this: "I discussed my findings with other managers after 3 months testing, and finally we chose a new one in time. Now we're quite convinced that we are on the right track", it's definitely a very good and strong evidence for his being proactive, good planning and effective execution.

During the behavioral interview, there are 3 tips for the interviewers.

First, the interviewers must be clear about the competencies or behaviors he wants to verify in the interview. It's better for him to have a list of the competencies and some prewritten questions that would elicit past examples of displaying the competencies desired. Regarding the "initiative" or "result orientation", there could be questions like "What have you done to ensure that you can lead your team to complete the stretched goal?" "Tell me one of the biggest obstacles you have overcome to get where you are today. How did you do that?"

Second, interviewers should listen proactively. That means you should listen attentively to gather in-depth information about the related experience of candidate's job, and keep focused on the STARs. If there are partial STARs, try to probe to get the example a complete picture. If there are only statements or opinions, try to lead the candidate to think of the real case from his past experience. Of course you should also respond with your empathy[8] instead of being too aggressive by just throwing questions. The interviewer should query and probe with respect, hence the rapport between the interviewer and the candidate could be built.

The last is about taking notes. It's not so easy to capture the whole example while listening, so interviewers may just record key words or sometimes use short hand[9]. But make sure you can recognize your handwriting an hour later. Also make sure you note down the STARS, not necessarily the candidate's answers, which can help you to make a confident conclusion based on facts instead of your feelings or pure memory.

It will of course take some time to practice for some interviewers who are not familiar with this behavioral interviewing skill. When the interviewers get used to this practice, they will soon find its advantage as being more objective and effective.

Behavioral interviewing has become more and more popular with employers. A December 2007 internet survey conducted by Equation Research polled more than 2,500 senior HR and training and development executives and they found that only 19% of employers don't use behavioral interviewing, while 25% plan to use that more often, rest of the pool plan to use as often as in the past, no company is to use that less often.

Vocabulary

definitely	ad.	明确地，确定地，绝对地
personality	n.	人格，个性，性格
assessment	n.	评估，评价，鉴定

Unit 3 How to Make an Interview Effective?

demonstrate	v.	表明，证明
notoriously	ad.	声名狼藉地
unreliable	a.	不可靠的
multiple	a.	多重的，多个的，多次的
in-depth	a.	深入的
initial	a.	最初的，开始的
desirable	a.	理想的，满意的
negotiation	n.	洽谈，磋商
confident	a.	自信的，沉着的
glance	n.	一瞥，扫视
stereotype	n.	成见，旧习
enhance	v.	增强，提高
innovation	n.	创新
clone	n.	克隆，复制品，一模一样的人
problematic	a.	有问题的，疑难的
conformity	n.	相似，一致
complementary	a.	补充的，互补的
supplemental	a.	补充的，增补的
innovative	a.	创新的，富有创新精神的
inevitable	a.	不可避免的
disagreement	n.	差异，分歧，不符合，不一致
conceivably	ad.	想得到地，想象地
perspective	n.	视角，角度，观点
viewpoints	n.	观点，看法，见解
dissimilar	a.	不一样的
unacceptable	a.	不可接受的
uniformity	n.	一样，一律，一致
advocate	n.	拥护者
alternate	a.	交替的，替代的
reasoning	n.	推理
appropriately	ad.	适当地

morale	n.	士气，精神
collaborative	a.	合作的，协调的
atmosphere	n.	氛围
collaboration	n.	合作
unfold	v.	展开
motto	n.	座右铭，箴言
tricky	a.	微妙的，复杂的，棘手的
background	n.	背景，出身，经历
behavioral	a.	行为的
diligent	a.	勤奋的，勤勉的
philosophy	n.	基本原理
volunteer	v.	自愿去做，自动请求去做
theoretical	a.	理论上的
vague	a.	含糊的，笼统的
obsolete	a.	陈旧的，过时的
proactively	ad.	积极地，主动地
persuasive	a.	有说服力的
elicit	v.	引出，诱出
initiative	a.	起始的，初步的
orientation	n.	导向，定向，定位，（对新环境的）适应
stretch	v./n.	伸展，延伸，扩展
obstacle	n.	障碍，妨害
overcome	v.	克服，战胜
attentively	ad.	注意地，留心地
probe	v.	探查，探究
empathy	n.	共情，同理心
aggressive	a.	进攻性的
query	v.	询问
rapport	n.	友好关系
handwriting	n.	笔迹
objective	a.	客观的

Unit 3 How to Make an Interview Effective?

1 mirror-hiring "照镜子招聘"
   指招聘人员倾向于录用与自己一样的人。这种招聘方式有积极的一面：可以确保企业自身的一些特性得到有效的保持和落实；同时，其也有消极的一面：企业将缺乏对其增长具有额外作用的人才，且容易导致企业内部"近亲繁殖（in-breeding）"，凸显其原有的缺陷。
2 JD   岗位说明，岗位描述（Job Descriptions）
3 behavioral interviewing   行为面试
4 quick learner   学东西很快的人
5 team player   有团队精神的人
6 STAR   人力资源管理中常用的原则，多用于招聘面试。STAR 为4个英文单词首字母的缩写，即："Situation, Task, Action, Result"。
7 root cause   根本原因，（问题的）根源
8 empathy   心理学术语，一般译为：共情、同理心、神入。其含义是：设身处地站在对方的立场上去理解对方。
9 short hand   速记

I Please answer the following questions according to the text.

1. What does the "must-have link" mean in the first paragraph?
2. What does the "nice-to-have steps" mean in the first paragraph?
3. Should the interviewer make decision by first impression?
4. What should be found or verified during the interview?
5. What is the behavioral interviewing?

II Please explain the following terms and phrases in English.

personality assessment   logical test   group discussion

first impression　　　　　effective interview　　　　job requirement
professional certificate　　job performance　　　　　experienced recruiter

III Please read the following statements carefully and give your choice: True or False.

1. Personality assessment is a must-have step in recruitment.
2. Plenty of advises are given to job seekers about how to dress and how to talk in an interview.
3. Most interview last for one hour, but many interviewers make their decision in 3 minutes.
4. Education background, working experience and professional certificates are sufficient for the recruiter to draw a conclusion.
5. The behavioral interviewing help the interviewer to know that the candidate possess the competencies needed.
6. "I'm a team player" is only a statement.
7. Interviewees should listen proactively.
8. The interviewer should query and probe with respect.

IV Please translate the following paragraphs into Chinese.

1. A typical job interview has a single candidate meeting with between one and three persons representing the employer; the potential supervisor of the employee is usually involved in the interview process. A larger interview panel will often have a specialized human resources worker. While the meeting can be over in as little as 15 minutes, job interviews usually last less than two hours.

2. In recent years it has become increasingly common for employers to request job applicants who are successfully shortlisted to deliver one or more presentations at their interview. The purpose of the presentation in this setting may be to either demonstrate candidates' skills and abilities in presenting, or to highlight their knowledge of a given subject likely to relate closely to the job role for which they have applied.

3. A common type of job interview in the modern workplace is the behavioral interview or behavioral event interview, also called a competency-based interview. This type of interview is based on the notion that a job candidate's previous behaviors are the best indicators of future performance.

4. Telephone interviews take place if a recruiter wishes to reduce the number of prospective candidates before deciding on a shortlist for face-to-face interviews. They also take place if a job applicant is a significant distance away from the premises of the hiring company, such as abroad or in another state or province.
5. In many countries, employment equity laws forbid discrimination based on a number of classes, such as race, gender, age, sexual orientation, and marital status. Asking questions about these protected areas in a job interview is generally considered discriminatory, and constitutes an illegal hiring practice.

V   Please do the following oral exercises with your partner.

1. Compare traditional interview with behavioral Interview.
2. Play the parts of the interviewer and the interviewee in a behavioral interview.

Unit 4

Retention from the First Day

"Cisco extends a warm welcome to new employees, starting with the recruiting process and extending to programs for new hires and employees of acquired companies. We want employees to experience the best that Cisco has to offer, beginning on their very first day."

Box 4-1

The First Day on the Job

A new employee may be anxious about starting a new job. Try to create a comfortable environment and remember not to overwhelm the new employee with too much information on the first day. Orientation is a continuing process, so there will be plenty of time to give the employee all the necessary information. On the first day, you should:

- Give a warm welcome and try to reduce any nervousness the new employee may feel.
- Discuss your plan for first day.
- Introduce the employee to other staff members.
- Arrange to have lunch with the new employee.
- Show the new employee around the office.
- Review the job description card and organizational charts with the employee.
- Explain ridesharing and transportation services.
- Review telephone, fax, e-mail, and Internet use.

Unit 4 Retention from the First Day

> - Give the employee the New Employee Benefits Packet. Be sure to discuss any questions or refer the employee to your Department Benefits Counselor. Remind the employee to fill out and submit benefits forms on time.
> - Explain that company policy and collective bargaining agreements call for most new employees to complete a probationary period before they become regular status employees. Discuss what the probationary period is all about and explain how and when the employee's performance will be appraised during the probationary period.
> - Have the new employee complete all the necessary personnel forms.

  This is the welcome message on Cisco's web. The leading network solution provider aims to shape each new hire fit to the organization in 90 days.

  The first 90 days are critical. Many companies miss this step or treat it with little attention. After the vacancies are closed, supervisors are keen to have new hires start working as soon as possible. Unfortunately, the sooner they want to have the new hires, the sooner the new comers may leave the organization.

  Exit interview[1] records show that people leave within 6 months partly because they haven't got sufficient information about their company and job, they don't know where to ask for resources, or they don't feel they are welcomed. There are comments like "Even on my first day or week, it didn't look like they were ready for my arrival." or "I didn't feel supported, even on my first day!"

  I still remember the first working day in my last company. After I met my boss, I was led to a work station. There was only a desk. No computer, even no chair. I then waited for maybe thirty minutes before I can sat down. At that time I was thinking: "Does the company really need me?"

  Retention measures are often too late when people you want have already started to think of leaving. Retention should starts from the first day of on boarding.

  How much time should companies spend on new employee orientation? What should be delivered during this program? No matter how different the schedules are, there are some common topics such as:
- talking about the history, structure, and culture of the organization;
- promoting the values and business strategies of the organization;

- presenting the code of conduct[2];
- explaining the compensation and benefits[3] items;
- teaching new employees how to use voice mail, e-mail, and file systems;
- emphasizing the safety and security guidelines;
- introducing the job description and objectives to be accomplished during the orientation period.

Box 4-2

New Employee Orientation: Starting off on the Right Foot

Remember your first day of school when you were just a youngster? It was a bit frightening, if you were like most kids. Lots of new people and a completely different environment. You weren't quite sure how you would be accepted.

New employees feel much the same way. They are coming into a new environment, meeting new people, and are not sure how they will be accepted. Employers can ease the transition and take advantage of the opportunity to get the relationship off to a good start.

Welcome your new employee. Smile, and tell them you are glad that they have come to work with you. You can make a big difference at this point. Show them around the facility, pointing out any important features along the way like emergency exits and hazardous areas, for example. Pretend you are showing a guest through your home. You want to make them feel comfortable and for them to relax as much as possible. Introduce them to people you meet along the way. Chances are your new worker won't be able to remember everyone's name when they are through with your tour, but you will at least have given other people the chance to learn who the new person is. As you introduce your new employee, explain what job they will be assigned and who they will be reporting to. This will help existing employees mentally fit the new person into what they know of your organization.

Introduce your new employee to the supervisor they will be reporting to, if they haven't already met. Show them their work station and where to get any supplies they might need. Talk briefly about important contacts they will want to

> remember, such as the person responsible for ordering supplies, the payroll person and any others you feel are key to the operation.
>
> Prepare a checklist of subjects which should be reviewed with each new employee and then set aside the appropriate amount of time so that can be done. Let everyone else know that you are not to be interrupted while you are orienting your new worker. You will want to convey to the new person that they are the most important item on your agenda at the moment.

There are not only training people who are involved in this process. Generally recruitment staff will ensure that contracts are ready for new hires, C&B staff[4] should start recording the attendance, and hiring managers should be prepared to welcome their team members by not only greetings but also work places, clear job instructions and so on. Therefore make sure that roles and responsibilities of each part are clearly defined so that the new employees can feel the consistent welcome message during the whole process. Otherwise, the new employee may think: "Is this messy place the right one I should stay in and contribute for?"

Some people travel when their new employee starts to work. That sends the wrong message—that they are not important enough for their supervisors to be there on their first day. When travel do happens, please call your new employee to explain that you feel regret that you cannot meet her on her first day of work. And you will schedule the meeting with her when you return. Or you may delegate the orientation to your colleague. Anyway make her feel that her first day of work is also an important day for you, and you care about her since the first day.

When the new employees arrive, make sure you have their work stations set up. There are telephone, computer, office furniture. They can open the computers immediately with necessary access ready to the e-mail accounts and file systems, etc. New employees often spend a lot of time hunting and pecking within a company's computer system to learn what is available on line. If enough lead time could be granted to appropriate parties, the new employees won't have to wait for the IT folks who are connecting wires under their work stations.

Some managers have to answer questions like "Where is the HR office?" and "Do we have the first aid box[5]?" many times after new employees join. In fact many companies will arrange office tours for the new employees to get familiar with their working environment. That's good but not enough. If there is always some buddy who can help the green hand[6] on how to deal with her new job, tell her when she can borrow books from company's library, what are the convenient bus routes between office and downtown area... she will definitely feel the safe launch[7]. The experienced staff rather than managers are the most suitable people to be the buddies.

When the new employees finally get to their new departments, managers must spend time with them reviewing their job descriptions, setting expectations; let them know the things that drive you nuts[8] as the manager, for example, showing up late, doing without thinking, postponing deadlines without notice in advance. And talk about what can make her successful in the organization, such as being proactive, going the extra mile[9], walking the talk[10]. Make her a par to the team and the company.

One of the reasons that people leave within the first 90 days is that they think they haven't got enough training. On one side absent of even talking about future training plans, employees aren't going to stick around and wait to see if there ever will be any training. On the other side, we shouldn't expect new employees to learn everything they need for the job in the orientation period. At this stage new employees need the training to enable them to be productive and happy members in the company—performing and living similar to those experienced staff. Therefore besides the documents, templates, and systems they are to use in their daily job, topics like how to use the instant messenger through company's intranet, how to claim travel expenses are also helpful in assisting them to grow in the unique environment.

There is never a perfect plan. Therefore check it frequently during the first weeks, months, and beyond. You might think it's too early to talk with the new employees about their career path and individual development approaches—they just start to learn how to become an independent performer. However employees like to know their organization supports their success. If your company has a formal development process, including formal performance evaluations with objectives, job rotations, or promotion philosophy, it's a great way to make the new employees think that they've chosen the right company and make up their mind to stay and make contributions.

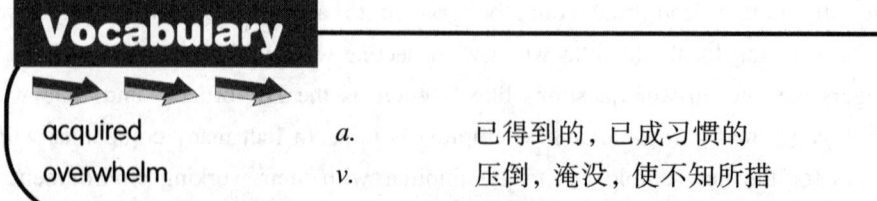

acquired	a.	已得到的，已成习惯的
overwhelm	v.	压倒，淹没，使不知所措

Unit 4 Retention from the First Day

nervousness	n.	紧张
ridesharing	n.	搭便车
counselor	n.	顾问
probationary	a.	试用的，见习的
shape	v.	塑造，使适合
critical	a.	关键的
youngster	n.	小孩子
facility	n.	设备，器材
hazardous	a.	危险的
mentally	ad.	内心里，精神上
appropriate	a.	适当的，合适的
orient	v.	使适应
convey	v.	传达，传递
peck	v.	啄，凿，用食指按键盘上的键打字
buddy	n.	伙伴，兄弟
description	n.	描述
expectation	n.	期望
proactive	a.	积极主动的，前瞻的
par	n.	同等，同价，同一水平
template	n.	模板
evaluation	n.	评估，评价体系
rotation	n.	轮换

1 exit interview   离职面谈
2 code of conduct   行为准则
3 compensation and benefits   薪资与福利（通常简写为 C&B）

4 C&B staff   分管薪资与福利的人力资源职员
5 first aid box   急救箱
6 green hand   新手
7 safe launch   安全启动，安全开始
8 drive you nuts   令你发狂
9 go the extra mile   多前进一步，多努力一点
10 walk the talk   言出必行

I Please answer the following questions according to the text.

1. What do you think about the title of the text?
2. How do you feel about the welcome message on Cisco's web?
3. Why did the author say that the first 90 days are critical?
4. How much time should companies spend on new employee orientation?
5. What do you think new employees need most?

II Please explain the following terms and phrases in English.

recruiting process	exit interview	retention measure
new employee orientation	recruitment staff	work station
office tour	working environment	job rotation

III Please read the following statements carefully and give your choice: True or False.

1. There is no warm welcome message on Cisco's web.
2. Many companies aim to shape each new hire fit to the organization in 90 days.
3. People leave within 6 months partly because they haven't got sufficient information about their company and job.
4. Retention should starts from the first day of on boarding.
5. One of the reasons that people leave within the first 90 days is that they think they haven't got enough training.

Unit 4 Retention from the First Day

6. The manager must tell new employees when she can borrow books from company's library.
7. We can expect new employees to learn everything they need for the job in the orientation period.
8. There is never perfect plan for retention of employees.

IV Please translate the following paragraphs into Chinese.

1. Effectively orienting new employees to the campus and to their positions is critical to establishing successful, productive working relationships. The employee's first interactions with you should create a positive impression of your department and the campus. The time you spend planning for the new person's first days and weeks on the job will greatly increase the chance for a successful start.

2. An effective orientation will: Foster an understanding of the campus culture, its values, and its diversity; Help the new employee make a successful adjustment to the new job; Help the new employee understand her role and how she fits into the total organization; Help the new employee achieve objectives and shorten the learning curve; Help the new employee develop a positive working relationship by building a foundation of knowledge about campus mission, objectives, policies, organization structure, and functions.

3. During your orientation discussion with the new employee, you want to take the opportunity to stress "how we do things around here". This is the best time for you to create the attitude you want your workers to have in performing their jobs. Remember that you can set the tone for the remainder of their employment with you. Make it positive and stress the things which are truly important to your organization. And, give the employee opportunity to ask questions along the way.

4. Make a special point of reviewing the organization's policy regarding sexual harassment. If you have five or more employees you must provide a copy of your policy to each employee in writing to meet the legal requirement.

5. How long should this process take? That depends on you and your organization. It will likely require an hour of your time at a minimum. It will be an hour which can clarify important information and avoid misunderstandings that could take you many hours to correct later on. An hour making people feel welcome, important and

giving them the information they need to succeed in your organization is indeed an hour well spent.

V Please do the following oral exercises with your partner.

1. Discuss the new employee orientation.
2. How will you want to be treated on your first day of job?

PART II

Compensation & Benefits
薪酬与福利

Unit 5
A General Compensation Structure

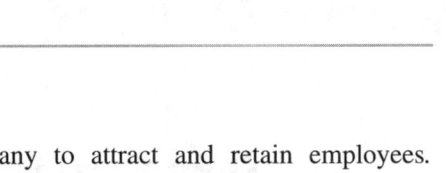

Compensation is definitely critical for a company to attract and retain employees. Companies view their remuneration system as a vehicle to achieve organizational growth and success, and always strive for a compensation structure[1] that is both externally competitive and internally equitable.

Box 5-1

Incentive Compensation

A standard base pay program offers fixed salary ranges for each position type for employees performing the standard duties of their jobs. Set up minimum and maximum levels within those pay ranges to account for variations in experience and skill levels. When setting the base pay structure, determine where your company falls within your own industry as well as competing industries that may also offer job opportunities for your employees. Set up the pay levels to be competitive, or else your company risk losing employees.

Once the base pay structure is in place, most companies then set up a merit pay[2] program that will take the employee through the salary range for their position at a performance-driven speed.

This comes into play when the employee's managers do annual employee performance reviews. The downside of this is that employees may begin to see it as a given that they will get a salary increase after each evaluation, and it ceases to be a motivation to perform better in their jobs. For this reason, more companies are moving toward more of a reward-based compensation style, also called incentive compensation.

Unit 5　A General Compensation Structure

> Incentive-based compensation is becoming much more common because of the increased emphasis on performance and competition for talent. This type of compensation structure significantly helps motivate employees to perform well. Hiring bonuses are also frequently used now, even for new
>
> college graduates. However, you might want to tie in a specific time period prior to the employee collecting this bonus—for example, one-half after six months and the remainder after one year of employment. Otherwise, you could run the risk of the employee departing after that first check, which would defeat your purpose. So does that mean incentive compensation is the way to go? Maybe so, if your company is in an industry where you really have to compete to get good employees.
>
> Setting up an incentive-based compensation program requires the same research into your industry as the base pay program. You'll still establish base pay levels, but it may be slightly lower and you will build into that base the annual or quarterly (or any other interval) bonuses, commissions, or other types of shared cash compensation.

In his book of *Human Resource Management*, Gary Dessler[3] defined compensation as "all forms of pay going to employees and arising from their employment". When somebody has found a new job, he usually expects the new job to bring him higher salary. However it happens frequently that although with a higher salary stated in his offer, the new hire realizes later that he gets no more money that what he was paid in previous job. He may have 10 percent increase in his base salary[4], but there is no quarterly bonus[5] to him at all, which was 20% of his annual salary in his last company.

Also when people would like to compare the compensation level of different jobs in different companies or industries, they find the compensation with "all forms of pay" is so complicated, and it's hard for them to compare something apple to apple[6]. Some companies distribute year-end bonus[7], some not. Some give 1 month salary as the year-end bonus, some give 2 months or more. Some provide transportation allowance[8], some offer gas subsidy[9]. Some buy supplemental insurance for employees, some grant stock options[10]. Some are guaranteed income, while some depend on the company profit and individual performance. So how could they be compared?

There are many categories developed for the comparison and further study about compensation. We can choose one popular methodology (as shown in Figure 5 – 1) to have a in-depth understanding. Mercer defines the annual based salary, which is the most basic part of the compensation, as the Component 1. Then Component 1 plus other guaranteed cash, e. g. the non performance related year-end bonus, the fixed allowance[11], is called Component 2 with the definition as Annual Guaranteed Cash. Similarly, some variable bonus[12] if any can be added to Component 2 and hence forms the Component 3, which is known as Annual Total Cash. Then long term incentives, stock options etc are items in Component 4. Some key benefits such as social insurance[13], medical plans or transportation subsidy etc belong to Component 5, which is the overall compensation package called Annual Total Compensation.

	Base Salary
+	Guaranteed Bonus
Component 1	Annual Base Salary
+	Fixed Allowance (Meal, Transportation, etc.)
Component 2	Annual Guaranteed Cash
+	Variable Bonus
+	Sales Incentive
+	Profit Sharing
+	Other Bonus
Component 3	Annual Total Cash
+	Stock Option
+	Long Term Incentive
Component 4	Annual Total Cash + Stock Option + Long Term Incentive
+	Pension, Housing, etc.
+	Medical Plan
+	Life/Accident Insurance
+	Mobile Phone
+	Other subsidy
Component 5	**Annual Total Compensation**

Figure 5 – 1   A General Compensation Structure Defined by Mercer

Base salary is always paid out monthly, and reflects the "value" of the position. It's also impacted by the position holder's background, e. g. experience, education, potential and performance record, etc. Employee's base salary normally is "fixed" for a certain period of time and to be reviewed on regular basis or when there is a change to the job.

Bonus is treated as one of the major elements of variable pay[14]. The payment of bonuses serves multiple purposes. One of the essential targets is of course directing behavior and recognition of outstanding performance. Sometimes when the base salary is to exceed the maximum of the salary band for that position, the lump sum bonus is to given to the position holder so that the base will be frozen and within the band till there is space for a base salary increase.

Although monetary bonuses are a very tangible means of showing recognition, they are generally considered to be poor long-term motivators and they cannot replace day-to-day leadership, recognition, motivation, and personal development. Managers are encouraged to find out the suitable non-monetary approaches to meet employees' motivation need. Otherwise, the increasing payroll cost will probably put the company in a non-competitive cost position, hence trigger the operation risk.

Benefits are issued either based on fixed structures (e.g. job class dictating eligibility for company car) or to fulfill a specific personal need/priority. The following are examples of typical monetary benefits.

- Car (including running cost).
- Transportation allowance.
- Medical insurance.
- Social benefits.
- Supplementary pension/housing subsidy[15].

Whenever possible, benefits should serve both the business and the individual's needs. Incorporating benefits in the total terms are important to obtain the "right" terms level.

Box 5-2

Variable Pay

Variable pay is employee compensation that changes as compared to salary which is paid in equal proportions throughout the year. Variable pay is used generally to recognize and reward employee contribution toward company productivity, profitability, team work, safety, quality, or some other metric deemed important.

The employee who is awarded variable compensation has gone above and beyond his or her job description to contribute to organization success. Variable pay is awarded in a variety of formats including profit sharing, bonuses, holiday bonus[16], deferred compensation[17], cash, and goods and services such as a company-paid trip or a Thanksgiving turkey.

It is very important to understand that the base salary and variable pay are two major components of the total cash compensation. Defining the proportion of these two parts in the total cash compensation is always based on the company business nature, background and compensation philosophy.

This methodology has been widely accepted by MNCs[18], especially those that participate the annual Total Remuneration Survey organized by Mercer. The companies guided by the same methodology provide to Mercer with accurate compensation data about each typical position in the organization, and then they get the benchmark reports for each position existing in the market after Mercer completes the analysis. Because the positions are also grouped according to Mercer's way, then it comes to be possible for companies to compare data apple to apple hence to determine their compensation strategy.

Companies eager to keep leading position in the industry may decide to give higher increase if they find others especially their potential competitors have positioned themselves at 75 percentile. Companies with abundant human resources supply may consider only mild increase because they don't need to offer too much.

Human resource professionals may not only use the estimated average increase ratio to negotiate with decision maker that they should put more budget for the coming merit increase, but also suggest a higher percentage of performance based variable pay for sales people to keep up with the trend if necessary. Also some new items showed in the survey can inspire the human resource people to think more broadly about how to design and update the remuneration system for the dynamic changes emerged in the company and the business.

Above information is salary structure related, and is not the only reference we can get from a quality market salary survey, nor is it enough for human resource professionals to make salary adjustment proposal. The salary structure is the foundation of a compensation system, based on which the comparison and analysis is practical and meaningful. Besides the salary structure, the company's pay positioning strategy, individual's pay position, employees' competency level, the company's development stage and business strategy are other information human resource professionals need to get from inside the organization. Also references from external world are to be considered, for example, the economic status and trend of the industry, the workforce statistics, the compensation trend of the labor market and so on.

One more thing to be emphasized again is that compensation is not the only way to retain people. In other words, people won't stay in a company only for the satisfactory payment.

Unit 5　A General Compensation Structure

Vocabulary

remuneration	n.	报酬，酬劳
vehicle	n.	媒介，手段，工具，载体
strive	v.	力求，努力，奋斗
externally	ad.	在外部，从外部
internally	ad.	在内部，从内部
equitable	a.	公平的，平衡的
minimum	a.	最小的，最低的
maximum	a.	最大的，最高的
downside	n.	缺陷，负面影响
defeat	v.	打破，击败，使无效
quarterly	a.	每季度的
interval	n.	时间间隔
commission	n.	佣金，提成
distribute	v.	分配，分发
essential	a.	本质的，必需的，主要的
motivator	n.	激励因素，推动力
motivation	n.	动机的形成，动机因素，动力
methodology	n.	方法论，研究方法
lump	a.	总共的
payroll	a.	薪资账册，发薪名单，薪资总额
dictate	v.	指挥，支配
eligibility	n.	资格，适合
metric	a.	公认的，习惯上的
percentile	a.	百分比的
abundant	a.	充足的，充裕的
mild	a.	温和的，轻微的
inspire	v.	激发，鼓舞，使产生灵感
quality	a.	优质的，高水平的
adjustment	n.	调整
practical	a.	实用的，可行的
meaningful	a.	有意义的

Notes

1. compensation structure　薪酬结构
2. merit pay　绩效工资
3. Gary Dessler　加里·戴斯勒（其著作《人力资源管理》是国际通用的人力资源管理专业经典教材）
4. base salary　基本工资，基础薪金（也可用 base pay）
5. quarterly bonus　季度奖
6. apple to apple　英语俗语，指将两个同类物品的各个对应方面一一进行比较。
7. year-end bonus　年终奖
8. transportation allowance　交通补助
9. gas subsidy　汽油补贴
10. stock option　股票期权
    很多公司在创业之初向员工提供本公司的股票期权，作为一种特殊的酬劳，这也是留住人才并激励员工与公司共命运的一种有效手段。
11. fixed allowance　固定津贴
12. variable bonus　浮动奖金
13. social insurance　社会保险
14. variable pay　浮动工资，浮动薪金，不固定薪酬
15. housing subsidy　住房补贴（也可用 housing allowance、housing reimbursement、housing benefit）
16. holiday bonus　假期红利，过节费
17. deferred compensation　递延薪酬，延期支付计划
18. MNCs　跨国公司（Multi-national Corporations/Companies）

I　Please answer the following questions according to the text.

1. Why should a compensation structure be externally competitive?

Unit 5 A General Compensation Structure

2. Why should a compensation structure be internally equitable?
3. What did Gary Dessler define compensation as?
4. Why is it hard to compare the compensation level of different jobs in different companies or industries?
5. What does a general compensation package include?

II Please explain the following terms and phrases in English.

remuneration system	organizational growth	compensation level
guaranteed income	company profit	cash compensation
long term incentive	annual total compensation	social benefit

III Please read the following statements carefully and give your choice: True or False.

1. Compensation is definitely critical for a company to attract and retain employees.
2. a compensation structure that is both internally competitive and externally equitable.
3. Every company distributes year-end bonus.
4. Some companies buy supplemental insurance for employees.
5. Base Salary is always paid out quarterly.
6. Monetary bonuses are generally considered to be good long-term motivators.
7. Transportation allowance, housing subsidy are examples of typical monetary benefits.
8. Compensation is the only way to retain employees.

IV Please translate the following paragraphs into Chinese.

1. Instead of continually ratcheting up base pay, manufacturing and service companies are adopting and expanding the use of incentive compensation programs, at all levels, to reward outstanding achievement without increasing fixed costs.
2. The key to the success of variable compensation is to have something you can measure and understand—something that is linked to creating economic value for the company.
3. Variable compensation is becoming a more common method for rewarding employees while linking their performance more closely to the employer's financial success. Some companies are allowing all levels of employees to participate in these programs. Executives of corporations have long been rewarded with bonuses for increased sales or productivity, the thinking runs, so why not bring this same

compensation method to middle management and even onto the shop floor?

4. Although money isn't everything, it certainly is one of the top issues potential employees look at when interviewing new companies. Whether you're offering a straight basic salary structure or an incentive-based pay structure may make or break your company in the eyes of top job candidates.

5. Compensation is a systematic approach to providing monetary value to employees in exchange for work performed. Compensation may achieve several purposes assisting in recruitment, job performance, and job satisfaction. It is a tool used by management for a variety of purposes to further the existence of the company. Compensation may be adjusted according the business needs, goals, and available resources.

V Please do the following oral exercises with your partner.

1. Discuss the general compensation structure mentioned in the text.
2. Which part do you think is the most important part of compensation? Why?

Unit 6
Intangible Reward

Managers may think of many forms of motivation and rewards to those good performers, high potentials or other staff they want to retain for different reasons.

Traditionally most rewards are compensation and benefits, such as salary increase, bonus, prize, some valuable souvenirs etc. The problem with these tangible rewards is that they are short-term motivators. The more people get, the more they develop an entitlement mindset. For example, give an employee 1,000 dollars for the successful project completion, and he or she will expect at least the same amount of money after the next project.

According to Herzberg's Two Factor Theory[1], money can't motivate employees to produce higher performance, and to some extent instead, it mitigates the influence of internal motive to pursue better result.

By Mercer's Total Reward Strategy concept[2], compensation and benefits are price for entry, while measures related to growth and internal environment can retain employees. Those include career development plan, exciting projects, leadership, organizational culture, recognition, work-life balance[3], interesting or challenging job itself.

Hewitt[4] also divides the rewards into extrinsic parts and intrinsic parts. The cash, pension, insurance, allowance, fund, or loans all belong to extrinsic rewards. Quality of work, culture, work-life balance, and some special recognition are defined as intrinsic rewards.

In some organizations, employees are encouraged to discuss with the leaders about the ways which can really motivate them. There are always internal drivers such as the opportunity of directing and influencing others, having more control on their own jobs, receiving appreciation or recognition, feeling the healthy balance between work and life and so on. On the other side, besides tangible rewards like bonus, external training courses, off site team building activities etc, there are external factors including opportunity to work with new people, variation in daily work, freedom from control, flexible working hours, public praise at staff meetings, team events where failures are openly shared...

Box 6-1

Internal Drivers and External Drivers

Internal Drivers
— directing and influencing others
— getting my arguments through
— having a high degree of control
— organizing the efforts of others to achieve the goal of the organization
— competition
— performing well in discussions and conflict
— responsibilities
— positive feedback
— personal interaction
— being appreciated
— proving myself
— complexity
— avoiding projects with high possibility of failure
— social harmony
— keeping friendly relationships with a high amount of trust

External Drivers
— teamwork
— sympathy to personal problems
— social events
— open office environment
— variation in daily work
— tight deadlines
— freedom from control
— clear work procedures
— bonus
— celebration

- small gratification (e. g. lunch, flowers)
- peer coaching[5]
- recognition posted on internal bulletin boards
- presenting to others
- job swap
- team events for practice sharing

Money is so important, but it can't replace other things people also in great need of. David in a well known IT company receives phone calls from head hunters every month with salary offers higher than his current level. He seldom considers the external opportunities simply because he has interesting new projects to do every time he finishes the previous one. He gets to know more and more people, and they all like working with him. "Everyday when I walk into the office, I expect to greet many lovely friends. We sometimes get together after work too. I don't need more money, but I can't lose my friends."

Someone may say: "Ok, he's got enough money, but I don't, so I need the money." Thinking about something else besides money, then you'll find some you need as well, although the external or internal drivers are probably different from those of others, but there should be some items on your wish list besides money.

Different people have different motivation, and the same person will be motivated by different things when he walks through different stages, which can be explained by Maslow's Hierarchy of Needs. That also reminds our leaders to frequently talk with the employees in order to understand their latest status and need so that there can be effective motivation.

Box 6-2

Maslow's Hierarchy of Needs

Abraham Maslow, a famous American professor in psychology. The Hierarchy of Needs model was developed between 1943 – 1954, and first widely published in *Motivation and Personality* in 1954.

At this time the model comprised five needs. The bottom one is physiological needs, then safety needs, love and belongingness needs, self-esteem needs and

> finally the need for self-actualization. In Maslow's most popular book "Toward a Psychology of Being" (1968), more layers of needs were added. However, the original five-layer-version still remains for most people.
>
> There are some limitations of the model.
> — In reality, people don't work necessarily one by one through these levels. They are much less structures in the way they satisfy their needs.
> — Different people with different cultural backgrounds and in different situations may have different hierarchies of need.
>
> Other researchers claim that other needs are also significant or even more significant. See McClelland, who identified needs for achievement, affiliation and power.

Apart from those tailor-made motivation solutions[6], there is also something in common. We may have found that giving verbal recognition is very effective to motivate one's morale. It is actually a proven format for giving sincere appreciation. The key is that we express the gratitude not just for what have been done, but also how it has been done because of his or her personal factors.

First, tell the person what you want to thank him or her for. For example: "Joan, what I really appreciate about you is that you're very proactive."

Then you give evidence, which is what she has done. You say, "You collect the needed information from different parties very quickly although you're new to this project. We manage to complete the project just in time."

The final step is an open question for her to demonstrate more of her competency. "How did you successfully identify all of the people you should turn to? I think we can all learn from you." Do you feel the difference? By asking these probing questions, the speaker emphasizes the appreciation again, and gives more time to Joan to absorb this gratitude. Furthermore, it's more sincere, not only Joan but others presenting feel the same. Even more important to a team, the good practice can be shared so that all can be stronger in dealing with similar cases, and the team required values are communicated vividly by this "thank you".

Cost saving has been a focus to many companies especially in tough time. When the layoff, salary freeze, and reduction on training happen frequently during the economic crisis, how should we retain the good employees? Try to find those intangible reward solutions.

Unit 6　Intangible Reward

Vocabulary

performer	n.	履行者，执行者，完成任务的人
potential	n.	有潜力的人
traditionally	ad.	按照传统地
compensation	n.	薪酬
souvenir	n.	纪念品，礼品
entitlement	n.	应得的权利
mindset	n.	心态，想法
motivate	v.	激发，促动
completion	n.	完成
mitigate	v.	减少，减轻，缓和
motive	n.	动机，动因
pursue	v.	追求，奉行
leadership	n.	领导能力，领导权
organizational	a.	组织的
interaction	n.	相互作用，互动
recognition	n.	认可，褒奖
extrinsic	a.	外在的
intrinsic	a.	内在的
pension	n.	养老金
allowance	n.	津贴
variation	n.	变化，变动
complexity	n.	复杂性，复杂状态
harmony	n.	和谐
teamwork	n.	团队工作，协调工作
sympathy	n.	同情
deadline	n.	最后期限，截止日期
gratification	n.	使人满足或喜悦的事物
peer	n.	同辈的人，同级别的人，同事，伙伴
swap	n.	互换，调换

hierarchy	n.	层次，层级，等级
psychology	n.	心理学
physiological	a.	生理的，生理上的
belongingness	n.	归属
self-esteem	n.	自尊
self-actualization	n.	自我实现
limitation	n.	限制，局限性
affiliation	n.	亲密关系
competency	n.	能力，胜任
emphasize	v.	强调
vividly	ad.	生动地，鲜明地

1. **Two Factor Theory 双因素理论**

   又叫激励保健理论（Motivator-Hygiene Theory），是美国行为科学家弗雷德里克·赫茨伯格（Fredrick Herzberg）提出来的，也称为"双因素激励理论"。20 世纪 50 年代末期，赫茨伯格和他的助手们在美国匹兹堡地区对 200 名工程师、会计师进行了调查访问。访问主要围绕两个问题：在工作中，哪些事项是让他们感到满意的，并估计这种积极情绪持续多长时间；又有哪些事项是让他们感到不满意的，并估计这种消极情绪持续多长时间。赫茨伯格以对这些问题的回答为材料，着手去研究哪些事情使人们在工作中快乐和满足，哪些事情造成不愉快和不满足。结果他发现，使职工感到满意的都是属于工作本身或工作内容方面的；使职工感到不满的，都是属于工作环境或工作关系方面的。他把前者叫做激励因素，把后者叫做保健因素。

2. **Mercer's Total Reward Strategy concept 美世公司的总体报酬体系**

   美世人力资源咨询公司（William Mercer）是世界上分布最广的人力资源管理咨询机构，总部位于美国纽约。其历史可以追溯到 1937 年的美国威达信集团公司（Marsh & McLennan Company）的一个部门。1959 年，威达信集团兼并了 William M. Mercer 有限公司（这是一家由 William Manson Mercer 于 1945 年在加拿大成立的公司）后，开始采用"美世"这个名字。美世独创了 TRS（Total Reward Strategy）

整体报酬体系。TRS 整体报酬体系不同于任何"传统"的工资或福利调查，它是一个独特的体系，提供人力资源专家所需的工资和福利数据，结合咨询要素和定制软件来确保客户全年使用。该项服务是一个全球项目，对 40 个国家进行调查，包括中国的 13 个城市。

3　work-life balance　工作与生活之间的平衡

4　Hewitt　翰威特

翰威特（Hewitt Associates LLC）是全球最大的综合性人力资源管理咨询公司之一，成立于 1940 年，总部位于美国伊利诺伊州，现已在 37 个国家开设 82 家分公司，拥有 12 000 多名员工。

5　peer coaching　同事之间的互相指导

6　tailor-made motivation solution　量身定制的激励方案

I Please answer the following questions according to the text.

1. What is intangible reward?
2. Why did the author say that tangible rewards are short-term motivators?
3. Is money the most important reward? Why?
4. Why does David seldom consider the external job opportunities?
5. How should companies retain the good employees during economic crisis?

II Please explain the following terms and phrases in English.

tangible reward　　　　organizational culture　　　　extrinsic reward
intrinsic reward　　　　internal driver　　　　　　　　external driver
effective motivation　　verbal recognition　　　　　　salary freeze

III Please read the following statements carefully and give your choice: True or False.

1. Traditionally most rewards are intangible.
2. The more people get, the more they develop an entitlement mindset.
3. Money can always motivate employees to produce higher performance.

4. Receiving appreciation or recognition, freedom from control are internal drivers.
5. Flexible working hours, public praise at staff meetings are external drivers.
6. Money can't replace other things people also in great need of.
7. The Hierarchy of Needs model was first widely published in *Motivation and Personality* in 1944.
8. Cost saving has been a focus to many companies especially in tough time.

IV Please translate the following paragraphs into Chinese.

1. Working in-groups may sometimes be time-consuming and unproductive, but there are also some tangible and intangible rewards that we benefit from. When you think of tangible rewards, you think of something you can see and feel. In a group environment, tangible rewards like merchandise and travel, the target group has the opportunity to see them and feel them and therefore form an emotional attachment to them.

2. Cash—unfortunately for those companies that attempt to motivate with it—is the least lasting type of reward, because it's typically confused with other compensation and therefore forgotten. That's the typical view of most call centre managers. However, this is not a question that's always 100% clear.

3. While money can be an important way of letting workers know their worth to the company, it tends not to be a sustaining motivational force to most individuals. In other words, salary raises and bonuses are nice, but they seldom motivate people to do their best on the job on an ongoing basis. Daily excitement for people's work is influenced more by how they are treated in the workplace-that is, by the softer side of management more than by what they are paid.

4. Money also has limitations as a motivator because in most organizations performance reviews-and corresponding raises-occur annually. To inspire employees, managers must recognize achievements and progress toward goals much more frequently than once a year. In fact, recognizing and rewarding performance should take place on a daily ba.

5. Intangible reward means non-monetary reward for performance; not always requiring recognition of others. An example is when the sales manager gives the salesperson recognition by a "pat on the back" to show appreciation for a job well done.

V Please do the following oral exercises with your partner.

1. Compare tangible reward with intangible reward.
2. Discuss Maslow's hierarchy of needs.

PART III

Performance Management

绩效管理

Unit 7

Implement a Successful Performance Management Process

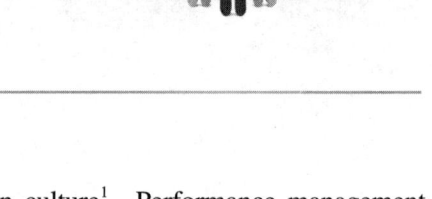

Many companies are promoting performance driven culture[1]. Performance management is perhaps one of the most effective management tools in different businesses. However it also universally understood that both managers and employees dread the performance appraisal[2] process for dozens of reasons.

Box 7-1

What Is Performance Management?

In their definitive text, Armstrong and Baron define performance management as "a process which contributes to the effective management of individuals and teams in order to achieve high levels of organizational performance. As such, it establishes shared understanding about what is to be achieved and an approach to leading and developing people which will ensure that it is achieved". They go on to stress that it is "a strategy which relates to every activity of the organization set in the context of its human resource policies, culture, style and communications systems. The nature of the strategy depends on the organizational context and can vary from organization to organization."

In other words performance management should be:
- strategic—it is about broader issues and longer-term goals;
- integrated—it should link various aspects of the business, people management, and individuals and teams.

It should incorporate:
- performance improvement—throughout the organization, for individual, team and organizational effectiveness;

Unit 7 Implement a Successful Performance Management Process

> - development—unless there is continuous development of individuals and teams, performance will not improve;
> - managing behavior—ensuring that individuals are encouraged to behave in a way that allows and fosters better working relationships.

Let's first hear the voice of employees.

"It's time consuming. I have pretty things to do in the year end. I can't afford the time!"

"My manager simply doesn't know the truth. They score just based on their gut feeling."

"My manager has never said anything that I should correct, but he eventually told me that I was performing not to the standard!"

"The KPIs[3] don't fit my job. How could I be evaluated that way?"

"It's unfair that I should be compared with a more experienced colleague."

"I don't know what to do, neither does my leader."

"What's the difference? No matter the score is good or bad, we have the same pay."

There are more to come if we have enough time and patience, and those concerns can never be completely eliminated in large and complicated companies. OnPoint Consulting surveyed United States managers and human resource professionals about their performance management systems. 56% of line mangers believe their performance management processes are not valuable. Only 43% agree that the performance management programs helps employees build their skills and competencies. 45% think it is consistently applied across the company. 45% say that it uses a rating scale that enables managers to differentiate levels of performance accurately. Less than 40% managers think it helps to build a high performance culture, or provides useful data for succession planning[4] or leadership development initiatives.

We have to admit that there isn't any perfect performance management system especially in this dynamic and complicated business world. However when we analyze the typical problems around the performance appraisal system, we can divide them into a few categories, and prepare the prevention approaches in advance so that we can mitigate the negative impact of the performance management tool and ease our life.

Generally there are problems found in the performance management system itself, or the people involved, or the implementation process. The specific problem can relate to just one category, or two or all the categories. Therefore the prevention approaches should be considered based on the whole performance management system.

The objective is the foundation of any performance management system.

If an employee says that he doesn't know what he should be appraised at the year end, then he should be asked first "what are you doing here for?" That problem probably lies on the sides of people and process. Leaders although know clearly what objectives they have set for the employees, they doesn't think there is the need to communicate with the employees. They take it for granted that the employees of course know their objectives.

Another common mistake is the alignment between the personal objectives and the organizational objectives. The failure of this alignment caused by either the lack of communication or the real existence of being not relevant makes employees lose the purpose and motivation for working hard to achieve excellent performance.

Many people also found during the performance appraisal interviews[5] that they just can't evaluate the past performance because some KPIs listed are out of date. Then there will be discussion or most likely disagreement first about the right objectives to be evaluated.

In order to combat those problems related to objective setting, we can, on people side, train the people about how to set SMART[6] objectives, and on process side, highlight the importance of objective setting as the right foundation for a effective performance management system. An easy way to bring more awareness to people about the objective setting step is just to separate the objective setting from the performance appraisal process on schedule. The objective setting for the coming year can be completed before current year end, while the performance appraisal for current year starts from the beginning of next year. By this approach, managers and employees can focus on the objective setting when they don't have to care the sensitive scores and constructive feedbacks.

The performance interview[7] sometimes is the most dreadful part in the performance management cycle.

Some young managers tend to wait till the appraisal time to tell the employee that she has been doing not so well. They are afraid to tell the truth to their subordinates when they spot the problems. They think that may hurt the feelings of the employees and the employees may do worse. The reality is the employees are overwhelmed by surprise during the appraisal interview, and they think they originally should have the opportunities to improve their performance. "Why don't you tell me earlier?" is the common response from a surprised and angry employee.

Some managers talk a lot during the appraisal interview, and then ask the employees to agree with him. Some employees feel uncomfortable to express their ideas in front of the dominating manager especially in this sensitive occasion. They then choose to agree whatever the manager believes. It looks like a cozy and productive interview until the manager in some time later is surprised by the negative feedback, worse performance or sudden leave from the same person. "Why don't you tell me earlier?" now is the voice from the manager.

When giving scores, managers sometimes tend to give high scores to all the objectives to an employee who is actually doing excellent on just one item. That's a kind of Halo Effect[8]. Sometimes manager feel rather comfortable to score all his team members around the middle point in spite of the different performance. The latter one can greatly damage the morale of the team. The excellent ones will feel unfair, the average ones will tease the situation, while the under-performing[9] ones will not improve. Soon the overall team performance will get down.

These problems can be solved by training programs. Both managers and employees should be trained on the proper behaviors during the interviews with perhaps different focuses. The lessons and best practices can be shared so that common mistakes are to be avoided with the right mindset and skills.

Follow-up is as important as the performance appraisal in the whole performance management system.

Some employee think performance appraisal is just formality, a waste of time. They see no difference if there isn't the appraisal at all. People get same salary increase, have same job assignment, no recognition or punishment. "Why should we make a fuss about it?"

Of course there are managers who feel the same. They don't know or care what they should do with all the scores and comments in hand. They're happy about the finish of this trouble work, and return to the daily work they are used to and without further thinking.

In fact performance appraisal is nothing if there is no proper follow-up. The performance appraisal system itself should consist of follow up actions as an integral part. The follow up actions may be action plans for performance improvement, the learning solution for personal development, the consequences caused by poor performance, etc. Managers should be trained to work with employees on the different follow-up actions. Which competencies are determining the performance? How should we bridge the performance gap? Is certain training course useful? What if the employee still misses the performance target? What reward should a star employee get?

Besides these immediate and individual follow-up, the company should also analyze the performance data of the whole organization and generate a company wide action plan to improve organizational performance. This could be the strengthening of training on objective setting because many not SMART objectives are found in the spot check. This could be the best practices sharing on regular performance review because some teams find it's hard for them to collect enough performance date at the year-end review[10]. This could be a general workshop to introduce the updates of the performance appraisal systems. They can take place before or after the performance appraisal. There is no restriction that we educate our staff on performance management only around the performance appraisal schedule.

Like what we require our managers to do—regularly review the team performance, we should reflect our performance management system from time to time, and before the real problem emerges. The system itself may have some problems, but more often the people and process side are what we have done wrong or haven't done enough. So don't just change or technically speak of update the performance management system when there is a performance problem. Look at the system, the people, and the implementation process all together to find the root cause.

Vocabulary

drive	v.	驱使，驱动
culture	n.	文化
universally	ad.	一般地，普遍地
dread	a.	害怕，担心
appraisal	n.	评价，鉴定
definitive	a.	明确的，确定的
strategic	a.	战略性的
integrated	a.	整体的，整合的
incorporate	a.	结合，合并
continuous	a.	连续的，不间断的
pretty	a.	很多的
score	v.	记分，评分
gut	a.	简单的，直觉的
eventually	ad.	最后，终于
experienced	a.	有经验的

Unit 7　Implement a Successful Performance Management Process

patience	n.	耐心
concern	n.	担忧，关切，关心的问题
eliminate	v.	消除，淘汰
complicated	a.	结构复杂的
valuable	a.	有价值的
consistently	ad.	一致地，协调地，不矛盾地
scale	n.	尺度
differentiate	v.	区别，区分
accurately	ad.	准确地
succession	n.	继任
initiative	n.	第一步，着手
especially	ad.	特别，尤其
dynamic	a.	动态的
category	n.	类别，类型
prevention	n.	预防
ease	v.	使轻松
involved	a.	有关的，相关的
appraise	v.	评价，鉴定
communicate	v.	交流，沟通，传达
alignment	n.	结合，组合
existence	n.	存在
combat	v.	搏斗，与……斗争
highlight	v.	突出显示，强调
awareness	n.	明白，了解
sensitive	a.	敏感的
constructive	a.	积极的，建设性的
dreadful	a.	可怕的
subordinate	n.	下级，下属
originally	ad.	原本，起初
uncomfortable	a.	不安的，不自在的
cozy	a.	舒适的，惬意的

tease	v.	取笑
proper	a.	正常的，适当的
formality	n.	形式，俗套
assignment	n.	分配，指定，委派，任务
punishment	n.	惩罚
fuss	n.	忙乱，小题大做
integral	a.	完整的，缺一不可的
improvement	n.	改进，进步，提高
consequence	n.	后果，影响
reflect	v.	反映
emerge	v.	出现，显露
technically	ad.	技术上，学术上
update	v.	更新，升级，使适应新形势

1. performance driven culture 绩效驱动的文化，指企业文化以提高绩效为总目标和推动力。
2. performance appraisal 绩效考核，绩效考评
3. KPIs 关键业绩指标（Key Performance Indications）
   KPI 是通过对组织内部某一流程的输入端、输出端的关键参数进行设置、取样、计算、分析，衡量流程绩效的一种目标式量化管理指标，是把企业的战略目标分解为可运作的远景目标的工具，是企业绩效管理系统的基础。KPI 是现代企业中受到普遍重视的业绩考评方法。
4. succession planning 继任计划，继任规划
5. performance appraisal interview 绩效考评面谈
   绩效考评面谈是在整项工作完成之后，根据下属绩效计划的贯彻执行情况，对其工作表现和工作业绩进行全面回顾、总结和评估，并将结果及相关信息反馈给员工。
6. SMART 目标管理原则
   SMART 分别代表 5 个以 S、M、A、R、T 开头的英文单词，但不同学者对这 5 个单

Unit 7 Implement a Successful Performance Management Process

词有不同的表述，但这 5 个字母所代表的中文含义一般都翻译为：S——明确性，M——可衡量性，A——可实现性，R——相关性，T——时效性。

7 performance interview 绩效面谈
绩效面谈是现代绩效管理工作中非常重要的环节。通过绩效面谈实现上级主管和下属之间对于工作情况的沟通和确认，找出工作中的优势及不足，并制定相应的改进方案。绩效面谈可以按发生的时间和内容分为三类，即初期的绩效计划面谈、进行中的绩效指导面谈、末期的绩效考评面谈。

8 Halo Effect 晕轮效应，光环效应
这是心理学术语，指对个人的总体评价成为了狭隘的对于某些特定特征的评判，这些特定特征就像月亮的光环一样，向周围弥漫、扩散，从而掩盖了其他的特征。

9 under-performing 业绩不达标
10 year-end review 年终检查，年终考核

I Please answer the following questions according to the text.

1. What is performance management?
2. Why do employees dread the performance appraisal process?
3. Why do managers dread the performance appraisal process?
4. What are the typical problems around the performance appraisal system?
5. Why is follow-up as important as the performance appraisal in the whole performance management system?

II Please explain the following terms and phrases in English.

management tool	performance appraisal process	performance improvement
managing behavior	implementation process	personal objective
organizational objective	performance gap	performance target

III Please read the following statements carefully and give your choice: True or False.

1. Many companies are promoting profit driven culture.

2. Performance management is perhaps one of the most effective management tools.
3. There isn't any perfect performance management system especially in the world.
4. The problems found in the performance management system are only relating to the implementation process.
5. The method is the foundation of any performance management system.
6. The performance interview sometimes the most dreadful part in the performance management cycle.
7. Some young managers are very glad to tell the truth to their subordinates when they spot the problems.
8. Follow-up is as important as the performance appraisal in the whole performance management system.

IV Please translate the following paragraphs into Chinese.

1. Performance management is the systematic process by which an agency involves its employees, as individuals and members of a group, in improving organizational effectiveness in the accomplishment of agency mission and goals.
2. In effective organizations, managers and employees have been practicing good performance management naturally all their lives, executing each key component process well. Goals are set and work is planned routinely. Progress toward those goals is measured and employees get feedback. High standards are set, but care is also taken to develop the skills needed to reach them. Formal and informal rewards are used to recognize the behavior and results that accomplish the mission.
3. Managing performance facilitates the effective delivery of strategic and operational goals. There is a clear and immediate correlation between using performance management programs or software and improved business and organizational results. For employee performance management, using integrated software, rather than a spreadsheet based recording system, may deliver a significant return on investment through a range of direct and indirect sales benefits, operational efficiency benefits and by unlocking the latent potential in every employees work day.
4. Performance management (PM) includes activities to ensure that goals are consistently being met in an effective and efficient manner. Performance management can focus on the performance of an organization, a department, employee, or even the processes to build a product or service, as well as many other areas.
5. Carrying out the processes of performance management provides an excellent

Unit 7 Implement a Successful Performance Management Process

opportunity to identify developmental needs. During planning and monitoring of work, deficiencies in performance become evident and can be addressed. Areas for improving good performance also stand out, and action can be taken to help successful employees improve even further.

V Please do the following oral exercises with your partner.

1. Discuss performance management process.
2. Play the parts of the manager and the employee in a performance appraisal interview.

Unit 8

What Should We Appraise?

Performance appraisal, as a method and process to identify, evaluate and develop individual performance, is a very important part of the performance management system, and is critical to the performance improvement of the organization as a whole. Different companies may have different appraisal systems measuring various items about the performance related items.

> **Box 8-1**
>
> ### Performance Appraisal
>
> A performance appraisal, employee appraisal, performance review is a method by which the job performance of an employee is evaluated (generally in terms of quality, quantity, cost, and time) typically by the corresponding manager or supervisor.
>
> A performance appraisal is a part of guiding and managing career development. It is the process of obtaining, analyzing, and recording information about the relative worth of an employee to the organization. Performance appraisal is an analysis of an employee's recent successes and failures, personal strengths and weaknesses, and suitability for promotion or further training. It is also the judgement of an employee's performance in a job based on considerations other than productivity alone.
>
> Generally, the aims of a performance appraisal are to:
> - give employees feedback on performance;
> - identify employee training needs;

> - document criteria used to allocate organizational rewards;
> - form a basis for personnel decisions—salary increases, promotions, disciplinary actions, bonuses, etc.;
> - provide the opportunity for organizational diagnosis and development;
> - facilitate communication between employee and administration;
> - improve performance through counseling, coaching and development.

The evaluation about the accomplishment of objectives set in the beginning of the year is the most popular item in any appraisal system. In this part, the actual historic performance usually in the past year is compared against the set targets. Managers and employees focus on the conclusion whether the past performance has missed, met, or exceeded the bar. This is also the part painful for many staff and supervisors. The staff are asked to present strong evidence to prove their past performance to be satisfactory, while the supervisor is to discuss with them about the figures and comments, and to provide both positive and negative feedback.

Sometimes there is disagreement about the actual performance. One reason is that some objectives were not SMART when they were set. A good objective is required to be Specific, Measurable, Achievable, Relevant, and Time related. Without those qualities, the objective is just something in written but hard to stick to, hence no way to be reasonably measured at the end of the year. Another quite common problem is that leaders regard the performance appraisal review meeting as the only suitable occasion to review performance. So they wait till the appraisal day and seriously point out to the staff that his/her performance is under the standard. The staff is of course shocked and asked "why don't you tell me earlier?" Regular review during the performance management cycle can greatly reduce that risk. Immediate feedback on poor performance is also a good approach. The year-end appraisal meeting is the very formal one, which presents the conclusion. However it's not the only element in the performance appraisal process.

We all know that it's impossible to quantify all the measurements, therefore sometimes when we evaluate the leadership or ethics, we use behavioral languages. Leaders are required to set clear goals to their team members, to monitor the progress regularly, to solve problems with certain ambiguity, to select right people for right positions, to reward good performance. Those behaviors behind the performance target showed in hard figures are in fact the major reason for the result. Therefore why not just appraise those behaviors and hence highlight the importance of those leadership characteristics which is equally important as the hard data?

Considering the behaviors of employee with no leadership roles, the ethics or the values promoted in the company can be evaluated during the performance appraisal process. Those ethics or values are the foundation for a company to compete in the fast changing world. Employees without enough buy in[1] to those properties are generally not engaged, and are under performing.

What we've mentioned including objectives, leadership, and ethics are all evaluated based on past facts. A successful performance management system should consist of both reflection about the history and aspiration about the future. Instead of putting a full stop after the scores, there should be remedy plan for the poor performance as a follow up to the past performance and a deliberate development plan for all to improve future performance of the whole organization.

The follow up to the past performance is quite necessary. Underperformers bring negative impact to the organization on culture and morale besides the daily performance loss. If the organization has slow respond to underperformers or even shows no differentiation to them from the stars, or inconsistent actions toward them, the poor performance of these few underperforming staff will become the new office norm and culture. An action plan agreed by both the supervisor and the underperformer defines the detailed steps to be taken in certain time frame (say three months), and the following action upon the outcome of this three-month remedy plan. Some underperformers return to the right track with the support from the team and of course their own efforts, some others may leave the company under such pressure. Whatever the case is, the lost productivity is restored, and the company saves the unjustified cost hence benefits the bottom line.

This kind of penalty system shouldn't be abused and should always be implemented on fact base with reasonable care to avoid the potential legal exposure or the damage to organization morale. Penalizing employees for using benefits is not a wise choice. Some leaders think that an employee on sick leave is less productive. Female colleagues returning from maternity leave sometimes find themselves to be ranked much lower than before. That's may sound logical, but it isn't. Staff shouldn't be penalized for taking sick leave[2] or vacation time. After all, employees with higher salaries are not necessarily expected to work longer hours. What should be penalized is the abusing of benefits.

The remedy and penalty are aimed to educate staff from wrong to right, while the personal development plan is the action plan directing them from good to better.

Generally the improvement plan is discussed and agreed between the employee and the supervisor. The aim of this personal development plan could be an even better performance in current role, or the necessary qualification for the new role wanted. When there is the gap between the desired result and the current status, there should be the action plans called personal development plan. The plan should have certain focuses generally within 3 targets to guarantee enough attention and efforts affordable by either the person or her supervisor. Therefore prioritizing is a must when evaluation all the solutions.

To be as specific as possible is also required in personal development plan setting. They are actually development objectives, therefore SMART also applies to them. Just that many leaders and employees don't pay enough attention to them, thinking those development objectives not so important as the performance objectives which is to be scored from 1 to 5.

An example for the meaningless development plan is not specific. Managers found that many staff should improve their communication skills. If that's the only conclusion, then it fails to provide tangible direction like: Which communication skills? How much improvement is needed? Through which approaches? Communication is a broad concept. Communication can be effective only through a series of steps. And it consists of different skill modules such as attentive listening, clear and succinct articulation, response to conflict, and public speaking ability and so on. Therefore the specific behavior flaw which makes the employee perform not up to the standard should be identified as "not to raise questions to clarify understanding". Then actions can be first a very relevant training course about the concept of communication, the information flow during the communication, the negative impact of less effective communication, and necessary skills to ensure the communication quality. Therefore from both mindset and behavior side, the employee has the opportunity to improve. After a few months practices, the leader can collect multi-source feedback about this specific behavior, then the improvement can be identified.

Further to the personal development plan, the preliminary talent identification is done in performance appraisal process in some of the companies. For those employees who have set their development plan to achieve higher level position, it's very natural that the leaders and the company consider and monitor the progress regularly. The career advancement can be the leader's role (sometimes we call that a generalist role[3]) and a specialist role[4] as well.

One thing we must bear in mind is the perception of the employees about this identification. From the company side, the communication must be clear and consistent that there are not guaranteed promotion for those who are identified as talents or being promotable during the performance appraisal process. When there is the organizational need, those identified people will be placed on the priority list, but the others also get the chance to be included. This is a dynamic name list, and the promotion is to be decided based on many internal and external factors.

Finally it comes to the conclusion part. The score of past performance is of course included. However some leaders tend to record this as the only item or result after the performance appraisal process. Actually the positive feedback and improvement area should also be highlighted since they are as important as the score. Remember we are not only looking at the past, but more importantly referring to the past performance. We aim to improve the future performance so that we as a whole can have sustainable development. That should not only be presented on paper, but also be remembered by the leaders and the employees.

By including those comments, the conclusion is also a tailor made summary for the employee. That makes her feel proud of her achievement, and be comfortable on the following actions to be taken. In one word the performance appraisal process shouldn't be just formality, or a process full of argument and painful memories. It is a powerful management tool, if used properly, it can greatly improve productivity and morale for both individuals and the company as a whole.

Vocabulary

appraisal	n.	评价，考核，鉴定
corresponding	a.	相应的，对应的
analyze	v.	分析
weakness	n.	弱点，缺点，短处，劣势
suitability	n.	适合，适宜，相配
disciplinary	a.	纪律性的
diagnosis	n.	诊断，判断
facilitate	v.	使便利，促进
counsel	v.	商议，劝导
accomplishment	n.	完成，履行
bar	n.	标准，合格线
ambiguity	n.	含糊，意义不明确
property	n.	性质，特征
aspiration	n.	渴望，志愿，抱负

Unit 8　What Should We Appraise?

deliberate	a.	深思熟虑的
underperformer	n.	考核不合格的员工
differentiation	n.	区别，不同，差异化
inconsistent	a.	不一致的，不符合的
underperforming	a.	表现不合格的
penalize	v.	使处于不利地位，处罚
exposure	n.	暴露，曝光，承受风险
maternity	n.	产假
qualification	n.	资格，资质
communication	n.	交流，沟通
module	n.	测量单位，系数，模量
preliminary	a.	预备的，初级的
generalist	n.	通才，知识渊博者，多面手
specialist	n.	专家，专业人才，精通某一专业的人
identification	n.	识别，鉴定
priority	n.	优先，优先权

1　buy in　本意为"买入、买进（证券）"，此处指"认可，接受"。
2　take sick leave　请病假
3　generalist role　通才职位（通常管理者需要的是通才，即知识面较为广泛的人才）
4　specialist role　专才职位（通常指某个专业领域的高级技术人才）

I　Please answer the following questions according to the text.

　　1. What is performance appraisal?

2. Which part of performance appraisal is painful for many staff and supervisors? Why?
3. How should a good objective be?
4. What should a successful performance management system consist of?
5. Why should the positive feedback and improvement area be highlighted?

II Please explain the following terms and phrases in English.

historic performance	positive feedback	actual performance
regular review	immediate feedback	poor performance
behavioral language	leadership role	organization morale

III Please read the following statements carefully and give your choice: True or False.

1. Performance appraisal is critical to the performance improvement of the organization as a whole.
2. Different companies have the same appraisal systems.
3. A good objective is required to be Smart, Measurable, Achievable, Relevant, and Time related.
4. Underperformers bring negative impact to the organization on culture and morale.
5. All underperformers return to the right track with the support from the team and their own efforts.
6. An employee on sick leave is less productive.
7. Staff shouldn't be penalized for taking sick leave or vacation time.
8. It's impossible to quantify all the measurements.

IV Please translate the following paragraphs into Chinese.

1. A common approach to assessing performance is to use a numerical or scalar rating system whereby managers are asked to score an individual against a number of objectives/attributes. In some companies, employees receive assessments from their manager, peers, subordinates, and customers, while also performing a self assessment. This is known as a 360-degree appraisal and forms good communication patterns.

2. As a distinct and formal management procedure used in the evaluation of work performance, appraisal really dates from the time of the Second World War—not more than 60 years ago. Yet in a broader sense, the practice of appraisal is a very

ancient art. In the scale of things historical, it might well lay claim to being the world's second oldest profession!

3. In many organizations (but not all), appraisal results are used, either directly or indirectly, to help determine reward outcomes. That is, the appraisal results are used to identify the better performing employees who should get the majority of available merit pay increases, bonuses, and promotions.

4. Performance appraisal systems began as simple methods of income justification. That is, appraisal was used to decide whether or not the salary or wage of an individual employee was justified. The process was firmly linked to material outcomes. If an employee's performance was found to be less than ideal, a cut in pay would follow. On the other hand, if their performance was better than the supervisor expected, a pay rise was in order.

5. A performance appraisal, employee appraisal, or performance review is a method by which the job performance of an employee is evaluated (generally in terms of quality, quantity, cost, and time) typically by the corresponding manager or supervisor. It is the process of obtaining, analyzing, and recording information about the relative worth of an employee to the organization. Performance appraisal is an analysis of an employee's recent successes and failures, personal strengths and weaknesses, and suitability for promotion or further training.

V Please do the following oral exercises with your partner.

1. Discuss performance appraisal system.
2. Imagine how you will feel if you are appraised as an underperformer in a company.

Unit 9

Make 360-degree Feedback More Effective

360-degree feedback[1] is also known as multi-rater feedback, which has been popular in the recently years and implemented in many Fortune 500[2] companies.

Box 9-1

360-degree Feedback

In human resources or industrial/organizational psychology, 360-degree feedback, also known as multi-rater feedback, multisource feedback, or multisource assessment, is feedback that comes from all around an employee. "360" refers to the 360 degrees in a circle, with an individual figuratively in the center of the circle. Feedback is provided by subordinates, peers, and supervisors. It also includes a self-assessment and, in some cases, feedback from external sources such as customers and suppliers or other interested stakeholders. It may be contrasted with "upward feedback[3]", where managers are given feedback by their direct reports, or a "traditional performance appraisal," where the employees are most often reviewed only by their managers.

The results from 360-degree feedback are often used by the person receiving the feedback to plan training and development. Results are also used by some organizations in making administrative decisions, such as pay or promotion. When this is the case, the 360-degree assessment is for evaluation purposes, and is sometimes called a "360-degree review". However, there is a great deal of controversy as to whether 360-degree feedback should be used exclusively for development purposes, or should be used for appraisal purposes as well. There is

Unit 9 Make 360-degree Feedback More Effective

> also controversy regarding whether 360-degree feedback improves employee performance, and it has even been suggested that it may decrease shareholder value.

It is a human resource intervention method that consists of feedback from the individual, her peers, superiors, subordinates, and customers. The feedback surveys are implemented to protect the confidentiality and the result is shared by the manager to help the individual to know how she is perceived by others. It's generally believed to be a highly effective evaluation tool for performance improvement and personal development.

By giving the individual feedback that might not usually be shared with her, HR blind spots[4] can be greatly reduced, which is quite essential for any change needed. She is able to set goals for to improve her performance and hence advances her career within the organization.

For a group of people working together, it's also a good way to have such feedback. The feedback can motivate others to change. A group's morale and effectiveness will improve dramatically after the members have had the opportunity to express freely and safely with honest, concrete and behavioral language.

The organization then of course is mostly benefited. Through the promotion of the common language from within, a signal can be send to employees about the wanted and expected behaviors, attitude, or working styles etc. The multi-source feedback system shows that all employees' opinions are important and actively sought. The exchange of valid information enhances work relationships and makes an organization more effective.

However there are many who doubt the benefits.

Tina, an experienced department head in a big multi-national company, was promoted when she was required to take charge of one more department. When the company launched the 360-degree feedback, she was very confident that she will get very favorable feedback because she has good reputation in the company and she believes she was leading a team very supportive to her. When the report was delivered to her, Tina opened the folder and had a very quick look. Then she turned to the cover to see if there was her name on the page. She was actually shocked. "Is that me?" After the doubt, then came the deep frustration. "How could they say that?"

She knew that sometimes she may make some people feel bad because of her differentiation on the star performers[5] and the poor performers. However that's the culture of the company and there was believed to be well communicated among all employees. Therefore she couldn't accept that it looked as if 2 or 3 respondents hated her, another 3 or 4 supported her absolutely, while others gave mixed views.

There should be only 2 or 3 negative feedback and all the rest were positive, as Tina previously expected. She wondered if she was still a good manager, and whether this would have any impact to her career development in the organization. Tina left the company one year later, which was regarded as an expensive talent loss by the top management of the company. There were other factors entered into that decision, but her experience with 360-degree feedback was definitely a major one.

Besides Tina, there were many more others who either think the 360-degree feedback as one of the HR tricks, or feel the risk of being betrayed by co-workers, or lose target after receiving contrary comments, or find it may be some tool for political games.

Dr. Johan Sullivan of San Francisco State University[6] says, "There is no data shows that the 360-degree feedback actually improves productivity, increases retention, decreases grievances or that it is superior to forced ranking[7] and standard performance appraisal systems. It sounds good but there is no proof it works other than a lot of companies have tried that."

Box 9-2

The Business Case for Forced Ranking

Forced ranking systems direct managers to evaluate their employees' performance against other employees, rather than the more common (and often grade inflated) measure of evaluating performance against pre-determined standards. The result of such a process is often brutally blunt: The top 20 percent of performers are amply rewarded, and the bottom 10 percent are shown the door.

Supporters such as former GE Chairman Jack Welch[8] argue that forced ranking creates a true meritocracy, while critics charge that a "rank and yank" approach is unfair to people performing at an acceptable level and creates an unhealthy cult-of-star[9] culture.

Unit 9　Make 360-degree Feedback More Effective

　　Forced ranking is the antidote to the problems of inflated rating and the failure to differentiate that many organizations have installed to help bring the truth into the performance management process.

　　By implementing a forced ranking procedure, organizations guarantee that managers will differentiate talent. While conventional performance appraisal systems may allow managers to inflate ratings and award Superior ratings to all, a forced ranking system ensures that distribution requirements will be met. Assuming that the system is wisely constructed and effectively executed, a forced ranking system can provide information that conventional performance appraisal systems can't.

　　But just ensuring differentiation, while valuable in itself, isn't the whole reason companies have gone to using forced ranking systems. Creating a forced ranking system forces a company to articulate the criteria that are required for success in the organization.

　　GE, for example, has identified its four Es (as the italics followed), the set of criteria it uses to rank its managers and executives: high *energy* level, the ability to *energize* others around common goals, the *edge* to make tough yes/no decisions, and the ability to consistently *execute* and deliver on promises. These criteria were determined over a period of several years and were the result of serious deliberation. Other companies have settled on different criteria. Some have used nothing more than "Good results, good behavior." Whatever the criteria the organization decides on, the deliberations that senior managers engage in determining these criteria help them to define and understand what they believe genuinely is important for success in the organization. The discussion of criteria often sparks significant, even boisterous, arguments about exactly what the measures and factors should be. There is value in this process even if no further action is taken. And simply knowing the criteria that senior executives use to assess talent increases the probability that organization members will alter their behavior in order to demonstrate more of the attributes that they now know will lead to success.

　　Based on the more and more practices in different companies, there are some tips for a more effective 360-degree feedback process.

At first, the individuals should have right attitude in giving and receiving feedback, and should own the responsibility of follow up.

It's understandable that people easily get defensive to negative feedback. The individuals should be aware that although the feedback sometimes seems to be not so objective, it does indicate what the individual is perceived by different people. Under some situations, what you are perceived is far more important than what you actually are. The gap between what the individual expects and receives provides the improvement space. The reflection and actions about the feedback then constitute the follow up plan.

When giving feedback, the behavioral language should be used instead of the description like "I think", "I feel", "they say". An easy tool here is the STAR method. That means you present a story by describing its Situation, Task, Action and Result so that it's more fact-based and more helpful.

The roles and responsibility of a manager in 360-degree feedback process is critical enough to determine it a success or a failure. The sufficient communication effectiveness, follow up support, and smooth implementation are the strong foundation of a valued 360-degree feedback process.

The manager must communicate clearly the purpose of this feedback and the benefits to the person receiving feedback. Also he or she should provide the feedback very tactfully with the good balance between non compromised confidentiality and the sound facts. Some recipients may ask to trace the source of the feedback for the defense purpose. If so the manager should bring them back to the right track in thinking the improvement area instead of the explanation for the specific story. Another side about the feedback is that the manager should not use this 360-degree feedback as the only way to assess one's behaviors. The direct communication between the manager and the individual is always needed, and can't be replaced by the multisource feedback.

The manager also should pay attention to the agreed improvement areas of the person. The person owns the action plans, and the manager can support him or her to realize it. Only with the follow up, the feedback system can be a meaningful learning process.

The implementation ownership generally lies in managers. According to the timetable and framework, managers should align their action with the guidelines so that the activities across the functions are consistent. The consistent format somewhat bring the sense of consistent mindset.

The managers and their subordinates can't implement a 360-degree feedback process

Unit 9 Make 360-degree Feedback More Effective

successfully without the right organization climate and guidance.

In a company that promoting open and two-way communication, it's more suitable for the implementation of 360-degree feedback. However even with such kind of company culture, employees are to be communicated to accept that the multi-source feedback is a tool for constructive opinions, and a system enhancing personal development.

The framework of the process should be designed to fit the company culture and management agenda. At first there should be a specific purpose. Generally performance improvement and personal career development are expected to benefit from the feedback system, but it is the development tool, and shouldn't be used as the evaluation tool for merit pay or promotion. Otherwise the feedback will be distorted by certain conflicts related to personal benefits. During the implementation process, the confidentiality should be emphasized and guaranteed by technology and logical actions to help people feel comfortable in giving constructive feedback. After all the employees get their feedback, there should be schedule for them to make follow up action plans. Also the company may evaluate the 360-degree feedback process effectiveness later when the comparison data is available.

Necessary training to managers and individuals are also part of the guidance the company should provide. The individuals should be trained on the skill in giving fact-based feedback, understanding the communication barriers, and encouraging themselves to face the dark side and be proactive in personal development. Managers should have additional courses on the right attitude towards information from multi sources, the necessary skill to keep confidentiality and protect the healthy feedback environment.

With the consistent mindset, careful practice and an open communication environment appreciating constructive feedback, the 360-degree feedback system can really add value to the development of the individuals and the organizations.

Vocabulary

intervention	n.	介入，干预
confidentiality	n.	保密，机密
administrative	a.	管理的，行政的
controversy	n.	争论，辩论，论战
dramatically	ad.	戏剧性地，引人注目地，剧烈地

concrete	a.	具体的，实际的
supportive	a.	支持的，赞许的
trick	n.	诡计，把戏
grievance	n.	不满，牢骚，悲叹
brutally	ad.	粗暴地，不讲理地，令人不快地
blunt	a.	钝的，呆板的，干脆的
meritocracy	n.	精英阶层
yank	n.	突然的猛拉
antidote	n.	解毒剂，矫正法
inflate	v.	使膨胀，使得意
energize	v.	加强，给以能量
boisterous	a.	狂风暴雨的，吵吵嚷嚷的
probability	n.	概率，可能性
understandable	a.	可理解的，容易理解的
tactfully	ad.	机智地，得体地，老练地，圆滑地
compromise	v.	妥协，折中
recipient	n.	接收者，感受者，接受者
trace	v.	追踪，追溯，追究
timetable	n.	时间表
align	v.	使结盟，使结合，使密切合作
distort	v.	扭曲，歪曲

1　360-degree feedback　360 度反馈
2　Fortune 500　财富 500 强
3　upward feedback　向上反馈
4　HR blind spot　人力资源管理中存在的盲点（盲区）
5　star performer　明星员工，业绩优秀的员工
6　San Francisco State University　旧金山州立大学

Unit 9 Make 360-degree Feedback More Effective

7 forced ranking   强制排名
8 Jack Welch   杰克·韦尔奇（通用电气公司前总裁）
9 cult-of-star   对星级的崇拜［指员工单纯追求名次（星级）］

I Please answer the following questions according to the text.

1. What is 360-degree feedback?
2. Why should the feedback surveys be implemented to protect the confidentiality?
3. What are the benefits of 360-degree feedback system?
4. What is the attitude of Dr. Johan Sullivan towards 360-degree feedback?
5. How could we make a 360-degree feedback process more effective?

II Please explain the following terms and phrases in English.

multi-rater feedback	feedback survey	evaluation tool
working style	multisource feedback	favorable feedback
negative feedback	contrary comment	political game

III Please read the following statements carefully and give your choice: True or False.

1. 360-degree feedback has been popular in many Fortune 500 companies.
2. 360-degree feedback is believed to be a highly effective evaluation tool for performance improvement.
3. No one doubts the benefits of 360-degree feedback.
4. 360-degree feedback is superior to forced ranking and standard performance appraisal systems.
5. There is no data the 360-degree feedback actually improves productivity.
6. People easily get defensive to negative feedback.
7. The manager must communicate clearly the purpose of this feedback and the benefits to the person giving feedback.
8. The feedback may be distorted by certain conflicts related to personal benefits.

IV Please translate the following paragraphs into Chinese.

1. Implemented with care and training to enable people to better serve customers and develop their own careers, 360 degree feedback is a positive addition to your performance management system. Started haphazardly, because it's the current flavor in organizations, or because "everyone" else is doing it, 360-degree feedback will create a disaster from which you will require months and possibly years, to recover.

2. 360-degree feedback is a method and a tool that provides each employee the opportunity to receive performance feedback from his or her supervisor and four to eight peers, reporting staff members, coworkers and customers. Most 360 degree feedback tools are also responded to by each individual in a self assessment.

3. 360 degree feedback allows each individual to understand how his effectiveness as an employee, coworker, or staff member is viewed by others. The most effective 360 degree feedback processes provide feedback that is based on behaviors that other employees can see.

4. When done properly, 360-degree feedback is highly effective as a development tool. The feedback process gives people an opportunity to provide anonymous feedback to a coworker that they might otherwise be uncomfortable giving. Feedback recipients gain insight into how others perceive them and have an opportunity to adjust behaviors and develop skills that will enable them to excel at their jobs.

5. Using a 360 degree feedback system for Performance Appraisal is a common practice, but not always a good idea. It is difficult to properly structure a 360-degree feedback process that creates an atmosphere of trust when you use it to measure performance.

V Please do the following oral exercises with your partner.

1. How can 360-degree feedback be used properly and effectively?
2. How will you feel if you receive negative feedbacks from your peers?

PART IV

Training Management

培训管理

Unit 10

To Start with Competency Modeling

Since the psychologist David McClelland[1] led the project to help the US Department of State identify the most suitable candidates for the diplomats in 1970's, the competency model[2] approach has been adopted by more than half of the Fortune 500 companies. More and more are catching up with the trend, with some of them do feel the need and the others simply would like to become the users of the fancy tool.

Box 10-1

What Is a Job Competency Model?

A job competency[3] model is a description of those competencies possessed by the top performers in a specific job or job family[4]. In effect, a competency model is a "blueprint for outstanding performance". Models usually contain 8 – 16 competencies with definitions, often grouped into "clusters" along with behavioral descriptors.

As an Individual, you can use job competency models to guide your own career development. Coupled with an accurate assessment of your own competencies, you will be able to identify competencies needing development and/or identify other jobs or careers that make better use of the competencies you possess.

As a leader in your organization, competency models and systems can help:
- improve the selection of people for jobs;
- develop skills and characteristics that lead to improved effectiveness and productivity;

Unit 10 To Start with Competency Modeling

- provide a consistent framework for HR applications;
- build alignment with organizational values and strategy.

There are many versions about what the competency really is. For Development Dimensions International (DDI)[5], the competencies can called as dimensions as well, and is defined as "Description of clusters or grouping of behaviors, motivations, and knowledge related to job success or failure under which data on motivation, knowledge, or behavior can be reliably classified."

Competencies are described as observable, measurable behaviors, but they are not simply concrete actions that are easily imitated. Instead, they can be manifestation of some underlying intent—driven by a person's basic motivations, personality, attitude, values, or self-concept. It is an enduring characteristic of a person that predicts behavior across many workplace situations.

The competency based human resources system is considered to be a good supplemental to the management system, with one objective is about "how" and the other is "what".

The focus on personal characteristics rather than the tasks, the concentration about outstanding performance rather than average performance also bring more interest to managers and human resources professionals.

Another reason is that competency can be a consistent base for all the other human resources applications or programs. The recruitment, performance management, learning and development, succession planning, talent management etc. can be set on the same sound base with competency as both evaluation criteria and development targets.

To set up the competency model in a company costs a lot of time, money and human resources. Generally the HR professionals are heavily involved in the process with or sometimes without the help from external consultants.

The first step in whatever case is the discussion with all stakeholders about:
- project background and objectives;
- work process and timeline;
- roles and responsibilities;
- company vision, mission, and values;
- short and long term business strategies;
- targeted outcomes.

Considering the objectives, a frequent met question is that whether we need to have an

HR application included in the phase one. Many organizations just build a competency model and then forget it. Or they still have it, but the competency model stands alone with no relation to other HR programs, which is absolutely a tool without any real value. With the intended HR application in our mind, e. g. for selection or development, we can monitor more accurately about the format of the model, and direct the following steps in the design process to the right track.

When there is an agreement on above items, the data collection should starts. Consultants and HR professionals always use a blend of approaches including focus group[6], critical event interview, generic competency dictionaries, and observation in action.

The focus group usually consists of job holder, the superior of the job holder, and training & development staff. Following a structured process, the group of people is to think systematically about the tasks and the personal attitude, skills, knowledge, and other characteristics needed for superior performance.

Critical event interviews with star performers will collect the answers about many in-depth questions to help the interviewer understand what competencies are needed for them to achieve the outstanding performance. The interviewers are required to be equipped with sound skill of probing strategy.

The generic competency dictionaries are conceptual frameworks of commonly encountered competencies and behavioral indicators. Generally there are twenty to forty competencies, each of which has five to fifteen behavioral indicators. It provides a general conceptual framework for the model building team to start with. Also the framework can be used as guidance to identifying the importance of a set of competencies in the focus group discussion or the critical event interview.

The method of observation in action is only suitable for some jobs, say cashier of the supermarket, call center clerk, etc. The needed behaviors and characteristics take place repetitively in a short time, and observation by the observer is very easy to be implemented during the working time.

The data can be collected by so many different ways. But how extensive should the data collection be? If the job is quite essential to the organization, if the budget for the project can afford, and if many HR applications are scheduled to be integrated with the competency model, more time is deserved to be put into the data collection period.

With the primary input, consultants and HR professionals will process the data, communicate with senior managers, and draft the competency lists and their proficiency stages. Furthermore, the competencies on the list are to be coded as behavioral descriptors and classified to fit the competency model structure based on the requirement agreed at the beginning of the project.

There are three major formats of behavioral descriptors. The most popular approach is the behavior indicators, which is the simplest one. Take "creative problem solving[7]" as an example. The competency is defined as the ability to apply lateral and analytical thinking and to seek alternative solutions for dilemmas and problem. The behavioral indicators are:

- challenging paradigms;
- leveraging diverse resources;
- thinking expansively;
- evaluating multiple solutions;
- encouraging innovation.

Box 10-2

What Is a Behavioral Indicator in an Assessment Centre?

A behavioral indicator is used in an assessment centre[8] to provide an objective description of the behavior that you might view from the candidate that provides evidence that they either have or do not have the competence that you are assessing. Behavioral indicators can therefore be positive or negative.

For example, if you were to assess the competence of "manages conflict well", having defined the actual competency to ensure it is fully understood by all assessors or observers, you would then need to produce a list of possible positive and negative behavioral indicators for this competency. In this example, some of the indicators might be:

• positive Behavioral Indicator—asks other people for their perspective, draws out the feeling of the group, listens to others before evaluating;

• negative Behavioral Indicator—makes decisions without considering the views of others, makes excessive "I" statements[9] rather than working towards satisfying mutual interests.

During the assessment or development centre, the assessors or observers will keep a list of which of these indicators arise and when; this will enable objective and easy scoring of the candidates on the competency under assessment.

The second method is to use evaluative competency levels. With this approach, a few key dimensions are identified for each competency, which is ranked in order of effectiveness. The highest level describes outstanding performance, and the lowest describes poor performance. The customer service clerk shows the highest level competency of understanding customer needs by "volunteer offer extra help", and lowest level by "don't listen to the inquiry of customers".

Another solution is to describe the extent to which a competency is required in a particular job. This is especially useful when the competency models are created for various positions in the company, and there is the need to compare the requirement of the different jobs for the sake of organizational analysis or the personal career planning. Let's look at the technical competency of Talent Management proficiency for HR professionals.

- The basic level requirement is "Understand the Talent Development Program process".
- The intermediate level asks for "Understand and apply the Leadership Pipeline to our Talent Development Program; proactively provide improvement suggestions in terms of Talent Management policy, process & administration."
- The advanced level is defined as "Develop and apply Talent Management principle, integrate both efforts of Succession Planning and Career Planning into Talent Management."

The draft competency models are then reviewed by senior managers and sometimes focus group, who provided most primary data. The revised competency set will finally be presented after consensus is reached among all stakeholders.

That is not the end of the process. Trainings should be delivered to users to know how to use the competency models in daily business, how to evaluate the proficiency level, and how to update the models. HR professionals may start to monitor the implementation of the competency model into other HR applications, and bear it in mind that a competency model alone doesn't mean anything but the waste of resources.

Box 10-3

Competency and Competence

You may find in your dictionary that the meanings of the above two words are the same. However, there are some people who believe that competency and

Unit 10 To Start with Competency Modeling

competence do not refer to the same thing.

They argue that: competency refers to the KSA (Knowledge, Skill, Attitude) that distinguish superior performers from average performers while competence is the ability to meet the basic requirements to perform a job or task. You are talking about the level of competence that a person has at a task when you use the word "competency".

Vocabulary

psychologist	n.	心理学家
diplomat	n.	外交官
fancy	a.	特别的，具有高度技巧性的
blueprint	n.	蓝图，设计图
cluster	n.	丛，组，团，群集
descriptor	n.	描述符号，描述者
version	n.	版本，说法
dimension	n.	维度
grouping	n.	集团，群集，编组
reliably	ad.	可靠地，确实地
observable	a.	可观察的，能观察到的
imitate	v.	模仿
manifestation	n.	表现，显示
underlying	a.	基础的，潜在的
intent	n.	意图，目的
self-concept	n.	自我概念，对自己的看法
enduring	a.	持久的，永久的
timeline	n.	时间表
vision	n.	愿景
mission	n.	使命
generic	a.	一般的，普通的

conceptual	a.	概念的，理论的
encounter	v.	遭遇，遇到
indicator	n.	指标，指示物
cashier	n.	收银员
supermarket	n.	超市
repetitively	ad.	反复地，重复地
extensive	a.	广泛的
deserved	a.	应当的，值得的
proficiency	n.	精通，熟练
lateral	a.	侧面的
analytical	a.	分解的，分析的
alternative	a.	替代的，可选的
dilemma	n.	困境
paradigm	n.	范例
leverage	v.	对……起杠杆作用
expansively	ad.	开阔地
intermediate	a.	中间的

1. David McClelland 大卫·麦克利兰（1917—1998，美国著名的社会心理学家，1987年获得美国心理学会杰出科学贡献奖）
2. competency model 能力模型
   也译作"胜任能力模型"或"员工素质能力模型"。国际知名企业大多基于能力模型构建培训体系，期望通过这种培训使员工胜任自己的工作。因此，建立能力模型是企业对员工进行培训的第一步。
3. job competency 工作能力，职业能力（也可用 occupational competency）
4. job family 一大类工作，属于同一类别的许多具体工作的集合
5. Development Dimensions International（DDI） 美商宏智国际顾问有限公司（成立于1970年，总部位于美国匹兹堡市，是国际知名咨询公司）

Unit 10 To Start with Competency Modeling

6 focus group 焦点小组讨论
这是一种通行的了解目标群体真实感受的方式，它也可以被理解为一种针对某一特定话题而进行的人数可控的定性讨论。这种方式有助于解决一些通过定量问卷无法得到反馈的问题，获得第一手的真实信息反馈。

7 creative problem solving 创造性地解决问题

8 assessment centre 评估中心（或评估中心方法）
一些企业或人力资源顾问公司会设立专门的评估中心进行人才测评，常见的评估方式是通过观察者对被评估者的行为进行观察而作出评估。在英文里，相应的人才测评方法也被称为 assessment centre。

9 "I" statements "我……" 的表述（即说话者只从自己的立场出发来进行表述）

I Please answer the following questions according to the text.

1. Why did the US Department of State need the help of a psychologist to identify the most suitable candidates for the diplomats?
2. Why did the author refer to the competency model approach as a fancy tool?
3. What is job competency?
4. How should we set up a competency model in a company?
5. Why does a competency model alone mean nothing?

II Please explain the following terms and phrases in English.

concrete action	basic motivation	workplace situation
personal characteristic	average performance	evaluation criteria
development target	behavior indicator	career planning

III Please read the following statements carefully and give your choice: True or False.

1. The US Department of State ask the help of a psychologist to identify the most suitable candidates for the diplomats in 1960s.
2. There are many versions about what the competency really is.

3. Competencies are not simply concrete actions that are easily imitated.
4. The competency based human resources system is considered to be a good supplemental to the management system.
5. Competency can be a consistent base for all the other human resources applications or programs.
6. To set up the competency model in a company costs little time and money.
7. Many organizations just build a competency model and then use it effectively.
8. A competency model alone doesn't mean anything but the waste of resources.

IV Please translate the following paragraphs into Chinese.

1. In every job, some people perform more effectively than others. Superior performers do their jobs differently and possess different characteristics, or "competencies", than average performers do. And the best way to identify the characteristics that predict superior performance is to study the top performers.
2. A competency is a personal characteristic (skill, knowledge, trait, motive) that drives behavior leading to outstanding performance. One of the examples of a competency is "conceptual thinking", defined as: finding effective solutions by taking a holistic, abstract or theoretical perspective.
3. Some scholars see "competence" as a combination of knowledge, skills and behavior used to improve performance; or as the state or quality of being adequately or well qualified, having the ability to perform a specific role. For instance, management competency might include systems thinking and emotional intelligence, and skills in influence and negotiation.
4. Competency has different meanings in different companies, and continues to remain one of the most diffuse terms in the management development sector, and the organizational and occupational literature.
5. The Occupational Competency movement was initiated by David McClelland in the 1960s with a view to moving away from traditional attempts to describe competency in terms of knowledge, skills and attitudes and to focus instead on the specific self-image, values, traits, and motive dispositions (i.e. relatively enduring characteristics of people) that are found to consistently distinguish outstanding from typical performance in a given job or role. It should be noted that different competencies predict outstanding performance in different roles, and that there is a limited number of competencies that predict outstanding performance in any given job or role.

Thus, a trait that is a "competency" for one job might not predict outstanding performance in a different role.

V Please do the following oral exercises with your partner.

1. Discuss the job competency of a qualified HR manager.
2. Talk something about your competency as a student.

Unit 11

Implementing the Four Levels Training Evaluation

Although it costs time and money to evaluate the training effectiveness, most companies are keen to have their training evaluation systems[1] so that the management will know whether certain training program should be continued, and how the program should be improved. Among those companies there are quite a lot of them using Kirkpatrick's four levels evaluation model[2].

The four levels are reaction, learning, behavior, and results. Reaction is Level 1. It evaluates to what degree the training participants react to the learning event. Level 2—learning—refers to the evaluation of the extent to which participants change their attitudes, or/and increase their skills and knowledge. Behavior as Level 3 measures the extent to which change in behavior occurred, i.e. to what degree participants apply what they learned during training when they are back on the job. Level 4—results—tends to know how the targeted outcomes have been achieved as the result of the learning event.

Level 1: Reaction

This level measurement is always presented in the form of a questionnaire asking how favorably the participants agree with several preset indicators about the training program facilitation. It is sometimes called the smiley sheet. Figure 11 – 1 is a simple sample of the sheet.

Please rate below items according to the defined scale.
5 Excellent   4 Good   3 Fair   2 To be improved   1 Poor

a) The course meets my expectation.
b) The trainer shows expertise in the subject.
c) The course materials are well prepared.
d) The course content can be applied in my job.
e) ...

Figure 11 – 1 A Sample of a Smiley Sheet

Besides the evaluation sheets, the face to face interview is also a direct way to gather the needed information. It is generally accepted that open questions should also be included in the questionnaire or interview to get detailed comments about some participants interested points that are not originally designed in the questionnaire or prepared by the interviewer.

100% immediate response rate is required, therefore we may find that the first thing after a trainer completing the course is to distribute the smiley sheet and collect them back within 5 minutes. With the technology development, some companies tend to use web based surveys in order to save the manual efforts in inputting paper results into the computer system.

The key to this level evaluation is to ask the right questions, which should be prepared in advance according to the training strategy of the organization and the target of the training program. In order to analyze the collected data, reasonable scale and acceptable standards for the training program is to be well defined so that the gap between the actual score and the norm can be found, and also the future improvement can be tracked back.

Every training program should at least have the Level 1 evaluation.

Level 2: Learning

Tests are used to measure the level of learning—how much participants have learnt to change their attitudes, or/and increase their skills and knowledge. Usually the improvement can be captured by the comparison of scores from a pre test before the learning course starts and a post test after the learning course completes. Figure 11 - 2 shows such a comparison.

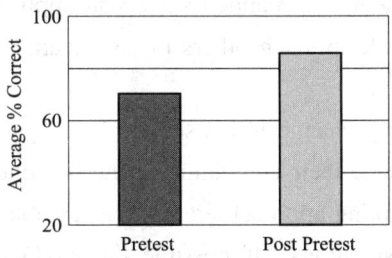

igure 11 - 2 Comparison of Test Performance

It is easy for trainers to organize the paper and pencil test in order to identify the learning gained in attitude or knowledge training, e. g. the customer service awareness, the processing steps of certain task, etc. For evaluating the skills trainings, a performance test should be arranged. For example, arrange a typing test to see if the clerk can improve his typing accuracy from 95% to 99% in the post training exercise, or a post training role play to see whether a sales person can be more persuasive.

This level evaluation is to be done for all participants, considering that it is not expensive and time consuming, while at the same time provides abundant information especially on the content of the training program. Not only the participants can provide the input about their learning, but also the feedback from the observations by their peers, customers, managers, or subordinates can be collected and analyzed.

Level 3: Behavior

A very common concern about the learning effectiveness is at Level 3. Most training programs get satisfactory results in Level 1 and Level 2. However, participants forget their learning after they complete the smiley sheet or post test. They return to work without carrying back what they've learnt as if learning happens in the classroom only. The Level 3 evaluation targets exactly whether and how much the learning has been transferred to workplace and applied to the daily job.

This evaluation is typically performed for three to six months after training because people need time to digest the learning gains, and the performance gains caused by that emerge even later.

Interviews, pre-survey and post survey, feedback from multiple sources are all good ways to evaluate behavior changes. Usually the evaluator will ask questions like:

- Did you use what you've learnt in your work?
- How much improvement has obtained since you apply the new technology?
- Was the participant able to teach others in your team about what he has learnt in the training program?
- Have you observed any change in his service level?
- Did our customer reduce their complaint on the hot line operation?

100% response or a sampling approach are both acceptable at this level depending on the cost and benefit in specific situations. If possible the evaluation can repeat later again at appropriate times to make sure that the learning has been launched and spread.

A very important factor that is frequently ignored about this knowledge transfer is the suitable learning climate within the company. Sometimes the application is to take place with certain conditions therefore the support from the team and company is needed. If the managers don't want to go an extra mile considering it may cost some additional expenses and efforts, they then tend to prevent the change or ignore the change initiative hence the application won't likely to happen. Just like a seed which you take back from the classroom, it becomes nothing after a while if there is no suitable soil, sunshine, or water.

In a learning organization, sharing after the training program is a mandatory following up step. There is a desire for change not only from the training participants, but also from their managers. Leaders encourage and support the behavior changes. Reward should be granted to the participants who improved their performance after learning.

Level 4: Results

Evaluation on results is rather difficult. The company wants to find the evidence that the training programs have really helped improve the product quality, raise the performance bar, provide better service to customers etc, which in the end benefit the bottom line. However for most of the cases, firstly it takes time to settle the benefit. Secondly it's not so easy to separate the training contribution from other management approaches.

Take the example from a sales skills training. After 6 months of the training, the sales revenue from the department A has grown for 20%. Then could we say the 20% is the result from the training? The marketing department may say that it's partly because they have implemented a very successful promotion on some products, and that's why these products occupy a big portion in the sales orders. The production department may say the process reengineering has reduced the human resource cost so that the prices of the products can be set a few percent lower than those of the competitors, and that's why sales people have more sold more. Sales people may argue too that they have been contacting the clients for a very long time even before the training program, and it's naturally that they get the orders at the right time to have the harvest.

There are some suggestions related to the issue.
- When the management team and the participants are sure that the training program is helpful, there is little need bothering leaning professionals to get a very accurate result.
- If the cost of getting the result is estimated much bigger than the benefit we get from the evaluation, just put it aside.
- Work with managers before the training program starts to agree what is the measurable result we want to get from the program. It could be a specific index such as the ratio of successful cold calls[3] in the next 3 months after the calling skills training, or the score of the customer satisfaction survey half a year later after the customer service training.

Summary

Evaluation is as important as the facilitation in learning. There are many good methods in evaluating the training effectiveness. Choose one according to your own situation, and adjust it to fit your organization. First ask what your purposes are. Then be careful about the data collecting process. Make quality analysis against established acceptable standards. Finally improve your training program through the evaluation.

Box 11-1

Approaches to Evaluation of Training

Commonly used approaches to educational evaluation have their roots in systematic approaches to the design of training. Evaluation is traditionally represented as the final stage in a systematic approach with the purpose being to improve interventions (formative evaluation) or make a judgment about worth and effectiveness (summative evaluation).

Six general approaches to educational evaluation can be identified as follows:

- Goal-based evaluation;
- Goal-free evaluation;
- Responsive evaluation;
- Systems evaluation;
- Professional review;
- Quasi-legal.

Goal-based and systems-based approaches are predominantly used in the evaluation of training. Various frameworks for evaluation of training programs have been proposed under the influence of these two approaches. The most influential framework has come from Kirkpatrick. Kirkpatrick's model follows the goal-based evaluation approach and is based on four simple questions that translate into four levels of evaluation. These four levels are widely known as reaction, learning, behavior, and results. On the other hand, under the systems approach, the most influential models include: Context, Input, Process, Product (CIPP) Model[4]; and Input, Process, Output, Outcome (IPO) Model[5].

Unit 11　Implementing the Four Levels Training Evaluation

Vocabulary

facilitation	n.	方便，助长，促进
preset	v.	预先设置
smiley	n.	笑脸符号
questionnaire	n.	问卷，调查表
trainer	n.	培训者
track	v.	拉纤，用纤拉
complaint	n.	投诉，抱怨
sample	v.	抽样
ignore	v.	忽视，不顾
mandatory	a.	强制的
reengineer	v.	重构，调整
formative	a.	形成的，构成的
summative	a.	概括的，总结的
responsive	a.	回复的，共鸣的，反应迅速的
quasi-legal	a.	准司法性的
predominantly	ad.	主要地，显著地，占优势地

1　training evaluation system　培训评估机制
2　Kirkpatrick's four levels evaluation model　柯氏四级评估模型
　　唐纳德·L·柯克帕特里克博士为美国培训与开发协会的前任会长、美国威斯康星大学教授。2004年，他获得工作场所学习与绩效终身成就奖。这一奖项是美国培训与开发协会的最高奖。他曾为众多公司和机构提供过管理培训和开发方面的咨询顾问服务，如可口可乐、通用电气、IBM、百事达等。其最知名的研究成果就是培训项目四级评估模式，这4个层级分别为：反应、学习、行为、结果。这一模式在世界各地得到了极其广泛的应用。

3　cold call　陌生电话，推销电话
4　Context, Imput, Process, Product (CIPP) Model　CIPP 评估模型
亦称决策导向或改良导向评估模式，它认为评价就是为管理者做决策提供信息服务的过程。背景评估（Context Evaluation）、输入评估（Input Evaluation）、过程评估（Process Evaluation）、结果评估（Product Evaluation）构成了 CIPP 评估模型。
5　Input, Process, Output, Outcome (IPO) Model　输入-过程-输出评估模型

Exercises

I　Please answer the following questions according to the text.

1. Why are most companies keen to have their training evaluation systems?
2. What are the four levels of Kirkpatrick's evaluation model?
3. What is a smiley sheet?
4. What are tests used to measure in the Kirkpatrick's model?
5. How should we use the Kirkpatrick's model properly?

II　Please explain the following terms and phrases in English.

training effectiveness	training program	training participant
training strategy	common concern	learning effectiveness
learning gain	learning organization	performance bar

III　Please read the following statements carefully and give your choice: True or False.

1. Most companies are keen to have their training evaluation systems.
2. The four levels in Kirkpatrick's model are reaction, learning, behavior, and results.
3. Level 1—reaction—tends to know how the targeted outcomes have been achieved as the result of the learning event.
4. The face to face interview is also a direct way to gather the needed information.
5. Every training program should at least have the Level 2 evaluation.
6. Tests are used to measure the level of results.
7. Most training programs get satisfactory results in all the four levels.

Unit 11 Implementing the Four Levels Training Evaluation

8. Evaluation on the level of results is rather difficult.

IV Please translate the following paragraphs into Chinese.

1. Since World War II, corporations have spent billions of dollars on worker training. As with any corporate investment, training directors are held accountable for the return on that investment; top management is looking for evidence that the dollars spent pay off. Budget justifications are in terms of potential savings generated through productivity gains or improved quality.

2. Companies are looking for cost-effective training strategies and seriously considering make-or-buy options. The portability and transferability of training materials are issues that multinational corporations wrestle with as global education networks take form and satellite communications proliferate.

3. Not only is top management becoming more demanding, but trainees are asking for and getting training materials geared to their requirements and delivered on demand. As computer-based training (CBT) and other instructional technologies become readily available (and cost-effective), the challenge for trainers is to deliver course materials in ways that ensure quality products at reasonable prices, tailored to end-user requirements.

4. Perhaps the best known evaluation methodology for judging training programs is Donald Kirkpatrick's Four Level Evaluation Model that was first published in a series of articles in 1959 in the Journal of American Society of Training Directors (now known as T + D Magazine). The series was later compiled and published in a book, Evaluating Training Programs in 1975.

5. Training is like selling. Instead of selling a tangible product, we sell ideas that are linked to improving performance at the organizations we represent. Like our sales colleagues, we want to show our products in the best possible light. To help us do that, we need to be conscious of the words we use to support these ideas. Two terms that are used over and over, and in my mind, minimize the value and intent of our training are "soft skills" and "smiley sheet".

V Please do the following oral exercises with your partner.

1. Discuss the significance of training evaluation.
2. Discuss the Kirkpatrick's four levels model.

PART V

Personal Development

个人发展

Unit 12

Three Steps to Personal Career Development

Based on the data collected from year 1999 till year 2008, Employee Engagement Survey[1] by Hewitt shows that for the employees in Asia Pacific, the career development opportunity is the top driver for their engagement. It's not always the compensation and benefits that counts. Of course we can't deny that more career development opportunities in fact bring more monetary reward in the near or far future. Nevertheless, it does indicate that both the companies and the employees are thinking further instead of restricting their insights at current stage only.

Box 12-1

Career Development

In organizational development (OD), the study of career development (CD) looks at:
- how individuals manage their careers within and between organizations;
- how organizations structure the career progress of their members, it can also be tied into succession planning within some organizations.

In personal development, career development is the lifelong psychological and behavioral processes as well as contextual influences shaping one's career over the life span. As such, career development involves the person's creation of a career pattern, decision-making style, integration of life roles, values expression, and life-role self concepts.

While many organizations are planning to invest more in constructing workplaces with more career development opportunities, the employees also should pay more attention to what they can invest on their side for a better career path within the organizations.

There is an easy and effective way for the employees to refine their thinking process about career development. We call it a 3 step method.

The first step is to know yourself.

First think of two or three events or experiences in your lifetime that you remember as being especially rewarding. No matter it relates to your job or not. What were you doing at the time, and what made these good experiences?

Then think of two or three events or experiences that were frustrating or unpleasant. What were you doing at the time, and made the experiences frustrating?

Ask a few people who know you well (could be your peers, supervisor, spouse or partner, friends, parents, etc.) what they have found you enjoy most, what you enjoy least, and what your particular strengths and abilities are.

Some people may find that they were really happy when they were promoted and they believed that they deserved more frequent promotions. Doing the same job at the same level makes them feel uncomfortable and think of leaving for better opportunities. Many employees may regard the achievement of finishing a difficult project something as their sweet memory, while easy work would bring them the regret of wasting their talent. Also there are people remember the birth of their kids as the most rewarding thing in their lives, while lack of time to take care of the family was what they hate most.

After collecting feedback from various resources, many people find that they are not what they think, while all the other people surrounding them are giving the same comments. Therefore it's time to look at oneself with a brand new perspective. A lady thinking herself being polite and tactful maybe regarded as aggressive and demanding since she always insists her idea without listening to others, and there is no compromise in her dictionary. She enjoys the heat from the debate, and she often wins the argument.

The difference between the self reflection and others' perception is not the key here although it does remind us about the blind areas we have. The key here is that the lady knows her strengths of being assertive and persuasive, and her passion in influencing others. Therefore it's naturally that she, working in a profit driven organization, is performing quite well as being very result-oriented. And she really enjoys the accomplishment when she gets things done.

We can imagine if the lady by nature hates to be the focus of the discussion, and doesn't want to express her idea openly and thoroughly, then she won't communicate so effectively and her influence span is to be limited to some extent. Consequently her achievements in the organization will be somewhat restricted.

The opposite scenario will be the lady with the passion of influencing others but unfortunately finds herself not so good at the influencing skills. Then of course her influence span is limited. Of course the influencing skills can be improved through training and practices. In previous case, the passion or attitude is not expected to be changed through any training.

Even the lady with perfectly matched passion and ability won't get the success if she is working in some workplace that value the harmony and layers instead of constructive feedbacks.

By far we can conclude that if a person possesses the passion and the ability that the organization needs, she or he is most likely to perform well and have a good career path. Some people may argue that the business changes always, so that the organizational requirement changes, then the person's passion and ability may miss the match. That is right if we don't consider the personal development at the same time. The ability can be trained and improved, while the passions can be explored. Therefore we can still expect the dynamic match between the person and the organization.

To make the things simple, study has been made to group the various preferences for best career into 5 categories.

There are people looking forward to advancement in their career with their passion for influence, impact and vision. The promotions are the best reward to them. Many successful business managers are the type.

There are people respecting loyalty and feeling honored when receiving long service award. They pursue security as the best career. Therefore public service, army, or other stable job without too many changes and risks are their favorites.

On the opposite, there are people love risks, excitement and challenges. They must stay networked with the people doing cutting-edge work[2]. They are eager to explore their distinctiveness to maximize their contribution. They always proactively sell their new ideas to change the way of living and doing. There are a lot of high tech talents in this group.

More and more young people in the eyes of the older generation are difficult to understand. They never think to have a job as a life-long job, which is the normal practice of his parents. They dare to cast away all the rules and principles. "This is my life" makes the person wants 100% percent of his work. However he can be a brilliant star as well if he is empowered to figure out his own way of getting things done. He is creative in problem solving. Many artists, business legends are those who fight for the freedom.

Unit 12 Three Steps to Personal Career Development

The last one to be introduced in the five categories is the balance type. Those people seek the equilibrium between work, relationships and self development. They like flexible working schedule so that they can take good care of the kids and at the same time do the job well. They are generally good at planning and organizing. They are not only junior level staff. Most of them are leaders in different areas because of their talent in organizing and leading people to success.

Employees may simply find which category they belong to by answering a questionnaire and then referring to the explanation of results. Combined the category briefing with the reflection on the first three questions, they can know what are the good jobs for them at certain point of career path, and what kind of job is to be avoided.

The second step is about how to find the organizational need.

If the employees are focusing on the promotion only, the job description or job advertisement for the vacancy tells clearly what the organizational need is. Generally there are several parts defining the responsibilities of the role, the qualification on education or working experience side, then the personal attributes—which is similar to what we mentioned as ability and passions. Take an HR Consultant[3] role in a bank as an example.

- Good communications and interpersonal skills with ability to interact with staff of all levels from senior executives to junior staff.
- A self-starter[4]; high energy level with a "Can Do" attitude[5].
- Highly independent. Ability to work independently with minimal supervision but a team player.
- Result-focused and service-oriented.

If the applicant doesn't have above characteristics, she is not likely to make her best career in this role. Instead she feels bothered by frequent oral contact with different types of people. She longs for a quiet corner to have a break. She hates to be pushed by tight schedule which is ridiculous in her eyes.

When there are no vacancies in the organization, employees could know the organizational need by:

- understanding the vision, values and company strategies;
- observing the behaviors and attitude of successful colleagues within the organization;
- talking with high level people about the career ambition;
- studying the criteria for entering talent program.

When the employees have fully understood what distinctiveness they have, and what the organization is looking for, they can start the third step to realize the best career.

This step is actually actions to bridge the gap between current ability and needed ability required by the organization. The organization need is out of individual control, and can be observed only with the mindset that it is dynamic for most of the organizations most time. The passion of the individual is something born with the person. With the growth of age and enlargement of life experiences, one may explore more interest. However it's hard to develop and time consuming. The only item one can change by time and efforts is the trainable ability.

Most training courses are targeted to improve certain ability. Besides the training courses, employees can also develop the needed skill through special assignment at work, or more directly by taking different jobs. Learning from superior and peers are also quite commonly used and effective learning method for ability improvement. Anyway this step is about the action, implementation, and realization. Turn to the thoughts into actions so that one achieves the best career in the end.

Many people may find sometimes they don't understand why others are selected to be promoted. The organization is always looking for people who can contribute more to the bottom line[6]. Today's winners are those who focus on developing their ability to make a difference in the organization. This is true for those in management or supervisory jobs—and especially for those in non-managerial jobs[7].

Box 12-2

Personal Career Development

Career development (CD) ought to be one of the primary responsibilities of individuals in organizations.

Career planning and development activities provide employees with assistance to develop realistic career goals and strategies to realize them. Individuals are best placed to develop their own action plan to achieve a particular career objective, as only the individual can answer these key questions:
- What is important to me?
- How hard am I prepared to work?
- Am I prepared to undertake further study?

Unit 12 Three Steps to Personal Career Development

- Am I prepared to make the necessary sacrifices to achieve my career goals?

While support is available from supervisors, ultimate responsibility for career management rests with the individual. This process does not happen automatically, and a conscious effort on the part of the employee is vital to ensure a successful career plan.

Vocabulary

insight	n.	眼光，见识
contextual	a.	联系上下文的，从前后关系来看的
psychological	a.	心理的，心理学的
refine	v.	精炼，提纯，改善，美化
lifetime	n.	一生，终生，有生之年
spouse	n.	配偶
surround	v.	围绕
demanding	a.	苛求的，吹毛求疵的
debate	n.	辩论，争论
assertive	a.	肯定的，断言的
passion	n.	热情，激情
thoroughly	ad.	全面地
span	n.	范围，跨度
consequently	ad.	因此，结果
scenario	n.	场景，情况
visibility	n.	能见度，可见性，显著性
loyalty	n.	忠诚
favorite	n.	喜欢的东西
excitement	n.	兴奋，刺激
distinctiveness	n.	独特性

maximize	v.	使最大化
brilliant	a.	明亮的，卓越的，杰出的
empower	v.	使有能力
artist	n.	艺术家
legend	n.	传说，传奇，传奇人物
equilibrium	n.	平衡
junior	a.	初级的，资历浅的
interpersonal	a.	人际的
minimal	a.	最小的，最低限度的
supervision	n.	监督，管理
ridiculous	a.	荒谬的，可笑的
ambition	n.	抱负，雄心
trainable	a.	可以培训出来的，通过培训可以形成的
supervisory	a.	监督的，管理的
sacrifice	n.	牺牲
conscious	a.	清醒的，自己知道的

1 Employee Engagement Survey 员工敬业度调查
2 cutting-edge work 尖端的工作，前沿的工作
3 HR Consultant 人力资源顾问
4 self-starter 做事主动的人
5 a "Can Do" attitude "一定能做到"的态度（指一种积极进取、充满自信的工作态度）
6 bottom line 财务报表最下面的盈亏结算线（指企业的利润）
7 non-managerial job 非管理岗位

Unit 12 Three Steps to Personal Career Development

I Please answer the following questions according to the text.

1. What does career development opportunity mean?
2. Why do many employees put more emphasis on career development than monetary reward?
3. What is the 3 step method mentioned in the text?
4. Why is it the first step to know oneself when thinking of career development?
5. Which step do you think most important in the 3 step method?

II Please explain the following terms and phrases in English.

career path	thinking process	self reflection
blind area	profit driven organization	influence span
constructive feedback	organizational requirement	stable job

III Please read the following statements carefully and give your choice: True or False.

1. More career development opportunities in fact bring more monetary reward in future.
2. All employees take promotion as the most rewarding thing in their lives.
3. Many employees may regard the achievement of finishing a difficult project something as their sweet memory.
4. Easy work would never bring employees the regret of wasting their talent.
5. Lack of time to take care of family was what everyone hates most.
6. An employee possessing the passion and the ability that the organization needs is most likely to have a good career path.
7. Some people pursue security as the best career.
8. Taking training courses is enough to improve performance.

IV Please translate the following paragraphs into Chinese.

1. Who is responsible for your career development? Many people think of it as a 50-50 arrangement. I carry 50% of the responsibility for my career development and my

employer carries 50%. Yes, in theory, but not in reality.

2. Many career experts agree that the best time to look for a new job is while you are still comfortably in your old one. If you're starting to feel unchallenged in your present position, you may be ready for a promotion to the next level. If there aren't many career advancement opportunities where you work, the best next job may be waiting for you elsewhere.

3. Career planning is a process of understanding oneself, exploring career options, making wise decisions and moving forward. What complicates it is that people, careers and organizations are constantly changing.

4. Career planning is not something done one time early in your career. Rather, it's an ongoing process throughout your life. It doesn't matter what's your profession, your industry or your place of employment. The reality is lives change, professions change, industries change, organizations change and so your career will change.

5. In HR management, career development is an organized approach used to match employee's goals with the organizational needs in support of workforce development initiatives. The purpose of career development is to: enhance each employee's current job performance; enable individuals to take advantage of future job opportunities; fulfill organization's goals for a dynamic and effective workforce.

V Please do the following oral exercises with your partner.

1. Discuss the concept of personal career development.
2. Talk something about your career planning.

Unit 13

Lucky George—A Typical Talent Development Program

George was very excited when he received the e-mail from the HR department one year ago saying that he had been enrolled in the talent development[1] program for that year.

Box 13-1

Talent Development

Talent development, part of human resource development, is the process of changing an organization, its employees, its stakeholders, and groups of people within it, using planned and unplanned learning, in order to achieve and maintain a competitive advantage for the organization. It is personal development for individuals but organizational development for companies.

The term "talent development" is becoming increasingly popular in many multi-national organizations, as companies are now moving from the traditional term "training and development". Talent development encompasses a variety of components such as training, career development, career management, and organizational development.

It is expected that during the 21st century more companies will begin to use more integrated terms such as talent development.

At that time, he had joined the company—a branch of a well known MNC with the headquarters in Europe—as a fresh graduate since no more than one year ago. "In fact I had little idea about what I should choose as my career after graduation from the university." George recalls that frustrating job searching experience. "I went to a job fair and simply noticed that there were many young people gathered in front of a few desks. I made the try, and was lucky enough to be selected."

After working in the company for almost one year, he learnt form both his manager and the internal bulletin board that the company was to have a talent development plan, and all the eligible staff—referring to those who met the performance, seniority, and other relevant standards—were encouraged to apply if they felt confident in both their capability and interest.

George submitted the application, and was arranged to have a panel interview first. A few senior managers asked him some very challenging questions. He still remembered some of them. "The questions were quite impressive. I didn't realize that I should think that way before I made any important decision." He was asked to evaluate his own performance and to think about the ways for improvement both from himself and his manager. "I seldom thought of improving further because my performance was quite good already. Neither did I consider the support I might request from my manager especially when standing in his shoes[2]."

The assessment center experience was also very impressive to George. He took that together with some other applicants in a big meeting room. They were provided with a folder of papers containing complicated information about a project background, and were required to present their own proposal ten minutes later one by one. At last a final proposal should be agreed by all the participants and be explained to the observers—mainly senior managers. "I was a bit nervous, and I thought some other participants shared the feelings. Of course at last we all overcame that and managed to show our ideas. The observers challenged each of us about our proposal, and it was very good that we can learn something immediately." George recalled.

Later he knew that besides the interview and the assessment center, there was also 360 degree feedback collected for each applicant.

After all those procedures, finally there was the short list. George had been waiting for a few weeks for the result, and he thought that even he couldn't be selected, it was still a kind of very valuable challenge and memory to him, because what he experienced in the selection process has made him to "start to think more and to do more" to strive for his ambition.

Talking about the reasons that he was picked out as "talent", George showed the Performance and Potential Matrix[3] (as shown in Figure 13-1) to explain. He was very proud that he was performing excellent and at the same time was evaluated to possess high potential in taking higher level positions.

Besides the sense of achievement and pride, George also felt the pressure. He was quite busy with his daily work as a supervisor. At the same time, he must spend extra time and

Unit 13 Lucky George—A Typical Talent Development Program

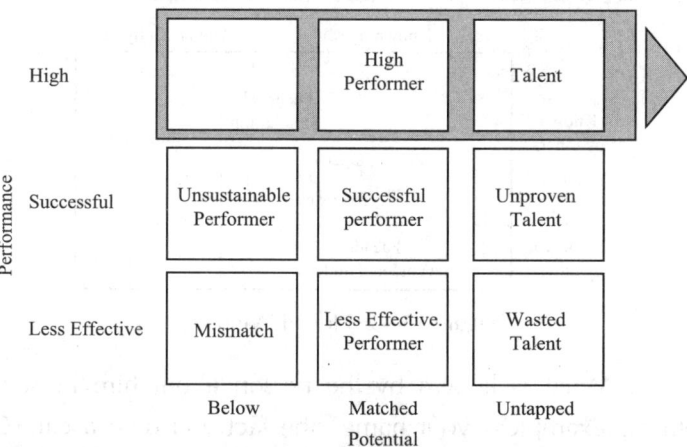

Figure 13-1 Performance and Potential Matrix

efforts to complete the required activities such as training courses, projects, and job rotation within a year. Fortunately there was a development plan tailor-made for him as a result of thorough discussions with his manager and HR. In this plan the exact schedule of all activities and resources needed were clearly stated and reviewed regularly.

The training courses cover from the time management, Johari Window[4] to Seven Habits[5], disclosing the major challenges a leader usually faces and introducing some basic management and leadership skills to conquer those issues. "Some of the courses are mandatory, while some are optional according to different needs from the participants." George explains. "I even chose PowerPoint because my work needs me to do effective presentations frequently."

Box 13-2

Johari Window

The Johari Window from Joseph Luft and Harry Ingham help us understand how we are giving and receiving information. It is shown as Figure 13-2.

It represents information including feelings, experience, views, attitudes, skills, intentions, motivation, etc. within or about a person in relation to their group, from four perspectives.

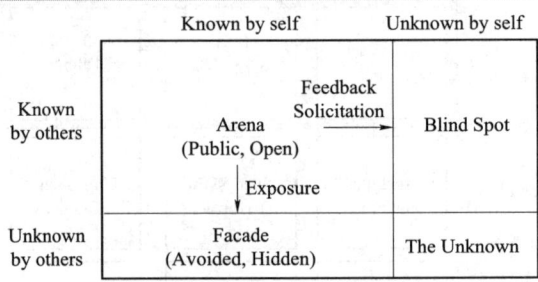

Figure 13-2　Johari Window

(1) Arena. What is known by the person about him/herself and is also known by others. Examples: your name, the fact you own a cat. One can and should increase the size of this region by increasing exposure and feedback solicitation.

(2) Blind Spot. What is unknown by the person about him/herself but what others know, for examples, your own manners, the feelings of other persons about you.

(3) Façade. What the person knows about him/herself that others do not know, such as your secrets, your hopes, desires, what you like and what you dislike.

(4) The Unknown. What is unknown by the person about him/herself and is also unknown by others. This information has an unknown potential to influence the rest of the Johari Window.

The Johari Window can help to illustrate and improve the self awareness between individuals and teams. It can also be used to change group dynamics within a business context.

The work project George did was a group project with other 5 colleagues from different departments. They worked for 2 months meeting regularly every week and asking for senior people's support. Eventually they came out a proposal to improve their operation system by a productivity gain of 15%. In George's eyes, he gained not only the recognition received in this project, but also the kind of rapport built with other departments through working together.

"I was very lucky. I also joined the rotation program. You know sometimes it's not so easy at certain point to find some suitable positions to swap between us. Therefore when there were only limited opportunities, only some of the talents could be selected for the job

Unit 13 Lucky George—A Typical Talent Development Program

rotation. I was picked out because I did well in the work assignment." George says. George then worked in another department for 6 months, and finally after he completed all the activities required by the talent development program, he was promoted to fill a vacancy of manager position in that department.

Not every participant was as lucky as George—to be promoted as soon as they completed the talent development program, which was thoroughly communicated by HR at the very beginning of the program.

"Indeed there is luck. However it's not all about luck." George has some advises to those who are still moving ahead in the talent development program. "You must make fully use of this platform the company has provided. Sometimes people are a bit shy or a bit lazy, and just waste those opportunities to know more and contact more. You shouldn't wait to be pushed. Instead you should take the ownership to lead yourself through till the target you desire. Furthermore, no pains no gains. I always believe in this old saying."

Vocabulary

enroll	v.	登记，使加入
unplanned	a.	未经计划的，随机的，意外的
encompass	v.	围绕，包含
eligible	a.	合格的
seniority	n.	资历
matrix	n.	矩阵
exact	a.	精确的，严格的
conquer	v.	征服，攻克，克服
optional	a.	可选的，非强制性的
solicitation	n.	恳求，恳请，征求

1 talent development   人才培养与发展

2　standing in his shoes　站在他的立场上考虑
3　Performance and Potential Matrix　绩效潜力矩阵
4　Johari Window　约哈瑞之窗（其中，Johari 的中文译法有多种，如乔哈里、约哈里等）
5　Seven Habits　七个习惯

1989 年，史蒂芬·R·柯维出版了《高效能人士的 7 个习惯》（*The Seven Habits of Highly Effective People*）一书，风靡全球。因此，Seven Habits 也成了非常经典的培训项目。

I　Please answer the following questions according to the text.

1. What do you think a talent development program is?
2. Why was George excited to be enrolled in the talent development program?
3. How did George feel about the assessment center experience?
4. Why was George picked out as "talent"?
5. Why did George think himself lucky?

II　Please explain the following terms and phrases in English.

HR department	fresh graduate	job fair
eligible staff	panel interview	senior manager
selection process	talent development	leadership skill

III　Please read the following statements carefully and give your choice: True or False.

1. George was very excited to be enrolled in the talent development program.
2. George had joined the company since more than one year ago.
3. Assessment center experience was very funny to George.
4. The selection process was a kind of very valuable challenge and memory to George.
5. George only felt excited about being pick out as "talent".
6. George gained not only the recognition received in this project but also the kind of

Unit 13 Lucky George—A Typical Talent Development Program

rapport built with other departments through working together.
7. George was selected to participate in the program because he was lucky.
8. Every participant will be promoted as soon as they completed the talent development program.

IV Please translate the following paragraphs into Chinese.

1. While talent development is reserved for the top management, it is becoming increasingly clear that career development is necessary for the retention of any employee, no matter what their level in the company. Research has shown that some type of career path is necessary for job satisfaction and hence job retention. Perhaps organizations need to include this area in their overview of employee satisfaction.

2. In today's challenging climate, the ongoing identification and motivation of talented people is as critical as ever. Ensuring that people feel their firm is still genuinely interested and supportive of their careers is essential to achieve sustained focus and high performance. It is also vital for the retention of talent when the upturn comes.

3. In truth, the HR function cannot run the talent development function. It requires the commitment and personal engagement of senior line management. Every time I've seen the system work well, the CEO has also been the Chief Talent Officer.

4. Training and development is usually the first casualty of budget cuts. Companies that do talent development well separate the talent development budgets from other training and development budgets so that one can be maintained while the other is cut back.

5. One of the most natural instincts of middle-level executives is to hoard talent — after all, they found it and developed it, why not use it? But if talent development is done at anything other than at the total corporate level, you sacrifice great opportunities for enrichment, cross-fertilization, and getting people the experience they want and need for later years.

V Please do the following oral exercises with your partner.

1. Discuss the concept of talent development.
2. What do you learn from George's story?

Unit 14

Leadership Development Approaches

There is no doubt that leadership development is quite critical to the success of organizations especially the future business target. There are also a lot of leadership development practices which are popular in many of the companies.

Box 14-1

Developing Individual Leaders

Traditionally, leadership development has focused on developing the leadership abilities and attitudes of individuals.

Just like people aren't all born with the ability to play football like Lionel Andrés Messi or sing like Luciano Pavarotti, people aren't all born with the ability to lead. Different personal characteristics can help or hinder a person's leadership effectiveness and require formalized programs for developing leadership competencies. Yet, everyone can develop their leadership effectiveness.

Achieving such development takes focus, practice and persistence more akin to learning a musical instrument than reading a book.

Classroom-style training and associated reading is effective in helping leaders to know more about what is involved in leading well. However, knowing what to do and doing what you know are two very different outcomes; management expert Henry Mintzberg is one person to highlight this dilemma. It is estimated that as little as 15% of learning from traditional classroom style training results in sustained behavioral change within the workplace.

A good personal leadership development program should enable an individual

> to develop a plan that helps him/her gain essential leadership skills required for roles across a wide spectrum from a youth environment to the corporate world. These characteristics include:
> - taking responsibility;
> - gaining focus;
> - developing life purpose;
> - starting action immediately;
> - developing effective and achievable goals and dreams.

Executive coaching and mentoring[1] are widely adopted development method. By matching the executive coach and high potential individual on a one-on-one[2] basis, it focus on enhancing a person's capability or skill development in a short term period (generally by coaching) or focus on longer term career advice and development (generally by mentoring). The coaching and mentoring help individual participant to identify solutions and actions by himself/herself through the exploration of situations, needs, motivations, skills, etc.

Therefore not only the individual receiving coaching or mentoring benefit from the interaction, but also the coach or the mentor learns from the one on one process. Of course a very tricky part here is that the effectiveness of this method varies a lot among different pairs. There is something chemical, or rapport that influences the trust between the pair and hence the effectiveness of communication till the final development outcome.

Most organizations emphasize that the owner of the career development is the individual himself/herself. It is very well demonstrated in the development method called learning resource guide. This is set up based on the competency gap for development. With each target competency, a list of development activities is provided to support the needed improvement. There could be seminars, trainings, workplace activities, action learning[3] projects, and books, magazines as references. This actually enlarges the concept of competency based training roadmap with the competency based development roadmap.

It's easy to implement in the organization, and it is an easy reference of learning resources for employees. It can be used for core, leadership, and technical competency development which is highly relevant to the organization's strategy. The key is the motivation of the individual, who may fully use this as the ladder for higher achievement in the organization or may keep it on the shelf as a newsletter only.

Action learning is very hot in recent years. An action learning project is a piece of research conducted within the organization, which has both strategic and business value, as well as learning value. Generally teams are formed around each carefully-chosen topic, comprising of a sponsor, leader, project manager and team members. Individuals are either full-time for an intense period (most effective), or "seconded" onto the project part time. Often facilitators are attached to each project—their role is to ensure individual and team learning occurs during the life of the project. The project process involves research, analysis, recommendations & action planning, and can extend to include implementation.

The action learning project has direct impact on organization success. It is effective as a "real time" development center[4] if well facilitated. It builds a range of leadership skills, including analysis and diagnosis as well as influencing. Participants also get an opportunity to build their reputation and profile within the organization. The senior management team sponsorship is quite important to the success of the action learning project. They should provide opportunity for project teams to present their findings for a "go" or "not go" decision. If several projects are run at once, there is the need to establish a project office to coordinate and extend learning between project teams.

Development center is sometimes integrated with assessment center by designing a set of work simulation exercises for individuals to participate and for professionally trained assessors to observe and giving feedback. But development center focuses on development, potential, and long term organizational needs instead of selection, current capability, and immediate organizational needs. Therefore a development center doesn't set any pass/fail criteria, and the assessors are rather facilitators than judges.

Development center can generate valid and reliable predictor of success—good for both selection and development. The realistic exercises reflect the future challenges and are tailored to organization's specific context. It is effective particularly in developing high-value jobs, such as leadership and key executive positions. The tool needs to be part of an overall development program and follow-up. Senior level sponsorship, time, and resources are heavily required.

A Leadership Practice Study by Mercer shows that overseas assignments[5], stretch assignments[6], and internal leadership coaching are top practices in China, and a combination of learning experiences with a predominant focus on on-the-job learning[7] is the most effective method for developing current and future leaders. Regional differences reveal that North Americans (64%) are more likely than their counterparts in Western Europe (46%) and Asia-Pacific (56%) to have identified the next generation of leaders and targeted them for development.

Unit 14　Leadership Development Approaches

Adobe, one of the leading software companies, when it started its leadership development program, identified that the successful leaders at Adobe are able to exemplify the company values, to influence and build relationships, to lead for exceptional results, to build strong global teams, and to develop others.

Based on those criteria, the leaders were at first assessed by 360-degree evaluation, and were assigned a coach who helped identifying existing strengths contributing to current performance and future development.

Then there were e-learning[8] courses for participants to understand further about Adobe's best practices across functions, and status in the industry as the common knowledge foundation.

The next step was the intense, off-site[9] classroom training course. For five full days, professors from UC Berkeley's Haas School of Business[10] teach sections on strategy, finance, marketing, innovation leading global teams, and more. Then Adobe executives, led discussions on how to apply what they have learned to their work in the company. At the same time participants broke into several teams, and using what they had leant competed with each other in a business simulation designed by an external consulting company. At the end of the course, the most successful team was selected based on pre-defined metrics related to growth and sustainability. Also feedbacks related to the leadership profile were provided throughout the course.

When the off-site study completed, the participants started to work on individual business challenges and had an opportunity to take part in a team business challenge with other participants. The individual business challenge lasted three months, helping the leader stretch his/her abilities and contribute more to the company. An executive sponsor would meet with the participant to tack progress. The team business challenge was decided by senior executives and related to a strategic project for the company. No more than ten participants set up a team to work for two months before they presented their recommendations for the further instruction from the senior executives.

According to Senior Vice President of Human Resources in Adobe, Donna Morris, the company was very pleased with the effect of the development program. "Last year (2009) 86 percent of our vice president and general manager positions were filled by internal candidates—up from 56 percent in 2007—and 92 percent of internal candidates taking the vice president and general manager positions were ALE (Adobe Learning Experience, name of the leadership development program) alumni." Besides the upward mobility, retention, and performance were measured as well to evaluate the program effectiveness.

Stewart D. Friedman, Director of the Leadership Development Center at Ford Motor Company, in his article "Leadership DNA", discloses the similar approaches applied there, such as action learning, e-learning, involvement of senior executives, generating business impact.

They have developed 5 strategic and 4 core programs. The core programs play a significant role in the identification, selection, and development of the company's next generation of leaders. The strategic ones are changing initiatives cutting across vertical and horizontal boundaries. All of their programs feature action learning.

E-learning tools are widely used. By this way participants invest time and energy trying out new ways of working that leverage synergies among work, home, and community, thus taking a total leadership development approach.

This total leadership is similar to most leadership approaches in that it aims to achieve superior result, and different from many of others because it emphasize your life at work, your life at home, and your life in the community as a whole life. Therefore the company is asking its leaders to pursue the triple bottom line of financial success, environmental protection, and social responsibility. It's amazing and it's wonderful.

Box 14-2

Leader Development & Leadership Development

More recently, organizations have come to understand that leadership can also be developed by strengthening the connection between, and alignment of, the efforts of individual leaders and the systems through which they influence organizational operations. This has led to a differentiation between leader development and leadership development, although few people has see it.

Leader development focuses on the development of the leader, such as the personal attributes desired in a leader, desired ways of behaving, ways of thinking or feeling. In contrast, leadership development focuses on the development of leadership as a process. This will include the interpersonal relationships, social influence process, and the team dynamics between the leader and his/her team at the dyad level, the contextual factors surrounding the team such as the perception of the organizational climate and the social network linkages between the team and other groups in the organization.

Unit 14 Leadership Development Approaches

Vocabulary

hinder	v.	妨碍，阻挠
formalize	v.	使成为正式，使具有形式
persistence	n.	坚持，持续，持久
akin	a.	同族的，同种的，类似的
associated	a.	联合的，联想的
spectrum	n.	范围，幅度，系列
mentor	v.	指导，当……的导师
mentor	n.	辅导教师，指导者
seminar	n.	研讨会
roadmap	n.	路线图，准则，指示
ladder	n.	阶梯，成功的手段
sponsor	n.	发起者，主办者
facilitator	n.	促进者，便利措施
recommendation	n.	推荐，介绍，建议
sponsorship	n.	保证人的角色
coordinate	v.	使配合，使协调
assessor	n.	评价者，评审员
predictor	n.	预言者，预报器
tailor	v.	量身定制，使合适
predominant	a.	突出的，最显著的
reveal	v.	显露，显示
counterpart	n.	对应者，相对应的人
exemplify	v.	举例证明，解释
exceptional	a.	例外的，特别多，优异的
sustainability	n.	可持续性
mobility	n.	移动性，灵活性，能动性
involvement	n.	包括，包含，牵连，相关事务
synergy	n.	协同，配合
community	n.	社区，社群，共同体
triple	a.	三倍的，三重的，三者的

environmental	a.	环境的
dyad	a.	二个的
linkage	n.	联系，连接

1. executive coaching and mentoring　高层管理训练与指导
2. one-on-one　一对一的
3. action learning　行动学习法
   行动学习法就是通过实际行动去学习，即在一个专门以学习为目标的背景环境中，以组织面临的重要问题为载体，学习者通过对实际工作中的问题、任务、项目等进行处理，从而达到开发人力资源和发展组织的目的。行动学习法是由英国管理学思想家雷吉·雷文斯（Reg Revans）在 1940 年发明的，并将其应用于英格兰和威尔士煤矿业的组织培训。
4. development center　人才发展中心（或发展中心方法）
   以培养组织所需要的重要人才为目的所建立的专门部门称为人才发展中心。一些跨国公司为了培养领导者，人为地"模拟"关键管理事件，以期在安全的环境中磨炼企业领导者，这种方法被称为 development center。
5. overseas assignment　外派任务，派往海外工作
6. stretch assignment　延伸任务，由本职工作延伸而来的其他工作
7. on-the-job learning　在工作中学习
8. e-learning　网络化学习，通过网络学习
9. off-site　离开基地的，离开工作场所的，脱产的
10. UC Berkeley's Haas School of Business　加利福尼亚州立大学伯克利分校哈斯商学院

I Please answer the following questions according to the text.

1. What is leadership development?

2. Why is leadership development quite critical to the success of organizations?
3. What methods are widely adopted for leadership development?
4. What is the key in leadership development?
5. Could anyone be developed to be a leader?

II Please explain the following terms and phrases in English.

business target	executive coaching	competency gap
development roadmap	team learning	future challenge
executive position	core program	leadership profile

III Please read the following statements carefully and give your choice: True or False.

1. Leadership development is quite critical to the success of organizations especially the current business target.
2. Executive coaching and mentoring are widely adopted development method.
3. Only the individual receiving coaching or mentoring benefit from the interaction.
4. Most organizations emphasize that the owner of the career development is the individual himself/herself.
5. Action learning has been very hot for centuries.
6. The action learning project has indirect impact on organization success.
7. Development center can generate valid and reliable predictor of success.
8. Every company may ask its leaders to pursue the triple bottom line of financial success.

IV Please translate the following paragraphs into Chinese.

1. Leadership development refers to any activity that enhances the quality of leadership within an individual or organization. These activities have ranged from MBA style programs offered at university business schools to action learning, high-ropes courses and executive retreats.

2. The success of leadership development efforts has been linked to three variables: Individual learner characteristics; The quality and nature of the leadership development program; Genuine support for behavioral change from the leader's supervisor.

3. Personal characteristics that associated with successful leadership development

include leader motivation to learn, a high achievement drive and personality traits such as openness to experience, an internal focus of control, and self-monitoring.

4. In the belief that the most important resource that an organization possesses is the people that comprise the organization, some organizations address the development of these resources, even including the leadership.

5. Most leadership development programs focus primarily on the objective, exterior factors involved in the situation, for example: behaviors, skills, strategies, structures, and processes. An integral approach combines a focus on the external, observable factors with an equal focus on interior factors such as thinking, feeling, and values—at both the individual and organizational levels.

V Please do the following oral exercises with your partner.

1. Discuss the difference between the two words "leader" and "leadership".
2. Do you want to be a leader? Why?

Unit 15
Identify the Right Leadership

Leadership development has been one of the key issues on the personal agendas of most CEOs. They notice that the shortage of the right leadership talent is a significant risk to successful business strategy execution and organization growth. Also the boards are paying more attention to their accountability for executive succession and are asking tough questions about the sustainable business development.

Box 15-1

What Is Leadership?

Leadership is theoretically defined by many scholars as the process of social influence in which one person can enlist the aid and support of others in the accomplishment of a common task.

However, for normal people, leadership can be considered as one's ability to get others to willingly follow.

Moreover, leadership has sometimes been described as taking people to a place that they would not normally go to on their own. Once a sound strategic planning process has determined what that place should be it is the leader's prime and fundamental responsibility to assure that there is cultural alignment with the vision and that the full resources of the organization are effectively brought to bear to achieve that destination.

However according to the data from the Global Leadership Imperative in 2006 research, although 75% global companies say business challenges uncover weaknesses in their organization's leadership pipeline[1], 72% are planning to take actions to close gaps, only about one-half of the companies have made sufficient investment to do so.

There are many reasons behind the data. A popular concern is that could leadership be developed? There is always a point saying that the leaders are born instead of developed. It may not be true, but at least it seems the higher the level, the more difficult to develop the leadership. Hence people then pay more attention to the selection of the right leaders.

Who are the right leaders we are looking for?

Hay Group[2] in 2007 developed an assessment center for a famous shipping company. They aimed to measure the competencies including customer relation, interpersonal skills, human resource development, teamwork & cooperation, creative problem solving, and result-driven.

Another leading consulting firm, Mercer, describes that the leaders need to be able to draw from the Head, Heart, and Guts. Head means providing purpose, direction, and strategy. Heart is understanding, working with and developing others. Guts refer to do the right thing based on clear values.

In fact each organization has its particular leadership profile, which means the requirements about capabilities, behaviors, attitudes, and values that leaders must exhibit in order to be successful within the organization. Some organizations also call this as leadership competencies, or leadership DNA etc. No matter what it is called, there must be a set of clear criteria within the organization in accordance with its business strategy, which provides a common language for discussing what leaders need to do for achieving business success and forms the basis of further leadership development activities. Consequently there are consistent collective leadership behaviors that are critical for the organization to implement its strategy and achieve target.

When this foundation is set up, it's time to select suitable tools and methods to assess those leadership competencies.

There are dozens of those things in the world, from small tests as easy as handwriting to the complicated activities like structured assessment center. And there will be more as the business world develops.

Interview is quite frequently used in any kind of selection. Regarding leadership identification, the behavior event interviews[3] are popular in leadership assessment practices. Those are targeted interviews conducted by trained interviewers, using behavior-based questions to gain a better understanding of a person's behavior in relation to possible future job requirement. Hence the interviewer will try to understand whether in the past the interviewee has demonstrated enough competencies related to the required leadership profile.

> ## Box 15-2
>
> ### Behavior Event Interview (BEI)
>
> Behavioral Event Interviews constitute a powerful tool for numerous organizational processes like recruitment, selection, performance management and even research.
>
> The interviews are backward looking and are based on the assumption that human behavior has patterns which repeat. Like the track record of a horse or sportsman, behavioral event interviews seek actual behaviors of a person and the underlying characteristics which power the behaviors, like attitudes, motives, intents, self image, world views or even drives.
>
> Based on the work of David McClelland and others, the Behavioral Event Interview presents a powerful tool for the professionals. This interview tool looks at critical incidents in a person's life or career and the behavior patterns.

Psychological tests are also widely used for being more objective than interviews and hence a persuasive supplement. Intelligence is always one of the focuses. Many test papers are designed for the participants to answer some questions related to figures, mathematics, logical reasoning, and verbal reasoning in a certain period of time in order to know how quick and how well the person can solve the problems. Raven's Progressive Matrices[4] is one of those. With the recognition of the importance of critical thinking, Watson-Glaser Critical Thinking Appraisal[5] has also been adopted in many organizations.

Besides intelligence, personality classification is also hot in leadership assessment. It is widely accepted that personal characteristics such as self-image, attitudes, values, traits, and motives shape the behaviors and they are rather stable. Therefore people are keen to search for the personalities a typical successful leader should have. Cattell 16 PF, MMPI, OPQ[6] are all well known personality assessment tools.

For most of the cases, due to the complexity of current business and the dynamic requirements for the right leadership profile, interviews, tests or assessment alone can't fully demonstrate the whole characteristics a candidate possesses against the pre-defined criteria. Assessment center approach, with a set of work simulation exercises individuals participate in and observed by professionally-trained assessors, then can identify most valid and reliable predictor of future success. During an assessment center, the individuals may go through steps like expert interviews, multi-source feedback, cognitive or personality test, case studies, and work related simulations. The assessment center is always deemed as objective due to assessment approach designed by external assessors, as realistic and challenging for being reflective of actual work situations. Furthermore, the powerful and objective behavior-based feedback can be used not only for leadership assessment, but also for future development.

Compared with assessment center, workplace assessment[7] is observations made by trained assessors on an individual's work abilities, demonstration of technical knowledge and skills and work performance in real workplace. Typically, a group of individuals are trained to observe the person in action as he goes about his work activities over a set time period, e.g., there could be two 1 – 2 hour observations over a 2 week period.

Box 15 – 3

What Is Workplace Assessment?

Workplace assessment is the final part of a structured learning program. A qualified workplace assessor measures and formally recognizes the skills and knowledge you have gained and are using on the job every day. It's about building your confidence to aim higher and gain even more experience.

You are assessed by one or more registered workplace assessors from your company or an external agency. If the assessors judge that your skills and knowledge meet the standards required, your skills will be formally recognized in a national standard. Once you have achieved all the standards required they will be recognized in a qualification.

The assessment can take place on or off the job. It could be an assessment of:

- what you already know and do in your job—your current skills;
- your new learning that you demonstrate in your everyday work.

So which assessment tool should we choose? And when?

It actually depends on what you want to assess, which validity level you will accept, how much time or efforts you can afford, and the understanding of the pros and cons of each assessment method.

Technical proficiency usually can't be identified in assessment center. But a expert technical panel can judge that. Workplace assessment is good for identifying both technical and core competencies, but it's hard to tell the leadership competencies.

Behavior event interview can search for evidences of all the three kinds of competencies—core, leadership, and technical. However, it's not so objective because its result heavily relies on the capability of the individual interviewer.

Workplace assessment and assessment center are much more objective than other assessment tools, while they are the most difficult to implement. The design of the assessment, the training for the assessors, and the participation of individuals are all time consuming. The check to external consultant is also something that makes the organization hesitate to move that way.

In general, the behavior event interview is useful for selection purpose for targeted jobs. It's effective at revealing insights into critical behaviors. Its level of being objective depends on the capability of trained interviewers. Interviewer can always get a sample of the interviewee's actual behavior on the job. On the other side, the interview reveals only the information the interviewee happens or chooses to present. There may be experienced interviewees, and also tactful interviewees who can decorate themselves as perfect candidates. One further point is that information about motives, traits, or self-image is hard to be disclosed through interviews.

As mentioned before the psychological tests about intelligence and personality are welcomed by many organizations for their high validity. They are comparatively easier to implement in the sense that most of them are paper and pencil format. The intelligence and cognitive tests are effective tools especially for assessing candidates for executive positions because they provide insight into critical thinking, numerical reasoning, reading comprehension, analytical reasoning, spatial relations, and ability to process information efficiently and accurately. Personality tests are effective tools for providing insight into personality, potential personality derailer, and common behaviors. However they can't provide much in-depth insight into job knowledge or experience. Also when people are still having concern that what the right personality profile is for the position, it's dangerous to use the test result as a screening tool only.

As for assessment center, it's accepted by many people that the tool is valid and reliable for providing powerful and objective behavior-based feedback, exposing potential personality derailer, reflecting actual work situations. The precondition for implementing assessment center is however that the competency framework must be in place. Besides the time and monetary expense, the complexity itself is always perceived as stressful for the individual. Hence although in the simulated situation, some participants may behave not the normal way as they do in actual job.

Workplace assessment has the similar advantage and disadvantages as assessment center has. However, without the assessment center as a lab to implement all assessment steps, it's much more difficult for the organization to prepare the assessment infrastructure in real working place and maintain it for maybe quite a long time.

Vocabulary

accountability	n.	负有责任
enlist	v.	争取，获得
imperative	n.	规则
uncover	v.	使露出，使知道，揭示
gut	n.	内在，实质
mathematics	n.	数学
trait	n.	特性，性格
cognitive	a.	认识的，认识力的
reflective	a.	反映的，反射的
demonstration	n.	表明，说明
derailer	n.	导致偏离正常轨道的因素
spatial	a.	空间的
stressful	a.	紧张的

Notes

1 leadership pipeline   领导力补给线

由斯蒂芬·德罗特（Stephen Drotter）、詹姆士·诺埃尔（James Noel）、拉姆·查安（Ram Charan）三位学者提出。他们认为，对于公司来说，有时候从外部选聘经理人员只能作为一时的权宜之计。作为长久之计，公司必须从内部构建、发展并保持

Unit 15　Identify the Right Leadership

一条高技能领导力的补给线。他们为此提出的领导力补给线（Leadership Pipeline）模型，通过关注和解释在领导人才培养的各个过渡阶段，那些诸如时间配置、工作技能及工作价值等发生的至关重要的变化，来帮助公司构建一条漏斗型管线的未来人才补给线。这一模型还能够帮助理解在不同的层级上对于管理者的不同要求

2　Hay Group　合益集团
1943年在美国费城成立，是一家全球性的管理咨询公司，在全球43个国家设有78个办事处。

3　behavior event interview　行为事件访谈法或面试法（BEI）

4　Raven's Progressive Matrices　瑞文推理测验
简称瑞文测验，是由英国心理学家瑞文（J. C. Raven）于1938年设计的一种非文字智力测验。

5　Watson-Glaser Critical Thinking Appraisal　华格二氏批判性思考评估（WGCTA）
这是一种以考察被试者的批判性思考能力为目的的心理测验。最早由美国著名心理学家华生（Watson）提出，后来由另一位美国心理学家格拉泽（Glaser）进行了改进。

6　Cattell 16 PF　卡特尔16项人格因素测验（Cattell 16 Personal Factors）
MMPI　明尼苏达多项人格测验（Minnesota Multiphasic Personality Inventory）
OPQ　职业性格问卷（Occupational Personality Questionnaire）

7　workplace assessment　工作场所实际操作评估

I　Please answer the following questions according to the text.

1. Why do most CEOs take leadership development as one of the key issues on their personal agendas?
2. Why are the boards paying more attention to the CEOs' accountability for executive succession?
3. Why does each organization have its particular leadership profile?
4. What psychological tests are mentioned in the text?
5. What tools and methods may be used to identify the right leadership?

II　Please explain the following terms and phrases in English.

leadership talent　　　sustainable development　　　leadership profile

leadership competency   leadership identification   psychological test
personality classification   leadership assessment   analytical reasoning

III Please read the following statements carefully and give your choice: True or False.

1. Leadership development has been one of the key issues on the personal agendas of most CEOs.
2. The boards tend to ask the CEO tough questions about the sustainable business development.
3. The leaders are born instead of developed.
4. Different organizations have the same leadership profiles.
5. Interview is quite frequently used in any kind of selection except for leadership identification.
6. Personality classification is also hot in leadership assessment.
7. Behavior-based feedback can only be used for leadership assessment.
8. Workplace assessment and assessment center are much more objective than other assessment tools.

IV Please translate the following paragraphs into Chinese.

1. A leader with vision has a clear, vivid picture of where to go, as well as a firm grasp on what success looks like and how to achieve it. But it's not enough to have a vision; leaders must also share it and act upon it.
2. There has been an explosion of literature about leadership lately. Leading is a very human activity—we're all human—so there are many people who consider themselves experts on leadership. Unfortunately, many people make strong assertions about leadership without ever really understanding a great deal about leadership. Understanding leadership requires more than reading a few articles or fantasizing about what great leaders should be.
3. Many people believe that leadership is simply being the first, biggest or most powerful. Leadership in organizations has a different and more meaningful definition. Very simply put, a leader is interpreted as someone who sets direction in an effort and influences people to follow that direction—the people can be oneself, another individual, a group, an organization or a community.
4. Some view leadership as a series of specific traits or characteristics. Others see it as

comprised of certain skills and knowledge. And some, me included, think of leadership as a process. This view of leadership, as a process, places an emphasis on social interaction and relationship. This is the idea that leadership is a type of relationship, one that typically includes influencing others in a certain direction. This leads to my current working definition of leadership: Leadership is a relationship that involves the mobilizing, influencing, and guiding of others toward desired goals.

5. Intrinsic traits such as intelligence, good looks, height and so on are not necessary to become a leader. Anyone can cultivate the proper leadership traits.

V Please do the following oral exercises with your partner.

1. What assessment tools and methods mentioned in the text are most impressive to you? Discuss about them.
2. Tell your opinions about the right leadership.

Organizational Development

组织发展

Unit 16
OD Basis

Many large multi-national companies nowadays have set up the organizational development (OD) function within or outside of human resources department, just like what happened to training function some years ago. More and more learning professionals also turn to the organizational development field to explore their further interest and career development.

What is organizational development? According to Thomas G. Cummings[1] in his book *Organization Development and Change*, organization development is a system-wide application of behavioral science knowledge to the planned development and reinforcement of organizational strategies, structures, and processes for improving an organization's effectiveness. Linda Holbeche[2] defines it as "the systematic application of behavioral science principles and practices to understand how people and organizations function and how to get them to function better within a clear value base. It is shamelessly humanistic and has strong value drivers." Of course we can find more in various books and articles. In general, the definitions tend to agree the following six common elements of organization development.

- It's always a planned effort.
- It consists of organizational wide activities.
- It should be managed from the top, i.e. get the top management support.
- It aims to increase organization effectiveness and health.
- The approaches are implemented through planned interventions in the organizational processes.
- The change is based on behavioral-science knowledge.

Although OD function sometimes is integrated with training function in many organizations, and training courses are frequently combined with OD activities, OD is definitely different from training. Training is short-term efforts, while OD is long term. Training intends to equip individuals with knowledge, skills and attitudes they need to do their jobs better, while OD aims to equip groups with the knowledge, skills and attitudes they need to interact more effectively. Training solutions usually are part of the OD framework, or we can say training is one of the OD interventions. Besides training, the introduction of enhance performance management, the business process re-engineering, coaching, delegating, mentoring, group meeting facilitation, team building etc are also typical OD approaches.

The need for OD approaches emerges when we are thinking questions like:
- What are the right skills to drive the company to a higher profit level?
- How should we define the criteria for the team managers when the company expands to its double size?
- How should we do to integrate the two cultures after the merge?
- How can we simplify the organization structure to respond quicker to our customers?
- How can we promote the company values among all the staff so that they do know what are the needed behaviors and attitude?

When the OD consultant, no matter she is from internal or external, turns to a piece of OD work, there are several steps to follow.

First, the OD consultant should be aware of who needs what kind of change by meeting project sponsor and stakeholders. Then it comes to contract stating the clear objectives of the project with clear roles clarification of the consultant and the client. It's usually helpful to use a structured client questionnaire to capture all the information needed for the project contract. The questions includes the overall operating context of the organization, the company values and strategies, the organization charts of a few layers, the competency requirement and current competency gap of the managers and employees, the major systems and processes in place, such as production management system, information platform, reward and recognition scheme etc.

Then the consultant determines what and how much data is needed via which collection process. Also she explores an appropriate mix of approaches to ensure the efficiency, objectivity, and validity of the data collection step. Anonymous questionnaires and surveys are always good ways to collect data especially when we have to get enough information before urgent deadline, and at the same time the respondents want to be safe from the risk of information leak. The consultant has to pay more efforts in designing the questions so that responses are more likely to be accurate for later analysis, and surveyed audience have the interest completing all the questions. A simple table called STEEPLES[3] provides an outline of the structure to collecting internal and external information influencing an organization's strength and weakness.

Box 16-1

STEEPLES Table

STEEPLES		
	Internal	External
S—Social		
T—Technological		
E—Environmental/ecology		
E—Economic		
P—Political		
L—Legal		
E—Ethic		
S—Something else		

  Interviews are considered when consultants want to fully understand someone's impressions or experiences, or learn more about their answers to questionnaires. The interviews provide more and deeper understanding, but they cost much time, and can be difficult for the consultants to analyze and compare the data.

  Consultants can get information from the review of files and documents like many financial experts do in a finance audit. This approach enables the consultants to have access to comprehensive and historical record, and doesn't need to interrupt the resource provider's routine work, which is quite helpful when the consultants expect quality information in the client's peak days. Of course the information kept in documents sometimes is too much to be fully searched, and there was reality of incomplete information, which means the interruption for clarification is still needed.

  Focus group is a common approach to get in-depth and common understanding about the topics such as the required competency for a typical position, the reactions to an organization change, the ways to improve team performance. An experienced facilitator is very necessary to keep the ball rolling or stop the discussion at the right time and wrap it as people are talking freely or argue fiercely so that quality time generates meaningful feedback. Another challenge to the approach is that it usually takes time and wisdom to analyze the responses.

Besides above mentioned methods, there are also case studies, observation, and so on, which help the consultants to collect enough information for assessing the organization as the second step in the OD project.

The following step is to determine the intervention approaches according to the project scope (size, complexity, type of change, level in organization, etc.), the time schedule, budget, and resources. Different consultants may have different ideas about the most suitable interventions. One possible reason is the organizational lens. Consultants view from different lens see different focus areas of the organization hence diagnose it in a different way. The impact of this is often underestimated. As an experienced consultant, one should always be aware of this personal preference and make sure she knows others lens as well.

Box 16-2

Organizational Lens

One of the most useful resources to explain these perspectives is *Reframing Organizations* (Bolman and Deal, Jossey-Bass, 1991). The authors depict four quite different and major organizational perspectives among researchers, writers, educators, consultants and members of organization.

Lens	Examples of What Is Noticed or Talked About from That Lens
structure	goals, objectives, roles, responsibilities, performance, policies and procedures, efficiency, hierarchy and coordination and control
human resource	participation, feelings, fulfillment, communication, needs of people, relationships, motivation, enrichment and commitment
political	power, conflict, competition, authority, experts, coalitions, allocation of resources, bargaining and decision making
symbolic	rituals, culture, values, stories, different perspectives, language, expressions, myths, commitment and metaphors

Note that these are horizontal lens regarding what different people notice across the activities in organizations. There are also many vertical lenses through which we view intra-personal dynamics, for example, the many perspectives put forth in the increasing amount of books on personal development.

At each level there are some options for intervention approaches. Organization assessment, succession planning, organization restructure, workflow redesign are typical organization level interventions. Team building, self directed work teams, department operational and performance improvement, interpersonal communications etc. are useful approaches at management or team level. The training and education to increase self-awareness and enhance personal development, the coaching for better individual performance are commonly used intervention approaches for individuals. Some of these interventions are classical tools, while some are comparatively new. Again, different consultants have different choices.

In the implementation of the interventions (the fourth step), consultants should be aware of the involvement extent of the stakeholders. For most of the cases, training programs, the best practice sharing or the enhanced coaching should be provided, on one side, to motivate participants, and the other side to equip them with necessary skills and knowledge in order to go through the change cycle.

The evaluation of an OD intervention is the final step within one OD project cycle. It usually contains steps to verify how the things are happened according to the project plan, to confirm management's view about the progress and achievement of goals, to produce data or verify results that can be used for benchmarking, comparisons, public relations, performance improvement, etc.

The five step methods can't guarantee that all the OD projects implemented that are to be successful. OD interventions are not magic.

When there is only OD consultant who feels a need for the OD change, while other stakeholders are willing to stay where they are, the project won't come to a desired end. That's easy to understand. People desire differently in the bottom of their hearts at the very beginning.

Since most OD interventions are long term efforts, for managers seek quick mend, the process is too time consuming and costly in their eyes. Therefore it's not likely for the consultants to get continuous support from the management team. That may later bring the suspension of an OD project.

Sometimes although managers express their eagerness for the feedback from OD project, they just refuse to listen to the data presented. Instead they think the unexpected data shows how lousy the consultants are doing their job! This kind of distrust cannot produce any productive result.

Box 16-3

The Ethics of Organizational Development Interventions

Organizational development should be beyond reproach. Based on the idea of working with organizational culture to bring out the best in people, the goals and ethics of organizational development are certainly laudable from a human perspective. It's hard to argue with the financial results, either. We have yet to hear of a true OD intervention being abused, though of course components of OD—the various tools used by OD practitioners—can easily be subverted or ineffective in the wrong hands.

Generally speaking, the ethical consultant or manager can do many things to make the lives of employees and managers better, and not just in financial terms.

A successful organizational transformation has several key components, whether it is called job enrichment, organizational development, continuous improvement, or quality.

First is empowering employees to do their jobs to the best of their ability. That requires pushing authority, responsibility, and information downwards.

Second is empowering employees to change the system. Drucker[4] is famous for noting that most problems are caused not by employees, but by systems, technologies, and processes. Since those are designed by people, it only makes sense that allowing people to fix problems in systems, technologies, and processes will have a tremendous impact in increasing productivity and quality.

Third is providing a clear vision to people and helping everyone to understand the organizational strategy. Giving people a common vision and strategy motivates people, because they are not working at cross purposes, and it avoids wasted effort. This may be the primary role of the organizational leader.

Any organizational initiative should be measured against whether it has these three components. Does an employee survey result in managers chastising employees for poor performance, or empowering managers and staff to do something about areas where there are gaps? Does a technology effort provide another way for managers to keep close tabs on[5] employee performance and enforce detailed regulations, or does it allow employees to see and improve their own performance, while spreading or learning from best practices?

Vocabulary

reinforcement	n.	增强，巩固
shamelessly	ad.	不知羞愧地
humanistic	a.	人性研究的，人本主义的
merge	n.	兼并
clarification	n.	澄清，说明
anonymous	a.	匿名的
audience	n.	听众，观众，读者
ecology	n.	生态
comprehensive	a.	综合的，全面的
peak	a.	顶点，峰值
incomplete	a.	不完整的，不完备的
interruption	n.	打断，中断，停止
depict	v.	刻画，描写，叙述
enrichment	n.	丰富，充实
coalition	n.	结合，联盟
bargain	n.	讨价还价
symbolic	a.	象征性的
myth	n.	神话
metaphor	n.	隐喻，象征
restructure	n.	重新组织，改组
redesign	n.	重新设计，调整
benchmarking	n.	基准评价
magic	a.	魔术的，有魔力的，不可思议的
mend	n.	改进，修复，加强，治愈

Unit 16 OD Basis

suspension	*n.*	悬吊，中止，搁置
eagerness	*n.*	渴望，热情
unexpected	*a.*	没想到的，意外的
lousy	*a.*	糟糕的
distrust	*n.*	疑惑，不相信
laudable	*a.*	值得称赞的
reproach	*n.*	责备，谴责，耻辱
practitioner	*n.*	实践者，从业者
chastise	*v.*	惩戒，惩罚

1 Thomas G. Cummings 托马斯·卡明斯
   美国南加利福尼亚大学教授，组织管理部主管，领导研究协会高级主管。其主要研究方向为高绩效组织的设计和战略变革管理。

2 Linda Holbeche 琳达·霍尔比契
   英国罗菲帕克学会（Roffey Park Institute）的研究主管。她的研究与其他活动的重点集中在能够让管理人员在工作中和他们广泛的生活中发挥最大的潜力。

3 STEEPLES "尖顶"表
   即 Social、Technological、Environmental、Economic、Political、Legal、Ethic、Something Else 几个词或短语的首字母。

4 Drucker 德鲁克
   即 Peter Ferdinand Drucker（彼得·费迪南·德鲁克，1909—2005），也译作：彼得·杜拉克，被称为"现代管理学之父"。

5 keep close tabs on 看守，检查，监督

Exercises

I Please answer the following questions according to the text.

1. Why do many large multi-national companies set up the organizational development function?
2. What is organizational development?
3. Why is OD definitely different from training?
4. What methods can help the OD consultants to collect enough information for assessing the organization?
5. What steps should the OD consultant follow when she turns to a piece of OD work?

II Please explain the following terms and phrases in English.

training function	organization effectiveness	organization health
organization structure	information platform	finance audit
routine work	organization change	team performance

III Please read the following statements carefully and give your choice: True or False.

1. The organizational development function should be set up within human resources department.
2. OD is shamelessly humanistic and has strong value drivers.
3. Training courses are never combined with OD activities.
4. OD is definitely different from training.
5. Training and OD are short-term efforts.
6. The OD consultant is always from an external agency.
7. To collect enough information for assessing the organization as the second step in the OD project.
8. Most OD interventions are long term efforts.

IV Please translate the following paragraphs into Chinese.

1. Organization development (OD) is a planned, organization-wide effort to increase

an organization's effectiveness and viability. Some scholars referred to OD as a response to change, a complex educational strategy intended to change the beliefs, attitudes, values, and structure of organization so that they can better adapt to new technologies, marketing and challenges, and the dizzying rate of change itself.

2. At the core of OD is the concept of organization, defined as two or more people working together toward one or more shared goal(s). Development in this context is the notion that an organization may become more effective over time at achieving its goals.

3. OD is a long range effort to improve organization's problem solving and renewal processes, particularly through more effective and collaborative management of organizational culture, often with the assistance of a change agent or catalyst and the use of the theory and technology of applied behavioral science. Although behavioral science has provided the basic foundation for the study and practice of organizational development, new and emerging fields of study have made their presence known.

4. Organization development is an ongoing, systematic process to implement effective change in an organization. Organization development is known as both a field of applied behavioral science focused on understanding and managing organizational change and as a field of scientific study and inquiry. It is interdisciplinary in nature and draws on sociology, psychology, and theories of motivation, learning, and personality.

5. "Interventions" are principal learning processes in the "action" stage of organization development. Interventions range from those designed to improve the effectiveness of individuals through those designed to deal with teams and groups, intergroup relations, and the total organization. There are interventions that focus on task issues (what people do), and those that focus on process issues (how people go about doing it).

V Please do the following oral exercises with your partner.

1. Discuss the concept of organizational development.
2. What should an OD consultant do?

Unit 17

Employee Engagement

Employee engagement[1] has attracted more and more attention from the managers and business stakeholders in contemporary world. It is directly linked to employee satisfaction, organizational performance, and bottom line result.

Researches about employee engagement were at first targeted to find whether the employees were satisfied with their job and the workplace. Later researchers found that with the employment satisfaction, the staff would promote the company to their friends and customers, and if there was vacancy in the company, they were willing to introduce other people to work here.

However, it's not necessarily that they don't think of looking for a better job. Therefore the researches then turned to study how to have committed staff who were really attracted by the company so that the company has less risk in attrition.

Today the staff commitment[2] has been gradually replaced by the concept of employee engagement. A committed employee is happy with his stay in the company, but an engaged employee goes the extra mile and contributes significantly differently for the success of the company.

To make it simple, Accenture[3] summarizes that it is all about say, stay, and strive. Say good things, stay as satisfied, and strive for excellence.

How's the employee engagement status in today's competing and dynamic business world? The American Society for Training & Development (ASTD) based on the survey data from around 800 high level human resource and training professionals, discloses that employee engagement is one of the most critical workplace issues of the day. However only one third of the workforce among the survey pool can be characterized as highly engaged. Most of the workforce is moderately engaged with the ratio of around 40 percent, while a forth of the workforce is minimally engaged or disengaged.

Gallup Q12 research presents similar data that at average companies, about 30 percent of

Unit 17 Employee Engagement

employees are engaged. It also estimates that disengaged workforce cost the US economy as much as $350 billion a year; the United Kingdom and Japan, $64.8 billion and $232 billion yearly respectively.

Box 17-1

Gallup Q12

The Gallup Q12 is a survey designed to measure employee engagement. The instrument was the result of hundreds of focus groups and interviews. Researchers found that there were 12 key expectations, that when satisfied, form the foundation of strong feelings of engagement. So far 87,000 work units and 1.5 million employees have participated in the Q12 instrument.

The 12 questions are:

(1) Do you know what is expected of you at work?
(2) Do you have the materials and equipment to do your work right?
(3) At work, do you have the opportunity to do what you do best every day?
(4) In the last seven days, have you received recognition or praise for doing good work?
(5) Does your supervisor, or someone at work, seem to care about you as a person?
(6) Is there someone at work who encourages your development?
(7) At work, do your opinions seem to count?
(8) Does the mission/purpose of your company make you feel your job is important?
(9) Are your associates (fellow employees) committed to doing quality work?
(10) Do you have a best friend at work?
(11) In the last six months, has someone at work talked to you about your progress?
(12) In the last year, have you had opportunities to learn and grow?

Besides above mentioned surveys provided by the professional consulting companies, the organizations can sometimes use simple questionnaire designed by internal training professionals if first the quality of the survey can be ensured, and second the company knows clearly what is its specific focus.

Customer's satisfaction about the service level is always a good indicator the to employee engagement level. Employees without much passion and morale to improve or even maintain the performance standard are not likely to provide satisfaction to the customers hence bring negative impact to the business bottom line. This can also be obtained by the customer satisfaction survey.

Attrition rate and feedback from exit interview are also symbols indicating the employee engagement level. Analysis on attrition rate and exit interview feedback always show that there are different motivation drivers for different group of people if they are classified by age, seniority, positions, performance and so on. That reminds the HR people and the direct managers that the engagement drivers are different, and there is no one-size-fit-all[4] approach to improve all employees' engagement level.

The Hewitt Associates Engagement Model[5], which is widely accepted by many companies, defines six categories of engagement drivers.

- People. Including senior leadership, superior, peers and clients.
- Competitive rewards consisting of compensation & benefits, other recognitions.
- Company practice which means company policies, company reputation, diversity and inclusion, performance assessment, etc.
- Quality of life meaning work-life balance, physical work, enforcement, safety and so on.
- Work itself including work activities, processes, resources, and internal motivation.
- Opportunities mainly referring to career development, learning within the organization.

As what has been mentioned previously, engagement is a very personal issue and it means differently for different people. That makes it natural that for many organizations, the most important approach to improve the employee engagement level is to strengthen the effective communication between the manager and the individual. The Hewitt Associates Engagement Model can frame a very good conversation structure for the manager and the individual to talk logically about which driver is the most important and which is the least, how the individual is satisfied about each of the aspects, and what efforts can be taken from each side to improve the satisfaction so that the overall engagement of the individual can be increased.

Some managers don't know how to continue the talk when the team members simply say that they want more salary.

Unit 17　Employee Engagement

　　The suggestion here is that the manager should just tell the employee that this is out of his control. Let the employee know that as the direct superior he can report the concern to the suitable level managers, and at the same time he could take some time to explain to the employee the company's pay philosophy—to bring the awareness of existing compensation fairness to the employee.

　　Then tell the employee that except the salary, there are more to be explored, which the employee looks forward to and the manager can provide within his control as well. For example, assign the challenging task to the employee who likes it, giving more responsibility to the one who likes more exposure, enroll the one as internal trainer who wants to share his learning with others, approve the flexible working schedule to the young mother who needs to pick up her kid, give more freedom to the subordinate who can do job independently with good quality, swap the jobs between two colleagues who would like to learn from each other, give more coaching time to the one who wishes to develop further in the organization, celebrate when the team gets good result . . .

　　The performance should also be one of the important topics between the manager and the employee. In fact frequent performance feedback itself can serve as an approach to improve employee engagement. When put into a bigger picture, performance talk is just a step regular taking place in the performance management cycle. A corporate culture driving performance can greatly improve the effectiveness of the performance management hence the employee engagement. Not in time performance feedback, not sufficient differentiation between top and bottom performance, no personal development plan, not feeling supported in achieving performance targets are typical performance related factors that drive the employee engagement to the lower side.

　　Many employees don't feel well differentiated in their pay partly because in most companies the individual compensation details are confidential, therefore the real differentiation just can't be showed as the evidence. At the same time, the benefits items are generally the same or sometimes are based on the position level or the service years in the company, for example, the supplemental commercial insurance. If the bonus is also not distributed against performance, then of course few employees will think the company pays for the performance, which is in fact opposite to what the company would like to promote among the staff.

　　Another improvement area for many organizations lies in the training solutions to young managers and employees. Being young here sometimes is beyond the physical condition of age, but more likely refers to the lack of enough maturity.

The newly promoted managers easily get lost in the pressure and deadlines of various tasks so that they ignore the morale of the team members. When there are problem symbols that they can spot, generally they have to devote much more efforts in fixing the problems. Therefore in time training organized by the training professionals and enhanced coaching from experience managers especially their direct superior will be a good prevention for the young managers to get too far away from the right track. These training and coaching should include the role transition from an individual contributor to a leader, the skills in time and resources allocation, the mindset and ability to give and receive feedback, the importance and necessary tips on communication and coaching...

The employees should also be trained to be aware of their responsibilities as well. Although managers are hold accountable in employee engagement, it doesn't mean that employees are free from any actions to strive for the higher engagement level. Employees should also be open to express in time their concerns and suggestions. Managers are not mind readers, and they shouldn't be the only ones to be blamed if they cannot get the meaningful feedback from their subordinates.

The employees should also be encouraged to think creatively to solve the performance issue or some other problems proactively. The ownership to the company helps a lot in employee engagement and vise versa.

Employees from different culture sometimes have very different perception to certain item. Some cultures tend to be more positive, while some tend to be more cynical. It's not a wise idea to do much to change the employees' culture difference, but the logical thinking process and the attitude of appreciation can be trained or influenced.

That's the employee engagement. It influences the business so deeply and not a single task can escape it. With the persistent efforts sticking to a learning organization, a performance driven culture, an open communication style, more and more employees will become highly engaged and lead others to improve the organizational performance to a higher stage.

Box 17-2

Signs of Low Employee Engagement

If you are wondering if employee engagement is a problem in your workplace, consider the following list of indicators of low employee engagement.

Unit 17　Employee Engagement

1. *The attrition rate is high.*

Whether staff is volunteering to leave or is being dismissed, only a small percentage of attrition is due to factors unrelated to employee engagement. The simple truth is that if employees are engaged and have high job satisfaction, they stay.

2. *Productivity is down.*

The statistics have been slipping for a while now. If you were to chart the decline it would be a slope downward.

3. *Deadlines are being missed.*

When employees are unmotivated and they are not working effectively as a team, deadlines get missed.

4. *Morale is low.*

Employees rarely walk around with a smile on their face. They are not interested in planning or being a part of social activities.

5. *Conflicts are happening frequently.*

You feel like a parent at times as their leader. One is complaining about another, so and so did this to that and so on. The conflicts are over small things but the emotions around them are magnified. The maturity level has dropped to a high school level.

6. *Lack of cooperation between staff or other departments.*

They complain about other departments and are blatant in their non-cooperation. It is to the point that the managers of other departments complain

7. *Employees leave the minute the clock turns 5:30.*

As soon as they can, they are out of there. They arrive when they must and leave when they can.

8. *Absenteeism is up.*

They call in sick, seem to be going to the doctor a lot, plan their vacation days carefully and use up all personal days.

9. *Punctuality is a problem.*

You may be seeing a problem with staff arriving late. It started off with one employee arriving late and now you are seeing others arriving late.

10. *Miscommunication is happening frequently.*

Miscommunications happen when staff are not listening carefully to each other and not taking the time to deliver their messages clearly and carefully.

Vocabulary

contemporary	a.	当代的
attrition	n.	磨损，消耗，减员，人才流失
moderately	ad.	中庸地，中等地，普通地
minimally	ad.	最小地，最低限度地
disengaged	a.	已脱离的，无约束的，不承担义务的
yearly	ad.	每年
respectively	ad.	分别
logically	ad.	逻辑地，合乎逻辑地
maturity	n.	成熟
cynical	a.	冷嘲热讽的，愤世嫉俗的
escape	v.	逃避，避免
unrelated	a.	无关的
slip	v.	滑落，下降
chart	v.	绘制图表
slope	n.	斜坡，斜度
blatant	a.	露骨的，喧闹的
miscommunication	n.	理解错误，沟通障碍

Notes

1 employee engagement 员工敬业度
2 staff commitment 员工忠诚度
3 Accenture 埃森哲公司
  埃森哲公司是全球性的管理咨询公司和技术服务供应商，在53个国家设立了分支机构。
4 one-size-fit-all 一刀切，普遍适用的方法
5 Hewitt Associates Engagement Model 翰威特咨询公司提出的敬业度模型

Unit 17 Employee Engagement

I Please answer the following questions according to the text.

1. What is employee engagement?
2. Why has employee engagement attracted more and more attention from the managers and business stakeholders?
3. What is the difference between the two concepts of staff commitment and employee engagement?
4. What are the main drivers for employee engagement according to Hewitt Associates?
5. How should a company make more and more employees become highly engaged?

II Please explain the following terms and phrases in English.

employee engagement	employment satisfaction	staff commitment
customer satisfaction	service level	exit interview
attrition rate	internal motivation	compensation fairness

III Please read the following statements carefully and give your choice: True or False.

1. Employee engagement is indirectly linked to employee satisfaction, organizational performance, and bottom line result.
2. Researches about employee engagement were at first targeted to find whether the employees were satisfied with their job and the workplace.
3. Today the employee engagement has been gradually replaced by the concept of staff commitment.
4. Customer's satisfaction about the service level is always a good indicator the to employee engagement level.
5. Attrition rate and feedback from recruiting interview are also symbols indicating the employee engagement level.
6. The Hewitt Associates Engagement Model is widely accepted by many companies.
7. Engagement means differently for different people.

8. Employee engagement influences the business so deeply and not a single task can escape it.

IV Please translate the following paragraphs into Chinese.

1. For several years now, "employee engagement" has been a hot topic in corporate circles. It's a buzz phrase that has captured the attention of workplace observers and HR managers, as well as the executive suite. And it's a topic that employers and employees alike think they understand, yet can't articulate very easily.

2. Employee engagement is a very big deal. There is clear and mounting evidence that high levels of employee engagement keenly correlates to individual, group and corporate performance in areas such as retention, turnover, productivity, customer service and loyalty.

3. Employee engagement, also called work engagement or worker engagement, is a business management concept. An "engaged employee" is one who is fully involved in, and enthusiastic about, his or her work, and thus will act in a way that furthers their organization's interests.

4. Employee engagement is the extent to which workforce commitment, both emotional and intellectual, exists relative to accomplishing the work, mission, and vision of the organization. Engagement can be seen as a heightened level of ownership where each employee wants to do whatever they can for the benefit of their internal and external customers, and for the success of the organization as a whole.

5. Employee engagement is a measurable degree of an employee's positive or negative emotional attachment to their job, colleagues and organization which profoundly influences their willingness to learn and perform at work. Thus engagement is distinctively different from satisfaction, motivation, culture, climate and opinion and very difficult to measure.

V Please do the following oral exercises with your partner.

1. Discuss the concept of employee engagement.
2. Discuss the significance of employee engagement to a company.

Unit 18
Succession Planning

In various surveys, succession planning always ranks the top five among the issues the senior management team is bearing in mind or worrying about.

Having a succession planning process in place is vital to the success of a company because the individuals identified in the plan will eventually be responsible for ensuring the company's sustainable development in the future.

When succession planning is accomplished, it enables the company to:
- build a leadership pipeline/talent pool to ensure leadership continuity;
- develop potential successors in ways that best fit strengths;
- identify the best candidates for positions;
- clearly define competency requirements along with strategies to develop both existing and new volunteer leaders to meet these needs;
- identify and transfer key knowledge and information that might otherwise be lost;
- ensure that the organization's current mission and vision are carried forward by future leaders.

The system must be proactive in the sense that it should include planning for both regular succession (retirement, planned promotions) and for eventualities, such as illness, fatalities and resignation.

Box 18-1

Leadership Pipeline

The Leadership Pipeline (as shown in Figure 18-1) idea was based on work originally done at General Electric in the 1970s by Walt Mahler[1], a HR consultant and teacher.

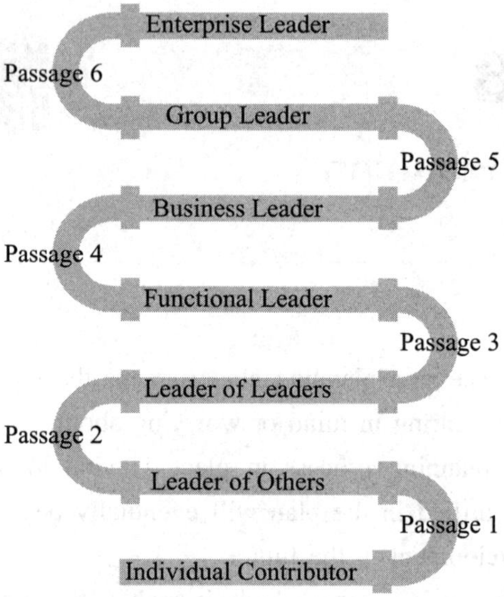

Figure 18 – 1   The Leadership Pipeline

(Pipeline levels from bottom to top: Individual Contributor — Passage 1 — Leader of Others — Passage 2 — Leader of Leaders — Passage 3 — Functional Leader — Passage 4 — Business Leader — Passage 5 — Group Leader — Passage 6 — Enterprise Leader)

Mahler set out to identify all the changes that were required to be successful at different leadership levels. Mahler also developed the crossroads model[2], suggesting that there were specific leadership crossroads in every organization, each with its own specific requirements. Drotter was a student and later a friend of Mahler and refined and adjusted the crossroads model into the leadership pipeline model. Executive Development and Coaching Consultant James Noel and Top-Level Succession Planning Consultant and Professor Ram Charan also contributed later.

Furthermore, succession planning should not be confused with replacement planning, which provides for temporary placement in key positions when an unexpected vacancy occurs. Succession planning is more about developing candidates for succession than identifying those who are coincidentally prepared. Growing talent within organizations yields leaders who, through their historical knowledge and experience in the organization, have earned the trust of the organization and are more likely to be accepted as capable leaders.

Some companies have very systematic approaches in succession planning, while some believe that a formal process is not necessary. No matter which way the company prefers, succession planning should take place in advance of its expected need. If done correctly, the company will have a cadre of qualified members who are more engaged and understand the company's core mission, vision and goals, and are ready to assume broader leadership roles.

However there are always pitfalls we meet in succession planning.

1. Lack of Management Support

A report of the Institute for Corporate Productivity[3], *Succession Planning Highlight Report*, found that 34 percent of organizations with more than 10,000 employees are not prepared to fill their leadership roles. The report also concluded that succession planning will be among the top five challenges executives will face in the future.

Among those companies with succession planning in hand, still some take the plans just as plans on the shelf[4], with few following up actions. During economic crisis, with the significant reduction on training budget, more than often the succession planning turns to be only name list showed in some reports.

In some companies there are concrete plans to develop those potential successors. However managers tend to avoid being deeply engaged into that since they are already overwhelmed by current daily work. To prepare for the future, or to deal with the present, it's always a question.

2. Not Effective Selecting

It's definitely a very difficult task to pick out those whom you believe are capable of handing future leadership job. Living in this fast changing world, we sometimes just can't forecast accurately what the criteria for successful leaders in the not so far future are. And no selecting tools can guarantee there is no discrepancy from the interviewers, seniors, or the tools themselves.

In his book *Know How*, Ram Charan[5] talks about non-negotiable criteria[6], which may give us some inspiration on selecting criteria.

Box 18-2

Non-negotiable Criteria

As you're moving leaders to new jobs, you have to know the person, but you also have to be sure you understand what each job really requires to succeed in it. Contrary to common belief, long lists of criteria don't clarify what's required. The opposite is true: lengthy lists indicate fuzzy thinking and are inherently too general to point to the person who has the best chance of succeeding in that job. Worse, when the criteria are too comprehensive, they eliminated people who may in fact be the best choice in favor of people who are so-so in many categories. The consequence is mediocrity for the organization and unhappiness for the person. You have to have a laser-sharp view of what is absolutely required for a person to do well in a job, and define the three or four non-negotiable criteria, things you cannot compromise on. After years of hiring people in the retail business, Ben Cammarata, the highly successful founder and CEO of the $15 billion off-price retail chain TJX, has had a high batting average over a thirty-year period recruiting, developing, and retaining leadership talent. His non-negotiable criteria are simple and clear. You must be street smart[7], have great people skills, and be intuitively good at merchandising—none of which, he believes, can be taught.

3. Lack of Flexibility

Many succession planning or talent development plans just can't end with satisfactory result.

Some of them fail when the candidates leave the organization before the development activities are completed. The long term investment gets poor ROI[8].

Box 18-3

ROI

ROI is the abbreviation for Return On Investment, also known as ROR (Rate of Return).

A performance measure used to evaluate the efficiency of an? investment or to compare the efficiency of a number of different investments. To calculate ROI, the benefit (return) of an investment is divided by the cost of the investment; the

> result is expressed as a percentage or a ratio.
>
> The return on investment formula:
>
> $$ROI = \frac{\text{Gain from Investment} - \text{Cost of Investment}}{\text{Cost of Investment}}$$
>
> Return on investment is a very popular metric because of its versatility and simplicity. That is, if an investment does not have a positive ROI, or if there are other opportunities with a higher ROI, then the investment should be not be undertaken.

There are frequent organizational changes. M&As[9] happening in today's business world, but the competencies needed are not identified up to date. Not starting with the right target then definitely brings wrong result.

Some traditional succession planning covers only very senior management level. However under different situation the company may find that the middle management is showing unhealthy turnover and it is hard to find those first line managers in a hurry.

There are usually a lot of development activities for a succession planning program. Some company tends to design a very complicated framework which aims to guide all the participants through the activities. The truth is that participants need to share the same principles that are suitable to all, but there must be individual development plan which fit the specific individual.

Vocabulary

continuity	n.	连续性
successor	n.	继任者，继承人
retirement	n.	退休
eventuality	n.	偶然事件，意外，不测
fatality	n.	命运，灾难，死亡（事故）
resignation	n.	辞职，辞呈
confuse	v.	混淆，弄错
coincidentally	ad.	符合地，适合地

yield	v.	产生，造就
cadre	n.	骨干
pitfall	n.	陷阱，风险，易犯的错误
forecast	v.	预测，预计
discrepancy	n.	差异，不符合，不一致
non-negotiable	a.	无商量余地的，说一不二的，不能讨价还价的
inspiration	n.	灵感，鼓舞
fuzzy	a.	模糊不清的
inherently	ad.	内在地，固有地，与生俱来地
so-so	a.	一般般的，不好也不坏的
mediocrity	n.	平凡，平庸
laser-sharp	a.	像激光一样精准的
batting	n.	击球
intuitively	ad.	直觉地
merchandise	v.	做生意
flexibility	n.	灵活性
turnover	n.	转换

Notes

1. Walt Mahler 沃尔特·马勒 [20世纪70年代在通用电气公司进行领导力补给线（leadership pipeline）模型的研究]
2. crossroads model 十字路模型（每一个组织内部都有其特定的领导力十字路口，对领导力的需求也各不相同）
3. Institute for Corporate Productivity 企业生产力研究机构（美国著名的咨询机构，其名称通常缩写为i4cp）
4. on the shelf 被搁置的，闲置的
5. Ram Charan 拉姆·查安（著名的管理咨询顾问和学者，领导力补给线的提出者之一）
6. non-negotiable criteria 必须绝对遵守的标准，不能讨价还价的标准

7 street smart 熟悉都市生活方式和世态的，在城市环境中有巧妙生存能力的
8 ROI （人力资源的）投入产出比率
9 M&As 并购，兼并与收购（Mergers and Acquisitions）

I Please answer the following questions according to the text.

1. Why does succession planning always rank the top five among the issues worried about by the senior management team?
2. Why is having a succession planning process in place vital to the success of a company?
3. What is the difference between succession planning and replacement planning?
4. What are the pitfalls in succession planning?
5. Should succession planning only cover very senior management level? Why?

II Please explain the following terms and phrases in English.

succession planning	leadership pipeline	leadership continuity
regular succession	replacement planning	capable leader
potential successor	senior management	middle management

III Please read the following statements carefully and give your choice: True or False.

1. Having a succession planning process in place is vital to the success of a company.
2. An effective succession planning ensure that the organization's current mission and vision are carried forward by future leaders.
3. Succession planning should include planning for both regular succession and for eventualities, such as retirement, planned promotions.
4. Succession planning provides for temporary placement in key positions when an unexpected vacancy occurs.
5. Every company believes that a formal process for succession planning is necessary.
6. Succession planning should take place in advance of its expected need.

7. In every company there are concrete plans to develop those potential successors.
8. Some traditional succession planning covers only very senior management level.

IV Please translate the following paragraphs into Chinese.

1. Succession planning is a process for identifying and developing internal people with the potential to fill key leadership positions in the company. Succession planning increases the availability of experienced and capable employees that are prepared to assume these roles as they become available.
2. Typically, succession planning entails three steps: a decision-making stage (choosing a successor), the gradual transfer of minority stock holdings and the transfer of ownership and management responsibilities to the successor.
3. It may not be vital to have a succession plan for every position in the company, but certainly there are some key areas of responsibility which must be considered.
4. Skillfully done, succession planning will bring the peace of mind that senior management should have, based on the understanding and expectations of its future leadership.
5. Recognize that all companies do not have to follow the same path either in the overall situation or even for each individual. Each situation should be analyzed and optimized in terms of the company's needs and the individual's needs. In addition, there should be enough time allowed to groom the successors. They should not be expected to learn the jobs/responsibilities overnight.

V Please do the following oral exercises with your partner.

1. Discuss the concept of succession planning.
2. How should a company avoid the pitfalls in succession planning?

Appendix 1
Glossary
词汇表

A

abundant	*a.*	充足的，充裕的
abuse	*v.*	滥用
accompany	*v.*	陪伴，陪随
accomplishment	*n.*	完成，履行
accountability	*n.*	负有责任
accumulate	*v.*	积累
accurately	*ad.*	准确地
achieve	*v.*	实现，达到
acquire	*v.*	取得，获得，学到
acquired	*a.*	已得到的，已成习惯的
adjustment	*n.*	调整
administrative	*a.*	管理的，行政的
advertisement	*n.*	广告
advocate	*n.*	拥护者
affiliation	*n.*	亲密关系
aggressive	*a.*	进攻性的
akin	*a.*	同族的，同种的，类似的
align	*v.*	使结盟，使结合，使密切合作
alignment	*n.*	结合，组合
allowance	*n.*	津贴
alternate	*a.*	交替的，替代的
alternative	*a.*	替代的，可选的
alumnus	*n.*	校友，以前的伙伴

ambiguity	n.	含糊，意义不明确
ambition	n.	抱负，雄心
analytical	a.	分解的，分析的
analyze	v.	分析
announce	v.	宣布，通告
announcement	n.	宣布，通告
anonymous	a.	匿名的
antidote	n.	解毒剂，矫正法
appointed	a.	指定的，约定的
appraisal	n.	评价，考核，鉴定
appraise	v.	评价，鉴定
appreciate	v.	感激，感谢
appreciation	n.	感激，欣赏
approach	n.	方法，手段
appropriate	a.	适当的，合适的
appropriately	ad.	适当地
arrangement	n.	安排，筹备，布置
artist	n.	艺术家
aspiration	n.	渴望，志愿，抱负
assertive	a.	肯定的，断言的
assessment	n.	评估，评价，鉴定
assessor	n.	评价者，评审员
assignment	n.	分配，指定，委派，任务
assistance	n.	援助，帮助
associated	a.	联合的，联想的
atmosphere	n.	氛围
attentively	ad.	注意地，留心地
attrition	n.	磨损，消耗，减员，人才流失
audience	n.	听众，观众，读者
awareness	n.	明白，了解

B

background	n.	背景，出身，经历

bar	n.	标准，合格线
bargain	n.	讨价还价
batting	n.	击球
behavioral	a.	行为的
belongingness	n.	归属
benchmarking	n.	基准评价
betrayal	n.	背叛，背信弃义
blatant	a.	露骨的，喧闹的
blueprint	n.	蓝图，设计图
blunt	a.	钝的，呆板的，干脆的
boisterous	a.	狂风暴雨的，吵吵嚷嚷的
bonus	n.	奖金，红利，额外津贴
briefing	n.	简报，简单告知
brilliant	a.	明亮的，卓越的，杰出的
brutally	ad.	粗暴地，不讲理地，令人不快地
buddy	n.	伙伴，兄弟
bulletin	n.	告示，公告

C

cadre	n.	骨干
calculate	v.	计算
capture	v.	捕获，获得
cashier	n.	收银员
category	n.	类别，类型
challenge	v.	质疑，质问
chart	v.	绘制图表
chastise	v.	惩戒，惩罚
clarification	n.	澄清，说明
clarify	v.	澄清，阐明
clone	n.	克隆，复制品，一模一样的人
cluster	n.	丛，组，团，群集
coalition	n.	结合，联盟
cognitive	a.	认识的，认识力的

coincidentally	ad.	符合地，适合地
collaboration	n.	合作
collaborative	a.	合作的，协调的
combat	v.	搏斗，与……斗争
commission	n.	佣金，提成
common	a.	通常的，常见的
communicate	v.	交流，沟通，传达
communication	n.	交流，沟通
community	n.	社区，社群，共同体
compensation	n.	薪酬
competency	n.	能力，胜任
competitor	n.	竞争者，竞争对手
complaint	n.	投诉，抱怨
complementary	a.	补充的，互补的
completion	n.	完成
complexity	n.	复杂性，复杂状态
complicated	a.	结构复杂的
comprehensive	a.	综合的，全面的
compromise	v.	妥协，折中
conceivably	ad.	想得到地，想象地
conceptual	a.	概念的，理论的
concern	n.	担忧，关切，关心的问题
concrete	a.	具体的，实际的
confidence	n.	信任，自信
confident	a.	自信的，沉着的
confidentiality	n.	保密，机密
conformity	n.	相似，一致
confuse	v.	混淆，弄错
connection	n.	关系
conquer	v.	征服，攻克，克服
conscious	a.	清醒的，自己知道的
consequence	n.	后果，影响
consequently	ad.	因此，结果
consistent	a.	一致的，协调的

consistently	ad.	一致地，协调地，不矛盾地
constructive	a.	积极的，建设性的
consume	v.	消耗，花费，浪费
contemporary	a.	当代的
contextual	a.	联系上下文的，从前后关系来看的
continuity	n.	连续性
continuous	a.	连续的，不间断的
controversy	n.	争论，辩论，论战
convey	v.	传达，传递
coordinate	v.	使配合，使协调
corporate	a.	公司的，法人的
corresponding	a.	相应的，对应的
correspondingly	ad.	相应地
counsel	v.	商议，劝导
counselor	n.	顾问
counterpart	n.	对应者，相对应的人
cozy	a.	舒适的，惬意的
critical	a.	关键的
crucial	a.	非常重要的，关键性的
culture	n.	文化
cynical	a.	冷嘲热讽的，愤世嫉俗的

D

deadline	n.	最后期限，截止日期
debate	n.	辩论，争论
defeat	v.	打破，击败，使无效
definitely	ad.	明确地，确定地，绝对地
definitive	a.	明确的，确定的
deliberate	a.	深思熟虑的
demanding	a.	苛求的，吹毛求疵的
demonstrate	v.	表明，证明
demonstration	n.	表明，说明
denial	n.	否认，拒绝接受

depict	v.	刻画，描写，叙述
depressed	a.	沮丧的，消沉的，忧郁的
deprive	v.	使失去，剥夺
derailer	n.	导致偏离正常轨道的因素
description	n.	描述
descriptor	n.	描述符号，描述者
deserved	a.	应当的，值得的
desirable	a.	理想的，满意的
diagnosis	n.	诊断，判断
dialogue	n.	对话
dictate	v.	指挥，支配
differentiate	v.	区别，区分
differentiation	n.	区别，不同，差异化
digest	v.	消化，领会，整理
dilemma	n.	困境
diligent	a.	勤奋的，勤勉的
dimension	n.	维度
diplomat	n.	外交官
disagreement	n.	差异，分歧，异议
disciplinary	a.	纪律性的
discrepancy	n.	差异，分歧，不符合，不一致
disengaged	a.	已脱离的，无约束的，不承担义务的
dissimilar	a.	不一样的
distinctiveness	n.	独特性
distinguish	v.	区别，区分
distort	v.	扭曲，歪曲
distribute	v.	分配，分发
distrust	n.	疑惑，不相信
downside	n.	缺陷，负面影响
dramatic	a.	戏剧性的，剧烈的，引人关注的
dramatically	ad.	戏剧性地，引人注目地，剧烈地，
dread	a.	害怕，担心
dreadful	a.	可怕的
drive	v.	驱使，驱动

dyad	a.	二个的
dynamic	a.	动态的

E

eagerness	n.	渴望，热情
ease	v.	使轻松
ecology	n.	生态
elicit	v.	引出，诱出
eligibility	n.	资格，适合
eligible	a.	合格的
eliminate	v.	消除，淘汰
emerge	v.	出现，显露
emergency	n.	紧急情况，非常时期
emotion	n.	情绪，情感
empathy	n.	共情，同理心
emphasize	v.	强调
empower	v.	使有能力
encompass	v.	围绕，包含
encounter	v.	遭遇，遇到
enduring	a.	持久的，永久的
energize	v.	加强，给以能量
enhance	v.	增强，提高
enlist	v.	争取，获得
enrichment	n.	丰富，充实
enroll	v.	登记，使加入
entitlement	n.	应得的权利
environmental	a.	环境的
equilibrium	n.	平衡
equitable	a.	公平的，平衡的
escape	v.	逃避，避免
especially	ad.	特别，尤其
essential	a.	本质的，必需的，主要的
evaluation	n.	评估，评价体系

eventuality	n.	偶然事件，意外，不测
eventually	ad.	最后，终于
exact	a.	精确的，严格的
exceptional	a.	例外的，特别多，优异的
excitement	n.	兴奋，刺激
executive	n.	执行官，总经理
exemplify	v.	举例证明，解释
existence	n.	存在
expansively	ad.	开阔地
expectation	n.	期望
experienced	a.	有经验的
explain	v.	解释，说明
exposure	n.	暴露，曝光，承受风险
extensive	a.	广泛的
externally	ad.	在外部，从外部
extrinsic	a.	外在的

F

facilitate	v.	使顺利，使方便，促进
facilitation	n.	方便，助长，促进
facilitator	n.	促进者，便利措施
facility	n.	设备，器材
fancy	a.	特别的，具有高度技巧性的
fatality	n.	命运，灾难，死亡（事故）
favorite	n.	喜欢的东西
feedback	n.	反馈
flexibility	n.	灵活性
forecast	v.	预测，预计
forefront	n.	前沿，最前面
formality	n.	形式，俗套
formalize	v.	使成为正式，使具有形式
formative	a.	形成的，构成的
freelance	n.	自由职业，独立职位

frustrate	v.	使挫败，使落空
frustrated	a.	有挫败感的，失意的
frustration	n.	失败，挫折
fuss	n.	忙乱，小题大做
fuzzy	a.	模糊不清的

G

generalist	n.	通才，知识渊博者，多面手
generic	a.	一般的，普通的
glance	n.	一瞥，扫视
glean	v.	搜集，拾遗，发现，查明
gradually	ad.	逐渐地，逐步地
gratification	n.	使人满足或喜悦的事物
grievance	n.	不满，牢骚，悲叹
grouping	n.	集团，群集，编组
gut	n.	内在，实质
	a.	简单的，直觉的

H

hall	n.	会堂，会议厅
handwriting	n.	笔迹
harmony	n.	和谐
hazardous	a.	危险的
hierarchy	n.	层次，层级，等级
highlight	v.	突出显示，强调
hinder	v.	妨碍，阻挠
honestly	ad.	诚实地，坦诚地
humanistic	a.	人性研究的，人本主义的

I

identification	n.	识别，鉴定

ignore	v.	忽视，不顾
imitate	v.	模仿
immediate	a.	立刻，即时
imperative	n.	规则
implementation	n.	执行，履行，贯彻，落实
improvement	n.	改进，进步，提高
incomplete	a.	不完整的，不完备的
inconsistent	a.	不一致的，不符合的
incorporate	a.	结合，合并
in-depth	a.	深入的
indicator	n.	指标，指示物
ineligible	a.	无资格的
inevitable	a.	不可避免的
inflate	v.	使膨胀，使得意
inherently	ad.	内在地，固有地，与生俱来地
initial	a.	最初的，开始的
initiative	a.	起始的，初步的
	n.	第一步，着手
innovation	n.	创新
innovative	a.	创新的，富有创新精神的
insight	n.	眼光，见识
inspiration	n.	灵感，鼓舞
inspire	v.	激发，鼓舞，使产生灵感
integral	a.	完整的，缺一不可的
integrated	a.	整体的，整合的
intent	n.	意图，目的
interaction	n.	相互作用，互动
intermediate	a.	中间的
internally	ad.	在内部，从内部
interpersonal	a.	人际的
interrupt	v.	打断，妨碍
interruption	n.	打断，中断，停止
interval	n.	时间间隔
intervention	n.	介入，干预

Appendix 1　Glossary

interview	n.	面试，面谈
intrinsic	a.	内在的
intuitively	ad.	直觉地
involved	a.	有关的，相关的
involvement	n.	包括，包含，牵连，相关事务

J

| jobless | a. | 没有工作的，失业的 |
| junior | a. | 初级的，资历浅的 |

L

ladder	n.	阶梯，成功的手段
laser-sharp	a.	像激光一样精准的
lateral	a.	侧面的
laudable	a.	值得称赞的
layoff	n.	裁员
leadership	n.	领导能力，领导权
legend	n.	传说，传奇，传奇人物
leverage	v.	对……起杠杆作用
lifetime	n.	一生，终生，有生之年
limitation	n.	限制，局限性
linkage	n.	联系，连接
logically	ad.	逻辑地，合乎逻辑地
lousy	a.	糟糕的
loyalty	n.	忠诚
lump	a.	总共的

M

magic	a.	魔术的，有魔力的，不可思议的
mandatory	a.	强制的
manifestation	n.	表现，显示

match	v.	匹配,适合
maternity	n.	产假
mathematics	n.	数学
matrix	n.	矩阵
maturity	n.	成熟
maximize	v.	使最大化
maximum	a.	最大的,最高的
meaningful	a.	有意义的
mediocrity	n.	平凡,平庸
mend	n.	改进,修复,加强,治愈
mental	a.	精神的,心理的
mentally	ad.	内心里,精神上
mentor	n.	辅导教师,指导者
	v.	指导,当……的导师
merchandise	v.	做生意
merge	n.	兼并
meritocracy	n.	精英阶层
metaphor	n.	隐喻,象征
methodology	n.	方法论,研究方法
metric	a.	公认的,习惯上的
mild	a.	温和的,轻微的
mindset	n.	心态,想法
minimal	a.	最小的,最低限度的
minimally	ad.	最小地,最低限度地
minimize	v.	使最小化
minimum	a.	最小的,最低的
miscommunication	n.	理解错误,沟通障碍
misconduct	n.	行为不当,渎职
mission	n.	使命
mitigate	v.	减少,减轻,缓和
mobility	n.	移动性,灵活性,能动性
moderately	ad.	中庸地,中等地,普通地
module	n.	测量单位,系数,模量
morale	n.	士气,精神

motivate	v.	激发，促动
motivation	n.	动机的形成，动机因素，动力
motivator	n.	激励因素，推动力
motive	n.	动机，动因
motto	n.	座右铭，箴言
multiple	a.	多重的，多个的，多次的
mutual	a.	彼此的，相互的
myth	n.	神话

N

necessarily	ad.	必需地，必要地，必定地
negative	a.	负面的，消极的
negotiation	n.	洽谈，磋商
nervousness	n.	紧张
non-negotiable	a.	无商量余地的，说一不二的，不能讨价还价的
notoriously	ad.	声名狼藉地

O

objection	n.	反对
objective	a.	客观的
observable	a.	可观察的，能观察到的
obsolete	a.	陈旧的，过时的
obstacle	n.	障碍，妨害
officially	ad.	正式地
opposite	a.	相反的，对立的
optional	a.	可选的，非强制性的
organizational	a.	组织的
orient	v.	使适应
orientation	n.	导向，定向，定位，（对新环境的）适应
originally	ad.	原本，起初
overbearing	a.	傲慢的，自大的
overcome	v.	克服，战胜

overwhelm	v.	压倒,淹没,使不知所措

P

par	n.	同等,同价,同一水平
paradigm	n.	范例
passion	n.	热情,激情
patience	n.	耐心
payroll	a.	薪资账册,发薪名单,薪资总额
peak	a.	顶点,峰值
peck	v.	啄,凿,用食指按键盘上的键打字
peer	n.	同辈的人,同级别的人,同事,伙伴
penalize	v.	使处于不利地位,处罚
pension	n.	养老金
percentile	a.	百分比的
performer	n.	履行者,执行者,完成任务的人
persistence	n.	坚持,持续,持久
personality	n.	人格,个性,性格
perspective	n.	视角,角度,观点
persuasive	a.	有说服力的
philosophy	n.	基本原理
physiological	a.	生理的,生理上的
pitfall	n.	陷阱,风险,易犯的错误
popular	a.	普遍的,流行的,受欢迎的
positive	a.	积极的,正面的
potential	a.	潜在的,可能的
	n.	有潜力的人
practical	a.	实用的,可行的
practitioner	n.	实践者,从业者
predictor	n.	预言者,预报器
predominant	a.	突出的,最显著的
predominantly	ad.	主要地,显著地,占优势地
preliminary	a.	预备的,初级的
presentation	n.	陈述,发言

preset	v.	预先设置
pretty	a.	很多的
prevention	n.	预防
priority	n.	优先，优先权
proactive	a.	积极主动的，前瞻的
proactively	ad.	积极地，主动地
probability	n.	概率，可能性
probationary	a.	试用的，见习的
probe	v.	探查，探究
problematic	a.	有问题的，疑难的
professional	n.	职业人士，专业人士，行家
professionalism	n.	专家气质，职业特质，职业水准
professionally	ad.	职业化地，专业化地
proficiency	n.	精通，熟练
profile	n.	形象，轮廓，人物简介
proper	a.	正常的，适当的
property	n.	性质，特征
psychological	a.	心理的，心理学的
psychologist	n.	心理学家
psychology	n.	心理学
punishment	n.	惩罚
purpose	n.	目的，作用
pursue	v.	追求，奉行

Q

qualification	n.	资格，资质
quality	a.	优质的，高水平的
quarterly	a.	每季度的
quasi-legal	a.	准司法性的
query	v.	询问
questionnaire	n.	问卷，调查表

R

rapport	n.	友好关系
reaction	n.	反应
reasoning	n.	推理
recipient	n.	接收者，感受者，接受者
recognition	n.	认可，褒奖
recommendation	n.	推荐，介绍，建议
recruiter	n.	招募人，招聘者
recruitment	n.	招聘，招募
redeployment	n.	转移，重新布置
redesign	n.	重新设计，调整
reengineer	v.	重构，调整
referral	n.	介绍，引荐
refine	v.	精炼，提纯，改善，美化
reflect	v.	反映
reflective	a.	反映的，反射的
regulation	n.	规章，制度
rehire	v.	重新雇佣，再次雇佣
reinforcement	n.	增强，巩固
reliably	ad.	可靠地，确实地
remedy	n.	补救措施，救治手段
remuneration	n.	报酬，酬劳
repetitively	ad.	反复地，重复地
reproach	n.	责备，谴责，耻辱
resignation	n.	辞职，辞呈
respectively	ad.	分别
responsibility	n.	责任，职责
responsive	a.	回复的，共鸣的，反应迅速的
restore	v.	恢复，重建
restructure	n.	重新组织，改组
retention	n.	保持，保留，留住
retirement	n.	退休

Appendix 1   Glossary

reveal	v.	显露，显示
ridesharing	n.	搭便车
ridiculous	a.	荒谬的，可笑的
roadmap	n.	路线图，准则，指示
rotation	n.	轮换
rumor	n.	传闻，流言

S

sacrifice	n.	牺牲
sample	v.	抽样
scale	n.	尺度
scenario	n.	场景，情况
score	v.	记分，评分
scour	v.	搜寻
screen	v.	筛选，甄别
selectively	ad.	选择地
self-actualization	n.	自我实现
self-concept	n.	自我概念，对自己的看法
self-esteem	n.	自尊
seminar	n.	研讨会
seniority	n.	资历
sensitive	a.	敏感的
shamelessly	ad.	不知羞愧地
shape	v.	塑造，使适合
sheet	n.	一张，纸张
slip	v.	滑落，下降
slope	n.	斜坡，斜度
smiley	n.	笑脸符号
solicitation	n.	恳求，恳请，征求
so-so	a.	一般般的，不好也不坏的
souvenir	n.	纪念品，礼品
span	n.	范围，跨度
	v.	跨越

spatial	a.	空间的
specialist	n.	专家，专业人才，精通某一专业的人
spectrum	n.	范围，幅度，系列
sphere	n.	范围
sponsor	n.	发起者，主办者
sponsorship	n.	保证人的角色
spot	v.	认出，找到，发现
spouse	n.	配偶
stereotype	n.	成见，旧习
strategic	a.	战略性的
stressful	a.	紧张的
stretch	v./n.	伸展，延伸，扩展
strive	v.	力求，努力，奋斗
stumble	v.	绊倒，蹒跚行走
subordinate	n.	下级，下属
succession	n.	继任
successor	n.	继任者，继承人
sufficient	a.	充分的，足够的
suitability	n.	适合，适宜，相配
summative	a.	概括的，总结的
supermarket	n.	超市
supervision	n.	监督，管理
supervisory	a.	监督的，管理的
supplemental	a.	补充的，增补的
supportive	a.	支持的，赞许的
surround	v.	围绕
suspension	n.	悬吊，中止，搁置
sustainability	n.	可持续性
swap	n.	互换，调换
symbolic	a.	象征性的
sympathy	n.	同情
synergy	n.	协同，配合

T

tactfully	*ad.*	机智地，得体地，老练地，圆滑地
tailor	*v.*	量身定制，使合适
teamwork	*n.*	团队工作，协调工作
tease	*v.*	取笑
technically	*ad.*	技术上，学术上
template	*n.*	模板
theoretical	*a.*	理论上的
thoroughly	*ad.*	全面地
timeline	*n.*	时间表
timetable	*n.*	时间表
trace	*v.*	追踪，追溯，追究
track	*v.*	拉纤，用纤拉
traditionally	*ad.*	按照传统地
trainable	*a.*	可以培训出来的，通过培训可以形成的
trainer	*n.*	培训者
trait	*n.*	特性，性格
transition	*n.*	转变，过渡期
trick	*n.*	诡计，把戏
tricky	*a.*	微妙的，复杂的，棘手的
triple	*a.*	三倍的，三重的，三者的
trivial	*a.*	琐碎的，细小的
turnover	*n.*	转换

U

unacceptable	*a.*	不可接受的
uncomfortable	*a.*	不安的，不自在的
uncoordinated	*a.*	不协调的
uncover	*v.*	使露出，使知道，揭示
underlying	*a.*	基础的，潜在的
underperformer	*n.*	考核不合格的员工

underperforming	a.	表现不合格的
understand	v.	理解，谅解
understandable	a.	可理解的，容易理解的
unemployment	n.	失业
unexpected	a.	没想到的，意外的
unfold	v.	展开
uniformity	n.	一样，一律，一致
universally	ad.	一般地，普遍地
unplanned	a.	未经计划的，随机的，意外的
unrelated	a.	无关的
unreliable	a.	不可靠的
update	v.	更新，升级，使适应新形势

V

vacancy	n.	（职位）空缺
vague	a.	含糊的，笼统的
valuable	a.	有价值的
variation	n.	变化，变动
vehicle	n.	媒介，手段，工具，载体
version	n.	版本，说法
viewpoints	n.	观点，看法，见解
visibility	n.	能见度，可见性，显著性
vision	n.	愿景
vividly	ad.	生动地，鲜明地
voluntarily	ad.	自愿地
volunteer	v.	自愿去做，自动请求去做

W

weakness	n.	弱点，缺点，短处，劣势

Y

yank	*n.*	突然的猛拉
yearly	*ad.*	每年
yield	*v.*	产生,造就
youngster	*n.*	小孩子

Appendix 2
Reference Translation for Texts
课文参考译文

第1部分　人员管理

第1单元　帮助你的员工找到新工作——你准备好了吗？

2008年开始的经济危机让很多人的生活发生了改变。财务专家建议人们缩减开支，预留6个月的生活费以应对紧急情况。在目前的全职工作之外，再找一份兼职工作，也是解决办法之一。然而，危机使得很多人失去了全职工作。因此，人们不只是需要财务建议，也需要寻找一份工作的方法。这些方法有时候会对人们很有帮助，尤其对那些从未想过会离开公司，却因为公司不得不通过裁员渡过经济危机而被迫离开的员工。

2009年年底，有一部好莱坞电影名叫《在云端》。在这部电影里，乔治·克鲁尼扮演一位专门负责解雇人的人力资源专业人士。然而，如果你想更加专业，你应该不只是解雇人，还应该帮助你的员工寻找一份新工作。

安妮是一家中型高科技企业的软件工程师，几个月前刚刚被解雇。当时她已经在那家著名的IT企业干了9年。她从一所一流大学获得理学学士学位之后，就加入了那家公司。她热爱公司的文化，也喜欢这份工作。她得到了她期望的提升。公司就是她的第二个家。

当裁员名单公布的时候，她觉得她的心都碎了。愤怒和疑惑让她泪流满面。在开始的几天里，她无法相信这是事实。这家IT公司为将要离开的员工开设了培训课程，指导他们如何控制自己的情绪和职业的变化。安妮从这些课程中受益匪浅，她逐渐摆脱了挫败感，并最终找到了现在这份新工作。每当谈起她的第一位雇主，她仍然很感激在那里工作的9年给了她丰富的工作经验，以及裁员之前的职业辅导课程。

帮助即将离开的同事寻找一份新工作，跟为他们精确地计算补偿方案一样重要。公司作为企业公民，应该承担起社会责任，将裁员给员工和社会带来的负面影响减少到最低限度。在裁员的时候，人力资源专业人员需要做的工作远比一张通知书要多得多。

在这种时候，有两个方面的问题需要关注：一个是心理方面，一个是程序方面。

Appendix 2　Reference Translation for Texts

　　裁员是公司面临的剧烈的组织变化，而失业对于员工个人生活的影响则更为严重。这时，（被裁掉的）员工在不同的阶段会有不同的情绪表现。

　　裁员名单公布的时候，他们的第一反应通常是震惊，并拒绝接受。"你在开玩笑吧？""我无法相信。"然后，在他们开始接受这一消息的时候，很多人因为遭受打击而变得愤怒和沮丧。他们会质疑为什么公司做出如此决定，会质问他们将来该怎么办。他们觉得受到了背叛，他们认为自己不再是公司的一部分，而把自己放在了公司的对立面上。在裁员的执行过程中，有些人会非常消沉，因为他们没有在这一过程中发现任何好的地方。他们没有任何新工作的保障，以前的同事一个一个地离开了，他们觉得自己是没有用的人。

　　在这个困难时期，从公司的角度，或者作为一个领导，能够给予这些员工的最大帮助就是提供充分的信息。这些信息包括：公司做出这种决定背后的原因，对被裁者的安置，给他们的赔偿。为了真正做到提供充分的信息，还应该反复地解释和澄清公司给予他们的其他支持。经理们应该充当真正的、优秀的倾听者，允许这些员工表达他们的愤怒和关切，并且给予迅速的反馈。有时候，经理们不得不说他们也不知道一些还没有最后敲定的细节问题。把话坦诚地说出来，并且确认你会尽快把问题的答案转达给员工。不要害怕那些质疑，因为这也是理解的一部分。

　　通常，在双方达成相互理解的时候，积极的对话就开始了，员工们会愿意配合公司进行后续的程序。现在，必要的培训可以开始了。这些培训可以帮助员工更多、更深入地了解公司能够为他们做些什么，以及他们自己需要做哪些改变。当他们重建自信之后，不一定要等到找到新工作，很多人就会最终接受现实。不同的人到达这一阶段需要花费不同的时间。给他们一些时间来应对。而且，毕竟这个过程的目标也是如此。当员工不得不离开公司的时候，应该让他们带着良好关系和感激之情离开。这是最后一个阶段。

　　我们始终考虑着心理方面问题的时候，就更容易将程序方面的问题设计好，使之与不同的心理阶段相配合。

　　在正式宣布裁员名单之前，召集经理们开一个简短的会议，是一个常用而且有益的方法。如果可能的话，在举行公开会议之前两三天召开这个简短会议。这样，经理们将有更多的时间来消化裁员信息，并准备好回答各种可能的问题。

　　在公开会议上，进行清晰的陈述有助于员工理解为什么要裁员及如何裁员。经理们应该做好随时被打断的准备，但是总的时间应该控制在 1～2 个小时之内。不要把陈述时间浪费在无休止的提问与回答上，只有基础性、标准性的信息需要在公开会议上正式宣布，其他涉及具体情况的问题应该在会议之后收集并解答。

　　会上公开宣布的标准信息及会后收集的问题与解答，都应该在公司的公告牌或者网站上公布，或者以两种方式同时公布。由于通常涉及法律问题，为了确保遵守相关的法律法规，同样的情况应该适用同样的标准，同样的问题应该给予同样的解答。

在那些不得不进行裁员的公司里，职业辅导项目也很流行。通常，会有一家外聘的顾问公司来帮助（被裁的）员工认识自己的情绪变化，并在他们寻找新工作的过程中提供支持。

很多公司都有重新雇佣政策：如果公司里有了新的职位空缺，他们将首先考虑那些以前因为组织变化而被裁掉的员工。对这种现实中发生的故事，我们也都听说过。所以，不要对那些离开公司的员工失去兴趣。这个世界很小（说不定很快他们又会回来）。

第2单元　发现候选人的新方法

找工作通常是耗费时间，而且多少会令人产生挫败感的事情。而事实上，对于招聘者来说，要找到一个合适的候选人也一样。

大多数公司把他们的招聘广告刊登在报纸上，或发到互联网上，然后就期待着潜在的候选人发现这些广告，并把他们的简历投递到指定地址。筛选和面试结束之后，招聘工作就完成了。录用部门的经理们祈祷他们真的找到了他们需要的人。

除了上述这种最常见的方法，公司还可能通过猎头公司去寻找高级职位的候选人，或者人才供给非常少的某些职位的候选人。那些猎头公司被认为在寻找和选择人才方面更加具有专业性。通常，这些职业代理机构拥有庞大的人才数据库，而公司内部的人力资源部门无法建立并维护这样的数据库。

公司也会经常采用内部推荐的方式选聘人才。同事比外部猎头公司，甚至比内部人力资源部门职员都更加清楚他们的朋友是否会喜欢这家公司，以及他们正在从事的这份工作。虽然那些成功地推荐了合适候选人的员工会得到额外的奖励，但是考虑到内部推荐方式更高的通过率，它被认为是一种非常高效而且经济的方式。

招聘经理们喜欢通过他们自己的关系网发布空缺职位和求职者的信息，比如：在互联网上发布招聘广告，发电子邮件，或者只是通过手机发送短信息。但是，最新的趋势是通过Facebook、LinkedIn、Twitter这样的社会关系网络来发布相关的信息。

这种新方法最令人惊奇的地方在于，只要你找到一个入口，就可以把如此多的人联系在一起。与传统的招聘方式相比，它的确是一种非常具有前瞻性的渠道。

从这些社交媒介上，我们能够得到的不只是显示教育背景和工作经验的正式简历，还可以发现言论背后的主题、建议、素质乃至价值观。西莉亚·皮卡斯是一家中型生产企业的招聘经理，她说："我曾经要招聘一位生产经理，当时有两个候选人条件相当，很难取舍。我设法找到了他们在网上发表的一些言论。然后我选择了那个说话很像我们经理的人。而且事后证明，这是个正确的决定。"

Appendix 2　Reference Translation for Texts

在不远的将来，这种方式是否会成为最流行的招聘渠道？根据 MRINetwork 招聘公司负责学习和人才培养的副总裁哈弗森女士的话，通过社会媒介寻找工作和人才，很可能"已经取代了传统的纸质简历方式"，招聘经理有时候不知道如何找到一位在网上不存在的人。"你必须在某个社交网站上有一个简介，这一点毋庸置疑。"

当然，它还不可能在目前成为唯一的方式。很多求职者从来没有想过有什么理由要在网上建立一种存在形式，也不知道该如何建立。这些人在制造业这样的行业工作，Facebook 和 Twitter 并不是他们日常生活的一部分。或者，他们几十年都坚持在同一家公司工作，从来不觉得有必要制作一份简历，在 LinkedIn 的个人主页上介绍他们的工作历史。这些人拥有新工作所需要的所有技能，但是却缺乏在求职过程中所需要的技能。

如何使用这些新工具不只是一个技术问题。更多的时候，它是关于如何以一种正确的、持续的方式宣传自己的问题。

雅各布·施密德是洛杉矶的一位 IT 顾问，2008 年，他失去了在一家德国技术公司的工作。这是他 20 年来第一次进入人才市场寻找工作。他像求职者通常所做的一样，发出简历，然后等待公司给他打电话。他没有等来任何回音。

在网上寻找工作信息的时候，他发现了几个网站和论坛，上面有一些关于如何在网上建立自己的"个人品牌"的建议。他开始在网上写关于工作的博客，并且通过 Twitter 联系那些同行。

他说："开始的时候，我很不顺手，有很多的磕磕碰碰。我不知我在干什么，也不知道该说些什么。"但是几个月之后，他习惯了——他在 Twitter 上写的关于工作的帖子更好了，他知道应该把他的帖子发给哪些正确的人。他开始持续地，但不是令人难以忍受地推销自己。

一位以前的同事注意到了施密德先生发的这些帖子，向他推荐了一家挪威技术公司的一个自由撰稿人的职位。

所有这些需要很多能量。很多求职者也并不清楚通过网络扩大他们影响面的重要性。这就是为什么指导人们如何利用社交网络正在成为职业顾问办公室里的顾问们最主要的工作之一。麻省理工学院的职业顾问和开发办公室的副主任南希·里奇蒙德说："我们向他们表明，使用社交媒介是让雇主知道他们正站在最新潮流的前沿的很好方法。这对他们的职业有着极其重要的意义。"

如果你正在寻找新的工作机会，你想过这个方法吗？

第 3 单元　如何让面试更加高效？

无论各行各业的公司的招聘程序有多么不同，与诸如人格测试、逻辑测验、小组讨论等那些"锦上添花"的步骤相比，面试都肯定是一个必要的环节。

这就是为什么求职者都希望得到通知面试的电话，为什么有大量的建议告诉他们如何着装、如何说话、如何表现得像一个充满自信的职业人士，以吸引面试官的注意。

听从这些建议有时候会有用。有调查显示，3秒钟之内的一瞥决定了第一印象。很多面试持续时间长达1小时，但是很多面试官在前3分钟就已经作出了决定。这种刻板印象，或者说"照镜子招聘"的背后存在着许多原因。

作为一名熟练的面试官，或者作为一名人力资源专业人士，我们应该尽力避免这样的面试。我们的目的是在高效面试的帮助之下，选聘合适的人到合适的职位上工作。

首先，在面试过程中，我们想要发现什么，或是证明什么？

这个答案很容易被接受：我们想要检验这个人能否获得这份工作，并做出令人满意的工作业绩。然后，很自然地，我们会想到岗位要求，这些通常就在手边的岗位说明书里写着。最棘手的部分是，我们从候选人那里获得的哪些信息能作为她是这个职位合适人选的证据。

我们很快就会想到教育背景、工作经验、职业资格证书等等东西。但是，这些还不足以做出决定。它们是技术或知识方面的证据，只有这些并不能保证良好的工作业绩。很多公司在它们的招聘广告中说，它们需要"结果导向型"的、"能够面对压力"的、"能够创造性地解决问题"的人。这些能力或行为其实就是高效面试的焦点所在。

我们怎样才能知道候选人具有我们需要的能力呢？答案是：行为面试。

还记得你要候选人描述他们自己的时候，他们是如何回答的吗？"我是一个负责任的人。""我很勤奋。""我学东西很快。""我工作努力。""我是一个有团队精神的人。"听起来不错，是吧？根据行为面试的原理，这些只是陈述，并不能提供真正的行为信息。在高效面试中，面试官应该做的是收集候选人以前言行的实例或证据，因为以前的行为预示着将来的行为。

迅速找出相匹配的行为的办法是：询问STAR。S代表形势，T代表任务。形势和任务描述了某种行为的产生背景。A显示了当时采取的行动，包括什么行动及是如何实施的。R指这种行为带来的结果。

当候选人在谈论他努力工作时，他可能会告诉你，当他们的团队在起草一份非常重要的投标文件时，有一位同事生病了，不得不去医院（形势）。他们必须在4个小时之内准备好所有材料（任务）。然后，他自告奋勇地顶替那位生病的同事，继续工作超过3个小时（行动）。最后，他们的投标文件按时完成了，并且最终中了标（结果）。

如果候选人这样说"我想我会在时间紧张的时候，加班工作以完成任务"，这只是想法，而非真正的行为。"我计划读更多的书，好让自己讲课讲得更好。""如果有人没有完成任务，我会和他一起寻找问题的根源。"这样的说法，也都不是行为，它们只是理论或对未来的陈述。

Appendix 2　Reference Translation for Texts

除了上述这些含糊的陈述、计划、理论和想法，我们经常会在面试中遇到的情况还有不完全 STAR。"我感受到了技术的快速变化，我觉得我们的软件包在 6 个月之内就会过时，所以我开始寻找替代品。我研读了所有可以获得的程序，并且测试其中的大部分。"这些话可能会让面试官觉得这个人确实在积极主动地做一些事情，但是，如果后面没有说明结果，这个例子就是无效的。

一位经验丰富的招聘者会问："你最终找到替代品了吗？"如果回答是"哦，全球 IT 部门比我早 3 个月开发出了很好的替代产品"，那么他的研究是否真的有意义就要打上一个问号。

如果他说："我没能继续下去，因为后来有太多更加重要的事情需要我去做。"那么，这个 STAR 本身就不具有说服力。

如果故事是："在测试了 3 个月之后，我跟其他经理探讨了我的发现，最终我们及时选用了一个新产品。现在，我们很自信地认为我们已经走上正轨了。"这的确是一个很好、很有力的证据，可以证明他是积极主动的、善于计划的、执行高效的人。

在行为面试中，面试官需要注意 3 个方面。

首先，面试官必须清楚他在面试中要证明的能力和行为是什么。他最好能够准备一份能力列表，以及一些事先写好的问题，这些问题能够引出可以展示候选人是否具备所需能力的以前的实例。关于"主动"和"结果导向"，可以问这样一些问题："你以前做过什么来确保领导你的团队完成延伸目标？"、"告诉我你达到今天这个水平之前，克服过的最大障碍是什么？你是如何做到的？"

第二，面试官应该积极主动地去听。这意味着你应该留心搜集候选人相关工作经验的深层信息，并且始终把重点放在 STAR 上。如果他说的只是不完全 STAR，那就尝试探究完整的实例。如果只是陈述和想法，那就尝试引导候选人去思考他以前工作经验中的真实案例。当然，你应该以你的同理心来回应，而不只是抛出一些咄咄逼人的问题。面试官应该带着尊重去询问和探究，这样面试官和候选人之间就可以建立起友好的关系。

最后一点是做笔记。在听的时候，很难抓住整个实例，因此面试官只能记录一些关键字眼，或者有时候使用速记方法。但是，要确保你 1 小时之后还能认出自己写的是什么。还有，要确定你记下的是 STAR，而不必是候选人的回答。这能够帮助你在事实而不是你的感觉或单纯的记忆基础上自信地作出决定。

行为面试在公司里越来越流行。Equation Research 在 2007 年 12 月进行了一次网上调查，调查了 2 500 位高级人力资源管理者和培训与发展主管。他们发现，只有 19% 的公司不采用行为面试，25% 计划更多地使用，其他人都计划像以前一样经常使用。没有公司准备减少使用。

第 4 单元　留住人才从第一天开始

"思科公司热烈欢迎新员工，从招聘程序开始，一直到为被收购公司的员工设计的项目，我们都希望员工在他们上班的第一天就体会到思科所能够提供的最好的东西。"

这是思科公司网站上的欢迎信息。这家领先的网络解决方案提供商要让每一位新员工在 90 天内适应公司。

开始的 90 天是非常关键的。很多公司没有这个步骤，或者只是漫不经心地对待。在空缺职位招来人之后，上司希望新人能够尽快开始工作。遗憾的是，他们越是希望快点指使新员工，新员工可能会越早地离开公司。

离职面谈记录显示，六个月内离开公司的人，一部分是因为他们没有获得有关公司和工作的充分信息，他们不知道到哪里去获取资源，或者他们觉得自己不受欢迎。有这样的一些评论："在我上班的第一天甚至第一个星期，他们好像都还没有为我的到来做好准备。"或者"我觉得缺少支持，即使是在上班第一天！"

我至今仍然记得我在前一家公司工作的第一天。在见过老板之后，我被带到工作台，那里只有一张桌子。没有电脑，甚至没有椅子。然后，我等了差不多 30 分钟才坐下来。在那个时候，我心想："这家公司真的需要我吗？"

在人们已经开始想要离开公司的时候才开始采取挽留措施已经太晚了。留住人才应该从他们上班的第一天就开始。

公司在新员工适应上应该花多长的时间？在这个项目期间，公司应该提供什么？不论各个公司对此的具体日程安排有多么不同，还是存在一些共同点：

- 讲述公司的历史、结构和企业文化；
- 宣传公司的价值观和商业战略；
- 提供行为守则；
- 解释薪酬与福利；
- 告诉新员工如何使用语音邮件、电子邮件和文件系统；
- 强调安全和保卫指南；
- 介绍岗位说明及在适应期内需要达到的目标。

在这一过程中，不仅仅涉及培训人员。通常，招聘部门的人员会为新员工准备好合同；薪酬与福利部门的人员会开始记录考勤；录用部门的经理会准备好欢迎新成员，不只是打个招呼，还要准备好工作场所、说明工作指导等。因此，确保各个部门的作用和职责井然有序，以使新员工感觉在整个迎新过程中受到了前后一致的欢迎。否则，新员工可能会想："我应该待在这样一个乱七八糟的地方，并且为之作出贡献吗？"

有些人在他们的新员工上班第一天刚好不在场。这样可能会给新员工带来错误的信

Appendix 2　Reference Translation for Texts

息——他们不够重要，所以他们的上司在他们上班第一天不在。如果确实出门在外，请给你的新员工打电话，说你为不能在她上班第一天见到她而感到遗憾，并且安排好时间，在你回来之后再见她。或者你可以委托你的同事进行新员工适应工作。总之，让她感觉到她上班的第一天对你来说也是很重要的一天，你从第一天起就关心她。

新员工到来的时候，确认你已经准备好了他们的工作台，那里有电话、电脑和办公家具。他们在经过必要的认证之后就可以马上打开电脑，并登录电子邮件账户和文件系统等。新员工通常要花费相当多的时间在公司的电脑系统里一点点地寻找有什么可以学习的资料。如果能够让相关方面提前足够的时间做好相关准备，新员工就不用等IT部门的人到他们的工作台下面接线了。

有些经理不得不在新员工加入后回答很多次这种问题："人力资源部办公室在哪里？""我们有没有急救箱？"事实上，很多公司会安排新员工参观办公场所，让他们熟悉他们的工作环境。这很好，但是还不够。如果还有某位伙伴总是能够帮助新手应付她的新工作，告诉她什么时间可以从公司图书馆借书、办公室到市中心的最方便的乘车路线……她肯定会感觉到她的新工作已经安全开始了。有经验的老员工，而不是经理，是这种伙伴的最佳人选。

当新员工最终进入他们的新部门时，经理们必须花时间和他们一起回顾岗位说明，设定对他们的期望；让他们知道作为经理，哪些事情会令你发狂，比如迟到、行动前不进行必要的思考、在没有预先通知的情况下推迟项目完成时间。还应该告诉她，什么能使她在公司里取得成功，比如积极主动、多付出一点努力、言行一致。让她和团队及公司站在同一水平线上。

员工在90天内离开公司的原因之一是，他们觉得他们没有得到足够的培训。一方面，在甚至没有谈起将来的培训计划的情况下，员工不会待在旁边，等着看到底会不会有培训。另一方面，我们不应该期望新员工在适应期内学会他们工作所需的一切。在这个阶段，新员工需要的培训是使他们成为公司里有生产力并且快乐的一分子——像那些老员工一样工作和生活。因此，除了他们日常工作中需要用到的文件、模板和系统之外，关于如何使用公司内部网的即时通讯工具、如何报销差旅费用等话题，也能够帮助他们在独特的环境中成长。

从来都没有完美的计划。在（新员工适应期的）前几周、前几个月，甚至更长的时间里，需要经常地检验计划。你可能会觉得现在就跟新员工谈论他们的职业上升通道和个人发展途径为时过早，他们还才刚刚开始学习如何成为一个独立的执行者。但是，员工希望知道他们的公司支持他们的成功。如果你的公司有一套正式的人才培养程序，包括按照目标进行的绩效评估、岗位轮换，或者升职原则，（告诉他们这些）将是一个很好的方法，能够让新员工认为他们选择了正确的公司，下定决心留下来并作出贡献。

第2部分　薪酬与福利

第5单元　一般薪酬结构

　　薪酬绝对是公司吸引和留住员工的关键因素。公司把他们的薪酬体系看做是实现组织增长和成功的一种手段，通常会努力建立一种对外具有竞争力、对内具有公平性的薪酬结构。

　　在他的著作《人力资源管理》中，加里·戴斯勒将"薪酬"定义为："由员工的工作所产生的、给予他们的所有形式的支付。"当人们找到一份新工作的时候，他通常期待新工作能带给他更高的薪水。但是，通常发生的情况是，尽管提供给他的薪水确实提高了，但是他后来发现他拿到的钱不如以前工作时多。他的基本工资可能上涨了10%，但是却完全没有季度奖金了，而在他以前的公司，这一部分占他每年薪资收入的20%。

　　还有，在人们想要比较不同公司或不同行业内不同工作的薪酬水平时，他们发现这个"所有形式的支付"的薪酬概念如此复杂，很难对它们进行一一比较。有些公司发放年终奖，有些不发。有些发放1个月的工资作为年终奖，有的发2个月的，甚至更多。有的提供交通补助，有的提供汽油补贴。有的为员工购买补充保险，有的给员工股票期权。有的提供保证收入，有的公司的薪酬取决于公司的利润和个人业绩。所以，它们怎么能进行比较呢？

　　关于薪酬，有许多分类方法及进一步的研究。我们可以选择一种流行的方法（如图5-1所示）来加深理解。美世公司定义的年度基本工资，是薪酬体系最基础的部分，我们称之为成分1。成分1加上其他保证现金，比如与绩效无关的年终奖、固定津贴，就是成分2，其名称是年度保证现金。类似的，如果有浮动奖金的话，加上成分2，就成了成分3，被称为年度总现金。然后，长期激励、股票期权等是属于成分4的项目。一些主要福利，比如社会保险、医疗计划、交通补贴等属于成分5。成分5就是总体薪酬，其名称是年度总薪酬。

　　基本工资通常按月支付，它体现了相应职位的"价值"。它还会受到拥有此职位者的背景的影响，比如经验、教育、潜力和业绩记录等。员工的基本工资在一定时期内通常是固定不变的，会规律性地或在工作发生变化的时候进行调整。

　　奖金被看做是浮动薪资的重要组成部分之一。奖金的发放有多重目的。最实质的目标之一当然是引导员工的行为和对优异的业绩表示认可。有时候，如果基本工资将要超过该职位的工资范围了，就会给该职位的拥有者发放一次性奖金，以使得基本工资可以被控制在范围之内，从而使得基本工资仍然有上涨的空间。

　　尽管货币奖金是一种表示认可的实质性的手段，但它们通常被视为糟糕的长期激励

Appendix 2　Reference Translation for Texts

```
                    基本工资
         +          保证奖金
成分1               年度基本工资
         +          固定津贴（餐费、交通补贴等）
成分2               年度保证现金
         +          浮动奖金
         +          销售提成
         +          利润分成
         +          其他奖励
成分3               年度总现金
         +          期权
         +          长期激励
成分4               年度总现金+期权+长期激励
         +          养老金、住房补贴等
         +          医疗计划
         +          人寿/意外保险
         +          移动电话费
         +          其他补贴
成分5               年度总薪酬
```

图 5-1　美世公司的一般薪酬结构

因素，它们无法取代日常的领导力、认可、激励和个人发展。经理们都被鼓励去发掘合适的非货币手段来满足员工的激励需要。否则，只是增加工资总成本，很可能让公司陷入不利的竞争地位，从而引发运营风险。

福利的提供可以按照固定的结构（比如，有资格使用公司车辆的员工），或者是为了满足某种特定的个人需要或优先权。以下是一些典型的货币化福利的形式：

- 配车（包括车辆行驶费用）；
- 交通补助；
- 医疗保险；
- 社会福利；
- 补充养老金或住房补贴；
- 其他。

在可能的时候，福利应当既服务于业务目的，同时也满足个人需要。将福利结合进总的工作条件当中，对于建立合适的工作条件水平非常重要。

理解基本工资和浮动薪资是总现金薪酬的两大主要成分是非常重要的。确定这两个部分在总现金薪酬里的比例通常要根据公司的业务性质、背景和薪酬原则。

上面的图表所示的方法被各个跨国公司广泛使用，尤其是那些参加了美世公司组织的年度"总体报酬调查"的公司。这些公司按照美世公司的方法，向美世公司提供公司每个重要职位的具体薪酬数据，然后在美世公司完成分析之后，它们会得到关于每个

职位在当前市场上的标准薪酬报告。由于这些职位按照美世公司的方法进行分类，使得将它们一一进行比较成为可能，从而帮助各个公司确定它们的薪酬战略。

渴望保持行业领先地位的公司可能会决定较大幅度地提高薪资水平，如果它们发现其他公司，尤其是它们的潜在竞争对手，把薪资水平定在 75 分位。那些拥有充足的人力资源供给的公司则可能只会考虑小幅提高薪资水平，因为它们不需要给的太多。

人力资源专业人士不仅可以用估计的平均（薪资）增长率来建议决策者们为即将到来的薪酬增长拨出更多的预算，也可能会建议在必要的时候提高销售人员绩效工资的比例，以跟上这一市场趋势。这份调查报告里的一些新项目也会让人力资源职员进行更广泛的思考：如何设计和更新报酬体系以适应公司和业务的不断变化。

上述信息只与工资结构相关，并不是我们可以从一份高质量的市场薪资报告中获得的唯一参考，也不足以作为人力资源职员提出工资调整建议的根据。这个工资结构只是薪酬体系的基础，在此基础上再进行比较和分析才有可行性和实际意义。除了工资结构，人力资源职员还需要从公司内部搜集诸如公司的工资定位战略、个人的工资定位、员工的能力水平、公司的发展战略和业务战略等其他信息。另外，还应该考虑来自外部世界的信息，比如经济状况和行业趋势、劳动力统计数据、劳动力市场的薪酬发展趋势等。

还需要再次强调的是：薪酬不是留住人才的唯一途径。换句话说，人们不会只是因为工资令人满意就留在某一个公司。

第 6 单元　无形报酬

经理们可能会因为有各种原因想留住某些员工（比如：业绩优异的、很有潜力的员工，或者其他员工），而想到给这些员工多种形式的激励和报酬。

传统上，大多数报酬是诸如涨工资、奖金、奖励及一些有价值的纪念品之类的薪酬与福利。这些有形报酬的问题是，它们是短期激励因素。人们得到的（有形报酬）越多，就越容易形成一种"理所应当"的心态。比如，因为一个项目成功完成而给了一位员工 1 000 美元的奖金，他或她在完成下一个项目之后就会期望得到至少同样数目的奖金。

根据赫茨伯格的双因素理论，钱不能激励员工作出更好的业绩；反之，在某种程度上，它会削弱员工追求更好效果的内在动机。

根据美世公司的"整体报酬体系"概念，薪酬与福利是招收员工进入公司的代价，而与增长和内部环境有关的措施才能够留住员工。这些措施包括职业发展计划、令人兴奋的项目、领导力、组织文化、认同感、工作与生活的平衡、感兴趣的或者具有挑战性的工作本身。

Appendix 2　Reference Translation for Texts

　　翰威特公司也将报酬分成了外在的和内在的两部分。现金、养老金、保险、津贴、基金或贷款都属于外在报酬。工作质量、文化、工作与生活的平衡及一些特殊的认可被定义为内在报酬。

　　一些企业鼓励员工跟领导讨论什么样的手段才能真正激励他们。通常有一些内部驱动力，比如：指导和影响他人的机会、对他们自己的工作有更多的控制权、得到欣赏或认可、感受到工作和生活之间的正常平衡等。另一方面，除了奖金、外部培训课程、业余团队建设活动等有形报酬之外，还有一些外部驱动因素，包括：与不同的人一起工作的机会、日常工作的变化、不受控制的自由度、弹性工作时间、员工会议上的公开表扬、共患难的团队经历等。

　　钱虽然如此重要，但它也不能替代其他那些人们也非常需要的东西。大卫在一家知名的 IT 公司工作，他每个月都会接到猎头公司的电话，给他开出的工资比他目前的要高。他几乎从未考虑过这些外面的机会，而原因仅仅只是因为他每完成一个项目之后，都会有下一个感兴趣的新项目去做。他认识了越来越多的人，他们都喜欢和他一起工作。"每天当我走进办公室的时候，都期待着跟那么多可爱的朋友打招呼。我们有时候在工作之余也会在一起。我不需要更多的钱，但我不能失去我的朋友。"

　　有的人可能会说：好吧，他的钱够用了，但是我不够，所以我需要更多的钱。想一想钱以外的东西，然后你会发现一些你也需要的东西，尽管对你而言，外部或内部驱动力很可能跟其他人的不同，但是你所期望的列表里应该有一些钱之外的项目。

　　不同的人有不同的激励因素，同一个人在不同的阶段也会被不同的事情所激励，这可以用马斯洛的需求层次理论来解释。这也提醒了我们的领导者，要经常与员工谈话，以了解他们最近的状态和需要，从而给予有效的激励。

　　除了量身定制的激励方案，还有一些激励措施是适合大部分人的。我们可能已经发现，给予口头的认可能够非常有效地鼓舞某个人的精神。这确实被证明是一种表示真诚感谢的形式。关键在于，我们表达感谢应该不只是出于他或她做了什么，还要表达因为他或她的个人因素而使得这件事情做成了。

　　首先，告诉他或她你为了什么而表示感谢。比如："琼，因为你非常积极主动，我真的要对你表示感谢。"

　　然后，你要给出证据，也就是她做了什么。你说："尽管你才刚进入这个项目，但你非常迅速地从不同的来源收集了需要的信息，使我们及时完成了这个项目。"

　　最后一步是一个开放性的提问，让她能展现出更多的能力。"你是怎样成功地确定你应该去找谁（收集信息）的？我想我们都能够从你这里学到东西。"你觉得有什么不一样吗？通过询问这些探究性的问题，说话者再次强调了感谢，也给了琼更多的时间去接受感谢。而且，这样更真诚，不只是琼，其他在场的人也会有同样的感受。这对一个团队来说更加重要，好的实践经验可以被分享，从而使得团队整体在处理类似情况时变得更加有力，团队所需要的价值体现通过"谢谢你"而得到生动的传递。

节约成本是很多公司的重点，尤其是在困难时期。经济危机之下，裁员、薪资冻结、减少培训的情况经常发生，我们应该如何留住优秀的员工？尝试从无形报酬中寻找解决办法吧。

第3部分　绩效管理

第7单元　绩效管理的成功推行

很多公司都在推行绩效驱动的企业文化。绩效管理可能是不同企业里最有效的管理工具之一。但是，也有这样一种普遍的认识：经理和员工出于多种原因，都对绩效评估程序心存恐惧。

让我们首先来倾听员工的声音。

"这是浪费时间。在年底我有很多事情要做，没时间做这个！"

"我的经理根本不了解情况。他们只是凭自己的感觉打分。"

"我的经理从来没有说过我应该改正什么，但是最终他说我的业绩不达标！"

"这些关键业绩指标并不适合我的工作。怎么能用这种方法来评估我？"

"我不知道该做什么，我的领导也不知道。"

"有什么意义呢？不管分数高低，我们的工资是一样的。"

如果我们有足够的时间和耐心，还会从员工那里听到更多类似的话。在大规模的、结构复杂的公司里，这些牢骚从来都不可能被完全消除。OnPoint 咨询公司就绩效管理体系向美国的经理和人力资源职员进行了调查，56% 的一线经理认为他们的绩效管理程序没有意义。只有 43% 认为绩效管理能够帮助员工提高技术与能力。45% 认为绩效管理在公司上下得到了一致的执行。45% 认为绩效管理采用的评估尺度可以使经理们准确地区分不同的业绩水平。不到 40% 的经理认为绩效管理有助于建立更好的绩效文化，或者为继任规划或领导力培养方案提供有用的数据。

我们不得不承认，不存在完美的绩效管理体系，尤其在现在这个不断变化而且非常复杂的商业世界里。不过，我们可以在分析有关绩效评价存在的典型问题的时候，将它们分成几个类别，并预先准备好预防措施，从而使我们能够减小绩效管理工具的负面作用，让我们的生活更加轻松。

通常，问题存在于绩效管理体系自身，或有关的人员，或执行程序中。某个特定问题只与一个类别有关，或者两个，或者涉及所有的类别。因此，预防措施应该建立在绩效管理体系的整体基础之上。

目标是所有绩效管理体系的基础。

Appendix 2 Reference Translation for Texts

如果一位员工说他不知道到了年底他的哪些方面将会被评估，那么首先应该问他："你来这工作是为了什么？"这个问题很可能存在于人员和程序方面。尽管领导们清楚地知道他们为员工设定的目标，但是他们并不认为有必要向员工进行传达。他们理所当然地认为员工应该知道他们自己的工作目标。

另一个经常出错的地方是个人目标与组织目标的结合。这种结合的失败，可能是由于缺乏沟通，也可能是由于两者之间的确不存在相关性，致使员工失去了目标和努力工作以取得良好业绩的动力。

很多人还发现，由于列出的某些关键业绩指标已经过时了，使他们在业绩考评面谈中无法对以前的绩效进行评估。然后就可能出现争论，最有可能首先出现的是关于评估目标正确与否的分歧。

为了克服这些与目标设定有关的问题，在人员方面，我们可以进行培训，教会人们如何设置"聪明的"目标；在程序方面，我们可以突出强调目标设定作为绩效管理体系基础的重要性。一个增加人们对目标设定了解程度的简单办法是：只是在时间表上把目标设置和绩效考核程序分离开。来年的目标设定可以在今年年底前完成，而对今年的绩效考核在明年年初开始。通过这种办法，经理和员工能够在不用操心敏感的分数和建设性反馈的情况下，专注于目标设定。

有时候，绩效面谈是绩效管理流程当中最可怕的环节。

有些年轻的经理倾向于等到考核的时候才告诉员工她做得不够好。他们不太敢在他们发现问题的时候就告诉下属事实情况。他们认为那样会伤害员工的感情，员工可能会做得更糟。现实却是，员工在考评面谈的时候极其惊愕，他们认为在开始的时候他们应该有机会改进。"你为什么不早点告诉我？"是一位惊愕而且愤怒的员工此时最常见的反应。

有些经理在考评面谈的时候说得很多，然后要求员工同意他的说法。有些员工在控制欲很强的经理面前难以表达自己的想法，尤其在这样一种敏感的场合。然后他们选择同意经理说的任何话。这看上去像是一次温馨且有效的面谈。但是之后，经理在某个时候会很诧异地从这位员工那里得到负面的反馈、更糟糕的业绩表现，或者突然离职。"为什么你不早点告诉我？"现在，这位经理想问这句话了。

在考核评分的时候，经理们倾向于给一位在某个方面确实很优秀的员工的所有指标都打高分。这是一种光环效应。有时候，经理很愿意给自己的团队成员都打一个跟平均水平差不多的分数，而不是根据不同的业绩打分。这样会极大地损害团队的士气。优秀的员工觉得不公平，一般的员工会冷嘲热讽，业绩不合格的不会改进。很快，团队的整体业绩会下滑。

在整个绩效管理体系中，后续工作与绩效考核一样重要。

有些员工认为绩效评估只是走形式，浪费时间。他们没有看到考核与否有什么不同。人们的工资涨幅一样，分配的工作任务一样，没有表彰，也没有惩罚。"我们干吗要小题大做？"

当然，也确实有些经理对绩效评估有同样的看法。他们不知道或不关心他们应该用他们手里的分数和评论去做些什么。他们只为完成这项棘手的工作而感到高兴，然后就回到他们习惯的日常工作中去，而不需要更进一步的思考。

事实上，如果没有正确的后续工作，绩效评估就没有任何意义。绩效评估体系本身就应该把后续行动纳入进来，成为其不可缺少的一部分。后续行动改进绩效的行动计划、个人发展的学习方案、业绩不合格带来的后果等。经理们应该接受培训，学会与员工一起开展不同的后续行动。业绩取决于什么能力？如何才能使业绩达标？特定的培训课程会有帮助吗？如果员工没有达到绩效目标，将会怎样？明星级的员工应该获得什么奖励？

除了这些即时的、个人的后续行动，公司还应该分析整个组织的绩效数据，提出一个公司范围内的行动计划，以改进组织绩效。这将增强目标设置培训的效力，因为通过这样的定位检查，能够发现很多不够"聪明"的目标。

就像我们要求经理们定期检查团队绩效一样，我们也应该在真正的问题出现之前，随时反思我们的绩效管理体系。这个体系本身可能会存在某些问题，但更多的时候是在人员和程序方面做错了，或是做得不到位。因此，在出现绩效问题的时候，不要只是改变或从技术上说更新绩效管理体系。要把体系、人员及执行程序放在一起去发现问题的根源所在。

第8单元 我们应该考核什么？

绩效考核，作为鉴定、评估和提高个人绩效的一种方法与程序，是绩效管理体系中非常重要的一个部分，对于改进组织的整体绩效具有关键作用。不同公司可能会有不同的考核体系，用来衡量与绩效有关的不同项目。

在任何考核体系中，对年初设置的目标的完成情况进行评估，都是最常见的项目。在这个环节，去年的实际历史业绩通常会与当初所设定的目标进行比较。经理和员工都最关注结果：过去的业绩是不合格、合格，还是优秀。这个环节也令很多员工和上司感到痛苦。员工被要求提供有力的证据证明他们过去的业绩令人满意，而上司要和他们讨论这些数据和评论，并给出正面和负面的反馈。

有时候对实际业绩会发生分歧。原因之一是有些目标在设置的时候就不够"聪明"。一个好的目标应该具有明确性、可衡量性、可实现性、相关性和时效性。没有这些特性，目标就只是一纸空文，很难朝着其前进，因此也没有办法在年终的时候被合理地衡量。另一个常见的问题是，领导们认为只有绩效考评面谈才是适合检查业绩的场合。所以，他们一直等到考核那天才严肃地指出员工的业绩不达标。这位员工当然感到震惊并且会问："你为什么不早点告诉我？"在绩效管理过程中，定期地检查业绩能够极大地减少风险。对不合格的业绩做出及时的反馈，也是一个好办法。年底的考评面谈是非常正式的、给出结论的环节。但是，它并不是绩效考核过程的唯一环节。

我们都知道，量化所有衡量指标是不可能的，因此，有时候，我们使用行为语言来衡量领导力或伦理道德。领导们应该为他们的团队成员设定清晰的目标，定期监督进程，解决某些模棱两可的问题，选择合适的人到合适的岗位工作，对优秀的业绩进行奖励。这些行为隐藏在通过确切数字显示的绩效目标背后，实际上它们是导致最终结果的主要原因。因此，为什么不只是衡量这些行为，从而强调这些与确切数据同等重要的领导力特征？

在绩效考核过程中，对于不在领导职位的员工的行为，可以评估企业伦理道德和价值观的推行情况。这些伦理道德和价值观是公司在快速变化的世界里进行竞争的基础。没有充分接受这些企业特质的员工，通常都是不敬业的，或者业绩不合格。

我们提到的这些目标、领导力和伦理道德，都是以过去的事实作为评估基础。一个成功的绩效管理体系需要既回顾历史，也应该展望未来。绩效考核不应在给出一个分数之后就结束，而是应该制订不合格业绩的补救计划，作为对过去业绩的后续跟进工作；同时，还应该为所有人制订周密的发展计划，以提高组织将来的整体绩效。

对过去的业绩进行后续跟进工作是非常必要的。业绩不合格的员工除了造成日常绩效损失之外，也对组织文化和士气造成了负面影响。如果企业对不合格者反应太慢，甚至没有将他们与优秀者区别对待，或者对他们采取的行动前后不一致，这些少数不合格者较差的绩效表现将成为办公室里的常态和风气。一个经过上司和不合格员工双方同意的行动计划应该明确在一个特定时期（比如3个月）内应当采取的具体步骤，以及根据这3个月的补救计划的效果而需要采取的行动。有些不合格员工在团队的支持之下，当然也在他们自己的努力之下，回到了正轨，而有些会迫于压力而离开公司。无论是何种情况，落后的生产效率被修复了，公司节约了不该发生的成本，从而对利润有利。

这种惩罚手段不应该被滥用，而且在执行过程中应始终以事实为依据，保持合理的谨慎，避免潜在的法律风险和对组织士气的损害。对享受福利的员工进行惩罚，不是明智的选择。有些领导认为休病假的员工是生产效率低下的。女同事在休完产假回来上班之后，发现她们的评级比以前降低了。这些听起来似乎很符合逻辑，但事实并非如此。员工不应该因为请病假或休假而受到惩罚。毕竟，不能指望工资越高的员工工作时间越长。只有滥用福利才应该受到惩罚。

补救和惩罚的目的是指导员工改正错误，重回正轨；而个人发展计划是指导他们从好变得更好。

通常，改进计划要经过员工和上司双方讨论同意。这个个人发展计划的目的可以是在目前职位上的更优异表现，也可以是想获得的新职位所需的资质。在期望的效果和目前的状态之间存在差距的时候，就应该制订被称为发展计划的行动计划。这个计划应该有特定的重点，通常在3个以内，以保证个人或者其上司能够为之投入足够的注意力和精力。因此，在评估方案时，必须确定优先顺序。

制订个人发展计划的时候，还应该尽可能具体。它们是实际的发展目标，因此也适用于"聪明原则"。只是很多领导和员工没有对它们给予足够的注意，他们认为这些发展目标不如那些要按1~5打分的绩效目标那么重要。

不具体的计划是一种无意义的发展计划。经理发现很多员工应该改进他们的沟通技巧。如果这就是唯一的结论，那么它就没能提供实际的方向，比如：哪方面的沟通技巧，需要多大程度的改进，通过什么方法。沟通是一个很宽泛的概念。有效的沟通可以只通过几个步骤实现，也可能需要不同的技能模块组合在一起，比如：留心倾听、清晰简洁的发音、对冲突作出反应、在公众场合说话的能力等。因此，导致员工绩效不达标的特定的行为瑕疵应该被确定，比如"不提出问题以加深理解"。然后，首先采取的行动可以是一项密切相关的培训课程，内容包括沟通的概念、沟通过程中的信息流、无效沟通的负面影响，以及确保沟通质量的必要技能。经过几个月的实践之后，领导可以从多个来源搜集关于这种特定行为的反馈，然后就可以确定是否有所改进。

在某些公司，在绩效考核过程中会进行比个人发展计划更深入的预备人才确认计划。对于那些把更高的职位作为发展计划的员工来说，领导和公司定期考虑并监督这一过程是自然而然的。职业的发展可能是领导职位（有时候我们称之为通才职位），也可能是专才职位。

我们必须关注员工对这种确认的感受。在公司这方面，信息的传达必须清晰且一致，要明确那些被确认为人才的，或在绩效考核过程中受到好评的员工并不一定能升职。如果组织需要的时候，这些员工会被列为优先考虑的对象，但是其他人也同样有机会被列入名单。这是一个不断变化的名单，升职会根据许多内部和外部因素来决定。

最后，到了结论部分。过去业绩的得分当然要包括在内。但是，一些领导倾向于在绩效考核过程之后只给出一个分数作为结果。实际上，建设性反馈和改进空间也应该被强调，因为它们和分数一样重要。记住，我们不只是在回望过去，更重要的是，要在参考以前业绩的情况下，提高将来的业绩，以使得整个组织得以持续发展。这不应只是写在纸上，还应该被领导和员工记住。

包含这些评语的结论，也是对员工的一个专门的总结。这能够使她为自己的成绩而感到自豪，对将要采取的后续行动感觉舒服。总之，绩效考核过程不应该只是形式，或是一段充满争论和痛苦的回忆。它是一个强有力的管理工具，如果正确使用，能够极大地提高个人和公司整体的生产效率和士气。

Appendix 2　Reference Translation for Texts

第9单元　让360度反馈更加有效

　　360度反馈也被称为多级反馈，近些年来颇为流行，在很多财富500强企业里应用。

　　它是一种人力资源干预方法，在向个人征求反馈意见的同时，也向她的同事、上司、下属和客户征求反馈信息。反馈报告会被保密，结果只有经理知道，以帮助她了解其他人对她的看法。它被公认为是一种高效的评估工具，可以实现绩效改进和个人发展。

　　通过给出一些平时不太可能让她知道的反馈信息，人力资源管理盲点可以大大减少，这对进行所需的任何改变都是非常重要的。在成员之间有机会自由地、安全地表达诚挚而具体的行为语言之后，群体的士气和效率将会得到巨大的提升。

　　然后，最受益的当然是组织。通过内部共同语言的增加，组织可以向员工传递出信号：哪些行为、态度或工作作风是被需要和期望的。这种多来源的反馈系统体现了组织非常重视并积极探询所有员工的想法。有效信息的交流增强了工作关系并使组织更高效。

　　然而，有很多人质疑这些好处。

　　蒂娜，一家大型跨国公司里一位经验丰富的部门领导，当她被要求多负责一个部门的时候，她获得升职。这家公司（对她）采用了360度反馈的方法。她非常自信一定能够得到很积极的反馈信息，因为她在公司里的声望很好，她相信她领导的团队非常支持她。当报告交给她的时候，她打开文件夹飞快地扫了一眼。然后，她翻回封面，去确认上面是不是她的名字。她的确被惊呆了。"这是我吗？"疑惑之后，是深深的挫败感。"他们怎么能这样说？"

　　她知道在她区分优秀员工和不合格员工的时候，有时可能会令人不愉快。但是，这是公司的企业文化，而且所有员工之间都进行了充分的沟通。因此，她无法接受这样的反馈：似乎2～3个人憎恨她，另外3～4个绝对支持她，而其他人都给出了混合的看法。

　　按照她之前的预期，应该只有2～3个人会给出负面的反馈，而所有其他人都应该给出正面反馈。她怀疑她还是不是一个好经理，这是否会影响她在这家公司的职业发展。蒂娜在1年之后离开了这家公司，这被公司高层看作是一个巨大的人才损失。她做出这个决定的原因也包括其他方面，但她经历的那次360度反馈绝对是最主要的原因。

　　除了蒂娜，还有很多其他人都认为360度反馈法不过是人力资源管理的小把戏之一，或者觉得这样有被合作伙伴背叛的风险，或者在得到负面反馈之后就失去了目标，或者发现它可能只是权术斗争的工具。

旧金山州立大学的乔汉·沙利文博士说："没有数据显示360度反馈确实能够提高生产效率、留住人才、减少不满，或是优于强制排名或标准的绩效考核体系。它听起来不错，但是没有证据证明，除了那些努力使之发生作用的公司之外，它在其他公司也会奏效。"

根据越来越多的不同的公司对360度反馈的实践经验，要使其过程更加有效，需要注意一些问题。

首先，个人在给出及接受反馈信息的时候，应当端正态度，并且对后续工作承担责任。人们容易对负面的反馈产生防御心理，这是很容易理解的。每个人都应该明白，尽管反馈信息有时候似乎不那么客观，但它确实反映了不同的人对他的看法。在某些情形之下，你是如何被看待的，比你真实的情况，要重要得多。个人的期望与其得到的反馈之间的差距，提供了改进的空间。对于反馈信息的反思和行动就构成了后续计划。

在给出反馈的时候，应该使用行为语言，而不是诸如"我想"、"我觉得"、"他们说"之类的描述。在这里可以使用一个简便的工具——STAR原则。这意味着你是通过描述形势、任务、行动和结果来讲述一个故事。这样可以使反馈信息具有更充足的事实根据，并且更加有用。

经理在360度反馈过程中的作用与职责是极其关键的，足以决定其成败。充分的有效沟通、后续的支持工作和顺利的执行，都是使一个360度反馈过程具有价值的重要基础。

经理必须清楚地传递这样的意思：这一反馈的目的及其对接收反馈的人的好处。另外，他或她还应该在不使其保密性和真实性打折扣的前提下，很有策略地（向接收人）提交反馈信息。有些接收者可能会追问反馈信息的来源，以进行辩解。此时，经理应该让他们回到正确的轨道，来考虑改进的空间，而不是去解释特定的故事。另一个方面，经理不应只是使用360度反馈法来评价一个人的行为。经理和这个人之间的直接沟通通常是必需的，不应该被多来源反馈所替代。

经理还应当关注经过员工同意之后的改进过程。员工自己主导行动计划，经理支持他或她去实现计划。只有配合以后续工作，这种反馈体系才是一个有意义的学习过程。

执行的主导权通常在于经理。根据时间表和提纲，经理应该将他们的行动和指导原则结合起来，以确保各项职能活动一致。形式一致在某种程度上会带来态度一致的感觉。

如果没有合适的组织氛围和引导，经理和他们的下属也无法成功地执行一个360度反馈过程。

在提倡开放的双向沟通的公司，更适合执行360度反馈。但是，即使是在这样的企业文化之下，也应该跟员工充分地沟通，让他们理解多来源反馈是获得建设性意见的一种工具及加强个人发展的一种制度。

Appendix 2　Reference Translation for Texts

360度反馈的过程应该被设计得符合企业文化和管理安排。首先应该有特定的目的。通常，绩效改进和个人职业发展是这种反馈体系的预期益处，但它是发展工具，不应当被用作绩效工资和升职的评估工具。在执行过程中，保密性必须被强调，并且通过技术和逻辑行为来加以保证，以使人们愿意给出建设性的反馈。在所有员工都得到反馈之后，应该为他们制订一个时间表以进行后续行动计划。另外，在得到比较数据之后，公司可以评估360度反馈过程的有效性。

对经理和个人进行必要的培训，也是公司应当提供的引导之一。个人接受的培训包括：以事实为依据提供反馈的技能、理解沟通障碍、鼓励他们面对负面效果、积极主动地进行个人发展。经理还应当学习额外的课程：关于对待多来源信息的正确态度、保密和保障健康的反馈环境的必要技能。

有了一致的态度、认真的操作，以及欣赏建设性反馈的开放的交流氛围，360度反馈体系才能真正为个人和组织的发展增加价值。

第4部分　培训管理

第10单元　从建立能力模型开始

自从20世纪70年代心理学家大卫·麦克利兰在美国国务院开展项目帮助选择最合适的外交官人选开始，能力模型方法已经被财富500强公司使用了超过半个世纪。越来越多的公司在追赶这个潮流，有些是真的觉得它们有需要，也有些只是想要使用这个奇妙的工具。

能力模型到底是什么，有很多个版本的解释。对于美商宏智国际顾问公司来说，这些能力被称为"维度"，被定义为"对与工作成功或失败有关的行为集合、动机和知识的描述，以使动机、知识或行为可以被可靠地进行分类"。

能力被描述成了可观察、可衡量的行为，但是它们并不仅仅是那些易于被模仿的具体行动。相反，它们能够显示某些潜在的含义——由个人的基本动机、性格、态度、价值观或自我概念驱动。它们是个人的一种持久特性，预示着（个人在）工作场所内各种环境下的行为。

这种建立在能力基础之上的人力资源系统，被认为是目标管理体系的有益补充，因为其目标一个是（说明）"如何"，另一个是（说明）"什么"。

这种系统的重点是特性而非任务，关注点是优异的业绩而非平均业绩，这也让经理和人力资源专业人士对其更加感兴趣。

另一个原因是，这种能力概念可以成为所有其他人力资源管理应用和项目的共同基础。招聘、绩效管理、学习与发展、继任计划、人才管理等，都可以建立在同样合适的基础上，能力既可以作为评估标准，又可以作为发展目标。

在公司内建立能力模型是耗费时间、财力和人力的事情。通常，人力资源职员首当其冲地需要付出很多努力，有时候得不到外来顾问的帮助。

无论在任何情况下，（建立能力模型的）第一步都是与各个利益相关方讨论下列问题：
- 项目背景和目标；
- 工作流程和时间表；
- 作用和职责；
- 公司的愿景、使命和价值观；
- 短期和长期的商业战略；
- 目标结果。

关于目标，一个经常遇到的问题是：我们是否需要在第一个阶段进行某个人力资源项目的应用？很多组织只是建立一个能力模型，然后就把它忘了。或者它们还在用它，但它只是一个孤立的、完全没有真正价值的工具，与其他人力资源项目没有任何关系。在我们头脑里已经有了想要应用的人力资源项目时，比如选拔或培养，我们可以更加精确地监督该模型的形式，并确保设计过程的后续步骤沿着正确的轨道进行。

就以上问题达成一致之后，数据搜集工作就该开始了。顾问和人力资源职员往往会结合使用多种方法，包括焦点小组讨论、关键事件采访、能力分类辞典、行为观察。

焦点小组讨论通常由某特定岗位的员工、其上司、培训与发展部门职员共同进行。按照结构性程序，小组成员要系统地考虑工作任务和个人态度、技能、知识，以及其他实现优异业绩所需要的特性。

对优秀员工进行的关键事件采访将收集员工对于很多深入的问题的回答，以帮助采访者理解他们实现优异业绩所需的能力。采访者需要懂得适当的探究策略和技巧。

能力分类辞典是指常见能力和行为指标的概念框架。通常会有 20~40 种能力，每一种能力具有 5~15 种行为指标。这可以为建立能力模型的团队提供一个基本的概念框架，作为着手点。同时，在焦点小组讨论或关键事件采访中，这个框架也被作为确定一系列能力重要性的指导原则。

行为观察的方法只适用于某些工作，比如超市收银员、呼叫中心接线员等。所需要的行为和特性在短时间内重复发生，让观察者非常容易在工作时间进行观察。

数据可以通过很多不同的方式进行搜集。但是，数据应该有多广泛？如果这项工作对组织非常重要，如果（能力模型）项目预算够用，如果预计有很多人力资源应用要与能力模型整合在一起，那么尽可能多的时间应该被投入到数据搜集阶段。

有了初步的资料，顾问和人力资源职员将处理数据，与高层经理沟通，起草能力列表及其熟练阶段。然后，列表上的能力将被转变成行为描述符号，并按照项目开始时各方同意的条件进行分类,以适应能力模型的结构。

主要有3种形式的行为描述符号。最流行的方法是行为指标,也是最简单的一种。以"创造性地解决问题"为例。这种能力被定义为:运用横向思维或逻辑分析,为困难或问题寻求替代解决办法的能力。其行为指标是:
- 挑战定势;
- 平衡利用各种不同资源;
- 思维开阔;
- 评估多种方案;
- 鼓励创新。

第二种方法是采用评估性能力评级的方法。使用这种方法时,为每种能力确定几个关键维度,然后把每种能力按照有效性进行排序。最高水平描述优异的绩效,最低水平即最低绩效。如果客户服务职员被描述为"自愿提供额外帮助",则说明其在理解客户需求方面的能力水平最高;如果被描述为"不听客户的询问",那么说明能力水平最低。

另一个方法是描述一种能力在某项特定工作中被需要的程度。如果能力模型是为公司里的多种职位而建立的,而且出于组织分析或个人职业发展的需要,要比较不同岗位对(不同能力)的要求,那么这种方法尤其适用。我们来看关于人力资源职员的"精通人才管理"这项能力。
- 最低水平的要求是"理解人才培养项目的程序"。
- 中间水平的要求是"理解并对我们的人才培养项目应用领导补给线模型;积极主动地就人才管理政策、程序和执行提出改进建议"。
- 高级水平被定义为"开发和应用人才管理原则,将继任规划和职业规划工作整合到人才管理当中"。

能力模型草案将由高层经理审查,有时候可能也会经过那些提供了基础数据的焦点小组讨论。所有相关各方达成一致之后,经过修订的能力模型将最终正式提出。

这并不是整个过程的终点。还需要对使用者进行培训,以使他们了解如何在日常工作中使用能力模型,如何评估掌握能力的水平,如何更新模型。人力资源职员可能要开始将能力模型结合到其他人力资源项目的应用之中,并跟踪执行情况;他们心里明白,孤立的能力模型没有任何意义,只是浪费资源。

第11单元 运用柯氏四级评估法进行培训评估

尽管评估培训的有效性费时又费钱,但大多数跨国公司都热衷于建立自己的培训评估机制,以使得管理层弄清楚某个特定的培训项目是否应该继续开展,以及如何改进该项目。这些公司大都采用柯式四级评估模型。

柯式四级评估模型的四级分别是反应、学习、行为和结果。反应是第1层。它评估接受培训者对学习事件的反应程度。第2层是学习，评估受训者改变态度、加强技能、增加知识的程度。行为是第3层，衡量所发生的行为改变的程度，即：受训者将他们在培训中学到的东西运用到工作中的程度。第4层是结果，是要了解作为学习实践的结果，预期效果的实现程度如何。

第1层：反应

这个层次的评估通常采用调查问卷的形式，问卷上有一些事先设置的关于培训项目的指标，用以调查受训者对培训项目的欢迎程度。这种问卷有时候被称为笑脸问卷。图11-1就是一个这种问卷的简单例子。

请根据给定的标准给下列项目打分。
5分表示"优秀"，4分表示"良好"，3分表示"还行"，2分表示"有待改进"，1分表示"差"
a) 课程符合你的期望。
b) 培训师传授了有关该学科的专业知识。
c) 课程材料的准备充分。
d) 课程内容能够应用到我的工作中。
e) ……

图11-1 笑脸问卷示例

除了评估问卷，面试也是收集信息的一个直接办法。通常认为，那些最初并没有被设计在问卷之内或由面试官提前准备好的开放性问题，也应该出现在问卷或面试中，以获取具体的评论。

这些问题需要100%的即时回答，因此，我们可能会发现，培训者结束课程之后的第一件事情就是分发问卷，然后在5分钟之内收回来。随着技术的发展，有些公司倾向于进行网上调查，以节约将书面结果输入计算机系统所耗费的人力。

这个层次评估的关键在于提出适当的问题，这些问题应该事先根据组织的培训战略和培训项目的目标进行准备。为了分析收集来的数据，应当确定培训项目的合理规模和可接受的标准，以发现实际得分和正常值之间的差距，并在将来缩小这一差距。

每一个培训项目都至少要进行第1层次的评估。

第2层次：学习

在学习这个层次（的评估中），测验被用来衡量学习水平——受训者学到了多少东

Appendix 2　Reference Translation for Texts

西去改变他们的态度、技能和知识。通常,通过比较学习课程开始之前和学习课程结束之后的测验得分,会发现有所改善。图 11-2 显示了这样的比较。

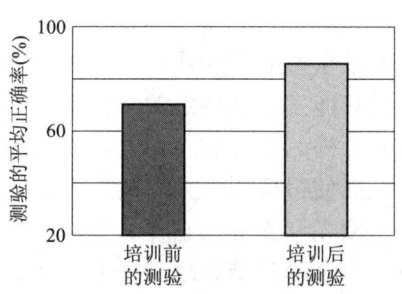

图 11-2　测验效果比较

为了确认在态度和知识培训中所学到的东西,培训者组织这种使用铅笔和纸的考试是非常容易的,例如对客户服务的认识、某项特定任务的流程等。对于技能培训评估,应该在培训之后的练习过程中安排操作测试,比如,通过打字测验,看一名职员能否将他的打字准确率从 95% 提高到 99%;或者通过培训之后的角色扮演,看一名销售员能否变得更具有说服力。

在不会耗费过多金钱和时间的前提下,应该对所有受训者进行这一层次的评估,同时要提供充足的培训信息,尤其是培训内容的信息。不只是受训者能提供有关他们学习的信息,还可以通过其同事、客户、经理及下属的观察来收集反馈信息,并进行分析。

第 3 层次:行为

对学习效果最为普遍的忧虑在第 3 个层次。很多培训项目在第 1 和第 2 个层次都获得了满意的效果。但是,受训者在他们完成调查问卷和测验之后,就忘记了他们学到的东西。他们没有把学到的东西带回到工作中去,似乎学习只发生在教室之中。第 3 层次评估的目标就是衡量有多少学到的东西被带回到了工作场所并应用到日常工作当中。

这种评估通常在培训结束之后的 3~6 个月进行,因为人们需要时间去消化学到的东西,而由此带来的绩效改进则出现得更晚。

面试、培训之前或之后的调查、多来源反馈,都是评估行为改变的好方法。通常,评估者会问以下问题:

- 你在工作中用到了你所学到的东西吗?
- 自从你使用了这项新技术之后,得到了多少改进?
- 你团队中的受训者能够向其他人传授他在培训项目中学到的东西吗?
- 你观察到他的服务水平发生改变了吗?
- 客服热线接到的客户投诉减少了吗?

在这个层次，100%地进行评估或者抽样评估都可以，取决于具体情况下的成本和利益。如果可能的话，可以在合适的时候重新进行评估，以确保真正的学习已经开始并且得到推广。

关于知识转化，有一个非常重要的因素往往被忽视，那就是公司内部合适的学习氛围。有时，应用所学到的知识只能发生在特定的条件下，因此公司和团队的支持是必需的。如果经理们考虑到要耗费额外的财力和精力，而不想多走一步的话，他们可能会阻止改变或忽视最初的改变，从而使得应用不太可能发生。就好像你从教室里带回了一颗种子，如果没有适宜的土壤、阳光和水分，它什么也长不出来。

在一个学习型的组织里，培训项目结束之后的分享环节是强制性的后续工作。不只是受训者有交流的渴望，他们的经理也有。领导鼓励和支持行为的改变。学习之后改进了绩效的受训者应该得到奖励。

第4层次：结果

评估结果是相当困难的。公司想要找到证据证明培训项目确实有助于改进产品质量、提高绩效水平、为客户提供更好的服务等。这些最终都对利润有好处。然而，在大多数情况下，首先利益的获得需要时间，其次要将培训的作用与其他管理工具的作用区分开来是不容易的。

以销售技能培训为例。在6个月的培训之后，A部门的销售收入增长了20%。那么，我们就可以说这20%是培训的结果吗？市场部可能会说，这一部分是因为他们对某些产品实施了非常成功的市场推广，因此这些产品在销售订单中占了很多的比重。生产部可能会说，生产流程的重新调整减少了人力成本，以使得产品价格跟竞争对手相比下降了几个百分点，因此销售人员才能卖出更多。销售人员也可能会争辩说，他们在培训项目开始之前就已经跟客户联系了很久，他们获得订单是自然而然的事情，是他们的辛勤耕耘恰好在此时有了收获。

对于这个问题，有下列建议。

- 只要管理层和受训者都确认培训项目有帮助，那就没有必要多此一举地要求参与学习的职员获得一个非常确切的结果。
- 如果获得结果的成本预计会比我们从评估中获得的好处高出很多，那么就不用管它了。
- 在培训项目开始之前，与经理们一起确定哪些是我们想要从中获得的可以衡量的结果。它可以是一个特定的指数，比如：在打电话技能培训之后的3个月内推销电话的成功率，或者客户服务培训之后半年内的客户满意度调查的得分。

Appendix 2　Reference Translation for Texts

总结

在学习方面，评估和推动同等重要。评估培训效果有很多好方法。根据你自己的情况，选择一种，并且加以调整，使之适应你的组织。首先问一下自己的目的是什么。然后对数据收集过程多加谨慎。根据已经建立的可接受的标准，（对数据）进行高质量的分析。最后，通过评估改进你的培训项目。

第 5 部分　个人发展

第 12 单元　个人职业发展的三个步骤

基于从 1999 年至 2008 年间收集的数据，翰威特公司的"员工敬业度调查"显示，对于亚太地区的员工来说，职业发展是他们敬业的最高动力。看来，薪酬与福利并非总是那么重要。当然，我们不能否认，更多的职业发展机会事实上会在或近或远的将来带来更多的货币报酬。不过，这确实体现了公司和员工都在作长远考虑，而不是只顾眼前。

在很多公司计划加强对工作环境建设的投入，以增加职业发展机会的同时，员工也应该更多地考虑他们自己应该进行哪些投入，以在公司内部开创一条更好的职业道路。

有一个简单而有效的办法，可以让员工改善他们关于职业发展的思维过程。我们称之为：3 步骤法。

第一个步骤是了解自己。

首先考虑你生活中经历的事件当中，哪几件（2～3 件）事情是你认为特别值得的，无论它是否与你的工作有关。当时你做了什么？什么使得它们成为美妙的经历？

然后考虑 2～3 件令你有挫败感或者不愉快的事情。当时你做了什么？什么使得它们成为糟糕的经历？

询问几位非常了解你的人（可以是你的同事、上司、配偶或恋人、朋友、父母等），他们发现你最喜欢的是什么，最不喜欢的是什么，你最独特的优势和能力在哪方面。

有些人可能会发现，当他们升职的时候他们确实很高兴，而且他们认为自己应该得到更多次的升职。从事同一级别的同一种工作，让他们感到不自在，想要离开（公司）去寻找更好的机会。很多人把成功完成一个艰难的项目作为甜蜜的回忆，而做简单的工作会让他们觉得自己的才能被浪费了。另外，有些人把孩子的降生当成一生中最值得回忆的事情，而缺少时间照顾家人是他们最不能忍受的。

从多种不同来源收集到反馈信息之后，很多人会发现他们并不是自己想象的样子，尽管周围所有其他人都给出了一样的评论。因此，是时候用全新的视角重新审视自己了。一位认为自己彬彬有礼、圆滑老练的女士，可能会被别人看成是具有侵略性而且吹毛求疵的人，因为她总是坚持自己的观点，不听取别人的意见，在她的字典里没有"妥协"这个词。她喜欢激烈的争论，而且她经常赢得争论。

自我印象和他人看法之间的差异不是这里的关键所在，尽管它确实提醒了我们自己存在的认识盲区。这里的关键是，这位女士知道她的优势是决断力和说服力，以及她想要影响别人的激情。因此，很自然地，在利润驱动的组织里工作的她会表现得很好，因为她的结果导向性非常强。在完成任务的时候，她的确享受成功的那一刻。

我们可以设想，如果这位女士本质上不愿意成为争论的焦点，也不愿意公开地、彻底地表达观点，那么她的沟通不会如此有效，她的影响范围也会在某种程度上受到限制。因此，她在组织里的成功也多少会受到限制。

相反的场景是，她有想要影响别人的激情，但是很遗憾地发现自己的影响能力不够强。那么，当然，她的影响范围是有限的。影响能力当然可以通过培训和实践得以加强。在以前的案例里，激情和态度一般被认为无法通过培训得到改善。

如果这位女士在某个重视和谐与等级，而不是建设性反馈的环境里工作，那么，即使她拥有完美匹配的激情和能力，她也无法取得成功。

到此，我们可以得出这样的结论：如果一个人拥有组织需要的激情和能力，她或他最有可能表现优异，并获得良好的职业发展道路。有人可能会说，业务总是在改变，因此组织的需要也在改变，那么这个人的激情和能力可能会不符合需要。这话没错，假如我们不考虑个人的发展也在同时进行的话。能力可以通过培训得以加强，激情可以被激发出来。因此，我们仍然可以期望在个人和组织之间保持动态匹配。

为了简化，有研究将多种多样的最佳职业取向参考分成了5大类。

有些人希望获得职业进步，他们有影响他人的激情，有冲劲和远见。升职是对他们的最好回报。很多成功的业务经理就是这种类型。

有些人看重忠诚，为获得长期服务奖而感到荣耀。他们把安稳视为最佳职业选择。因此，公共服务、军队或其他变化和风险较小的稳定工作是他们最喜欢的。

相反，有些人喜欢冒险、刺激和挑战。他们必须和从事尖端工作的人待在一个圈子里。他们渴望挖掘自己的特性，以使他们的贡献最大化。他们总是积极主动地推销他们的新想法去改变生活方式和工作方式。在这个群体里，有很多高科技人才。

越来越多的年轻人在老一辈人的眼里显得难以理解。他们从没想过要拥有一份终生工作，而这正是他们父辈的习惯做法。他们敢于摒弃所有的规则和约束。"这是我的生活"（这种想法）使得这样的人想要百分之百地拥有对自己工作的控制权。如果他被授权可以用自己的方式完成任务的话，他可能成为一颗璀璨的明星。他在解决问题方面富有创造性。很多艺术家、商界传奇人物就是那些为自由而战的人。

Appendix 2　Reference Translation for Texts

　　5 种类型中的最后一种是平衡型。这类人寻求工作、关系和自我发展之间的平衡。他们喜欢弹性工作时间，以使得他们能够照顾孩子，同时也把工作做好。他们通常善于计划和组织。他们不只是初级职员。他们中的大多数是不同领域的领导，因为他们具备组织和领导人们取得成功的才能。

　　通过回答问卷，然后参照得分的解释，员工可以很容易地发现他们自己所属的类型。结合这个类型的简介，并回顾开始时的 3 个问题，他们可以了解在职业发展道路的某个特定时刻，什么样的工作对他们来说是好工作，什么样的工作应该避免。

　　第二个步骤是如何发现组织的需要。

　　如果员工的重点只是升职，那么岗位说明或者空缺职位的招聘广告就清晰地说明了组织的需要。通常，岗位说明包括几个部分：职位的职责、学历或者工作经验、个人特质（这与我们前面提到的能力和激情类似）。以银行的人力资源顾问职位为例。

- 良好的沟通和人际关系技能，能够与从高层管理者到初级职员的所有级别人员进行互动。
- 做事主动，精力充沛，充满自信。
- 重视结果，以服务为导向。

　　如果申请者没有上述特质，她就不太可能以这个职位作为她最后的职业选择。相反，她会为与不同类型的人频繁进行口头交流而感到烦恼。她渴望有一个安静的角落可以休息一会。她不喜欢被紧张的工作日程推着走，这样的日程安排在她看来是荒唐的。

　　组织没有空缺职位的时候，员工可以通过下列方法了解组织需要：

- 理解公司的愿景、价值观和战略；
- 观察组织内部那些成功同事的行为和态度；
- 跟那些具有职业抱负的高层次的人进行交谈；
- 研究进入人才培养项目的标准。

　　在员工对自己的特点有了充分的理解，并知道组织需要什么样的人才的时候，他们就可以开始实现最佳职业选择的第 3 个步骤了。

　　这个步骤是实际行动，以弥合自身目前的能力和组织需要的能力之间的差距。组织的需要是不由个人来控制的，观察组织需要的时候要保持正确的心态：大多数组织在大多数时候的需要都是动态变化的。个人的激情有时候是天生的。随着年龄的增长和生活经验的丰富，一个人可以开发更多的兴趣。但是，这是很困难的，而且耗费时间。唯一可以通过时间和努力去改变的，就是通过培训可以获得的能力。

　　大多数培训课程的目标都是提高某种特定的能力。除了培训课程，员工还能够通过在工作时承担特殊任务，或者直接从事不同的工作，来培养必需的技能。向上司和同事学习，也是非常常用且有效的提升能力的学习方法。不管用何种方法，这个步骤就是关于行动、执行和实现的。把想法转化成行动，才能最终实现最佳的职业梦想。

很多人可能会发现，有时候他们不理解为什么其他人被选中升职了。公司通常在寻找那些能够为利润作出贡献的人。今天的胜利者是那些重视培养自己的能力，以使得自己在公司里脱颖而出的人。这对那些从事管理和监督工作的人来说是事实，对那些从事非管理工作的人来说，更是事实。

第13单元 幸运的乔治———一个典型的人才培养项目

一年前乔治收到人力资源部的邮件，通知他被选入当年的人才培养计划，他非常兴奋。

那时，他作为应届毕业生，才刚进入公司不到一年。这是一家总部在欧洲的著名跨国公司的分公司。"事实上，毕业之后我对应该选择什么作为我的职业，几乎没有想法。"乔治回忆起令人沮丧的求职之路："我去了人才市场，看见那么多年轻人挤在几张招聘台前面。我努力尝试了，而且很幸运地被选上了。"

在公司工作了将近一年之后，他从他的经理和内部公告牌得知公司将要开展人才培养计划，所有符合条件的职员——指那些业绩、资历和其他相关方面符合标准的人——都被鼓励申请参加，只要他们对自己的能力和兴趣都有自信。

乔治提交了申请，首先被安排参加了小组面试。几位高层经理向他提了一些非常具有挑战性的问题。他还记得其中的几个问题。"这些问题让人印象深刻。我没有认识到在做出重要决定之前应该那样进行思考。"他被要求评价自己的表现，并从自己和上司的角度考虑继续进步的方法。"我很少想到继续进步，因为我的业绩已经相当好了。我也从没想过我可能需要来自经理的支持，特别是站在他的立场上考虑。"

评估中心的经历也让乔治印象非常深刻。他和其他一些申请者在一间大会议室里参加了评估。他们拿到了一个文件夹，里面有几页纸，上面的信息是关于某个项目的各种复杂信息。他们被要求在10分钟之后逐一发言，提出自己的建议。最后，所有人要达成一致，形成一份最终的项目计划书，并向观察者（主要是高层经理）进行解释。"我有一点紧张，我想其他的参加者也跟我有同感。当然，最终我们都克服了紧张并成功地给出了我们的建议。观察者就我们的计划书向我们每个人提出挑战性的问题。那种方式能够使我们当场就学到东西，这非常有好处。"乔治回忆说。

后来他了解到，除了面试和评估中心，对每一位申请者还会采用360度反馈法搜集信息。

所有这些程序结束之后，就该公布入选名单了。乔治几个星期之后知道了结果，他想，即使他没有被选上，这对他也是非常有意义的挑战和记忆，因为他经历的选拔过程让他"开始想得更多并且做得更多"，为实现自己的抱负而努力。

谈到被选为"人才"的原因，乔治借用了绩效潜力矩阵来说明。他非常自豪自己

Appendix 2   Reference Translation for Texts

业绩优秀，同时被评估为在承担更高级别职位方面具有较高的潜力。

除了成就感与自豪感，乔治也感觉到了压力。作为一个主管，他的日常工作非常忙碌。同时，他必须付出额外的时间和精力来参与一些规定的活动，比如培训课程、项目，以及一年之内的轮岗工作。幸运的是，在他的经理和人力资源部门充分讨论之后，（公司）为他安排了一个量身定制的培养计划。在这个计划里，所有活动的准确时间表和资源都清楚地列了出来，并且会定期评议并调整。

培训课程内容从时间管理、约哈瑞之窗到高效能人士的 7 个习惯，体现了领导经常会面临的主要挑战，介绍了一些基本的管理和领导技能来应对这些问题。"根据参加者的不同需要，有些课程是必修的，有些是选修的。"乔治解释说，"我甚至选择了 PowerPoint 课程，因为我的工作需要我经常进行有效的演示。"

乔治的工作项目是一个集体项目，和来自不同部门的其他 5 位同事一起进行。他们工作了 2 个月，每周定期开会，寻求高层的支持。最终，他们提交了一份提案，用来改进他们的操作系统，使效率提高 15%。在乔治看来，他从这个项目所获得的不只是认同，还有通过共同合作而与其他部门建立起的良好关系。

"我非常幸运。我也参加了轮岗计划。你知道有时候在我们之间找到合适的岗位进行轮换不是那么容易的。因此，机会有限的时候，只有某些人能够被选择进行轮岗。我被选上了，因为我的工作任务完成得不错。"乔治说。之后他在另一部门工作了 6 个月。最后，在他完成了人才培养计划要求的所有活动之后，他被提升到了那个部门一个空缺的经理职位上。

不是所有参加者都像乔治这么幸运，能够在完成人才培养计划之后尽快被提升，而且其培养计划能够在刚开始的时候就经过人力资源部门的充分沟通。

"这确实是运气，但也不全是运气。"对那些还没有完成人才培养计划的人，乔治有一些建议，"你必须充分利用公司提供的平台。有时候，人们有一点害羞，或者有一点懒惰，浪费了可以理解更多、联系更多的机会。你不应该被推着走，而是应该主导你自己的行动，直到实现你希望的目标。而且，没有耕耘，就没有收获。我一直相信这句老话。"

第 14 单元   领导力培养方法

领导力的培养对于组织的成功来说，无疑是相当关键的，尤其是对于将来的商业目标。在许多公司，有很多流行的领导力培养方法。

高层管理训练与指导是一种被广泛采用的方法：在一对一的基础上，为每一位具有高潜力的个人配备一位高层管理者作为"教练"。这种方法的重点是在短期内加强个人的能力或技能培养（一般是通过训练），或者加强长期职业指导及发展（一般是通过指导）。这种训练与指导能够帮助接受者通过调查形势、需要、动机和技能等，自己确定解决办法和行动方案。

不只是接受者个人能够从这种互动中获益，教练或导师也能从这个一对一的过程中学到东西。当然，非常微妙的是，对于不同组合，这种方法的效力大不相同。有一些化学反应，或者友好关系会影响到彼此间的信任，从而影响到沟通的效率，并最终影响到这种方法的效果。

大多数组织强调，职业发展的主导权在于个人自己。这一点在被称为"学习资源指导"的方法中得到了很好的证实。这一方法的建立基础是，培养存在不足的能力。针对每一项目标能力，都列出了一系列培养活动以支持所需的改进。这些活动可能是研讨会、培训、工作场所活动、行动学习项目，以及参考书籍和报刊。这实际上扩充了以能力为基础的培训计划，加入了以能力为基础的培养计划。

这种方法在组织里执行起来较为简便，而且员工很容易将其作为学习资源参考。它可以用来培养核心能力、领导力和技术能力，这些都与组织战略高度相关。关键因素是个人动机，个人可以充分利用该方法，将其作为通向更高成就的阶梯，也可能只是将其放在一边，仅仅作为一种信息来源而已。

行动学习法在近些年来非常热门。一个行动学习项目就是组织内部开展的一项研究，具有战略价值、业务价值及学习价值。通常由发起者、领导、项目经理和团队成员，就一个仔细选择的主题进行行动学习。这些人通常在很短的时间内全职投入这个项目（这样最有效率），或者在业余时间兼顾。通常，每个项目都有促进者——他们的作用是确保个人和团队在项目过程中确实进行了学习。项目过程包括研究、分析、建议及行动计划，并且可以扩展到执行阶段。

行动学习项目对组织成功具有直接影响。如果实施得当，它就像是一个"实时的"人才发展中心。它会加强（参与者的）一系列领导技能，包括分析和判断，以及影响。参与者还有机会提高自己在组织内的声望和形象。高层的发起对于行动学习项目的成功至关重要。他们可以提供机会让项目团队自己做出"进行下去"或"不进行下去"的决定，并说明其理由。如果有几个项目马上要开始进行，则需要成立一个项目办公室来协调各个项目组并交流学习心得。

有时，发展中心（方法）会与评估中心（方法）相结合，设计一系列的工作模拟练习让个人参与其中，同时由经过专业培训的评估者进行观察并给出反馈。但是，发展中心的重点是发展，是潜力和长期的组织需要，而不是选拔、目前的能力和组织的即时需要。因此，发展中心不会设定任何合格与否的标准，评估者更像是促进者，而不是评判者。

发展中心方法可以产生有效且可靠的成功预测指标，这对于（人才）选拔和培养都有利。现实的练习是根据组织的特定环境而设计的，反映了将来可能面临的挑战。在

Appendix 2   Reference Translation for Texts

高价值职位（比如领导职位或关键管理岗位）的人才培养方面，这种方法尤其有效。这种工具需要成为整体发展计划的一部分，并且有后续工作进行配合。高层的发起、时间及资源都是非常必要的。

美世公司的领导实践研究显示，在中国，外派、延伸任务，以及领导力训练是最常采用的方式；以在工作中学习为重点，结合学习经历，是最有效的培养现任及将来领导的方法。地区差别显示，北美企业（64%）比西欧和亚太企业（56%）更喜欢确定下一代领导人，并把他们作为培养目标。

Adobe 是一家世界领先的软件公司。它开始领导培养计划的时候，确定公司的成功领导者应该能够彰显公司的价值观，影响和建立关系，领导公司实现特殊的效果，建立强有力的全球团队，并培养其他人。

除了这些标准，领导者还要首先通过 360 度反馈法被评估，被指定一名教练来帮助其确认自己所具有的、有利于目前业绩和将来发展的优势。

然后就是网络学习课程，使参加者进一步理解公司各项职能的最佳实施情况、在行业中的地位等基础性的常识。

下一步是高强度的脱产培训课程。整整 5 天的时间，来自加利福尼亚州立大学伯克利分校哈斯商学院的教授们讲授关于战略、金融、市场、创新领导全球团队等方面的课程。然后公司的执行官们会主持讨论会，讨论如何将他们所学到的知识运用到他们在公司的工作中去。在课程最后，按照之前确定的与增长和可持续发展有关的标准，选出最成功的团队。另外，在培训课程过程中，还会给出关于领导形象的反馈。

脱产学习结束后，参加者们开始着手解决个人面临的业务挑战，并有机会参与其他人的业务挑战项目组。这一个人业务挑战项目持续 3 个月，帮助领导者延伸其能力，为公司作出更多贡献。一位高层发起者会与他们会面，以跟踪项目进展。这个业务挑战项目目由高层管理者决定，与公司的某个战略项目有关。不超过 10 个参加者组成一个小组一起工作 2 个月，然后提出他们的建议，并等待高层管理者的进一步指令。

根据 Adobe 公司主管人力资源的副总裁唐纳·莫里斯的说法，公司对培养计划的效果非常满意。"去年（2009），我们的副总裁和总经理职位，有 86% 都是由内部候选人担任的，这个比例在 2007 年是 56%。其中，92% 的内部候选人参加过 ALE 计划。"除了向上的流动，留住人才和绩效也被用来衡量这个计划的有效性。

斯图尔特·D·弗里德曼，福特汽车公司领导力发展中心的主任，在他的文章"领导力 DNA"中，阐述了其他可以应用的类似方法，比如行动学习法、网络学习、高层管理者的介入，这些方法都会对业务产生影响。

他们开发了 5 种战略计划和 4 种核心计划。核心计划在甄别、选拔和培养公司下一代领导者方面意义重大。战略计划是改变垂直或水平边界的行动方案。他们所有的项目都具有行动学习的特征。

网络学习工具被广泛应用。通过这种方式，参加者投入时间和精力，尝试对工作、家庭和社会进行新的平衡与协调，从而采用一种全面的领导力培养方式。

这种全面的领导力与大多数领导力培养方法类似，以实现更优的效果为目标，但又与其他很多方法不同，因为它强调你的工作生活、家庭生活，以及你的社会生活是一个整体。因此，公司要求领导者追求财务成功、环境保护和社会责任三重的利益。这是令人惊叹的，也是奇妙的。

第 15 单元　确定正确的领导力

领导力的培养是大多数 CEO 个人日程里最为重要的问题之一。他们注意到，缺乏合适的领导人才，是组织增长和商业战略执行所面临的一个重大风险。另外，董事会也越来越关注管理者对继任问题的责任，会询问一些关于可持续商业发展的难点问题。

根据 2006 年的全球领导力规则研究，尽管 75% 的全球公司都说商业挑战揭示了公司领导力补给线的不足，72% 的公司计划采取行动弥合差距，然而只有大约一半已经对此进行了充分的投入。

数据背后的原因有很多。最普遍的担忧是，领导力能够被培养吗？总是有人说：领导是天生的，而不是被培养出来的。这未必是事实，但至少看起来，越是高级别的职位，领导力越是难以培养。因此，人们更加注重选择合适的领导。

谁是我们寻找的合适的领导？

合益集团 2007 年为一家著名的船务公司开发了一套评估中心方法。它们的目标是衡量能力，包括客户关系、人际关系能力、人力资源发展、团队合作、创造性解决问题和结果驱动这些方面的能力。

另一家领先的人力资源顾问公司——美世公司，认为领导可以通过"头脑、心灵和精神"来确定。"头脑"是指能够提供目的、方向和战略。"心灵"是指能够理解他人，和他人合作，并培养他人。"精神"是指遵从清晰的价值观，做正确的事情。

事实上，每个组织都有其特定的领导形象，即领导为了在组织内取得成功所必须具有的能力、行为、态度和价值观。有些组织也称之为领导能力，或者领导力 DNA 等。不管被称为什么，它都必须是根据组织的商业战略所确定的一系列清晰的标准，为使组织内部人员在讨论领导为实现商业成功而需要做什么的时候具有共同语言，它构成了后续的领导力培养活动的基础。因此，一致的集体领导行为对组织执行战略并实现目标至关重要。

确立了基础之后，就该选择合适的工具和方法来评估领导能力了。

世界上有很多这种方法，简单的有诸如字迹分析一样的小测试，复杂的有像结构性评估中心这样的方法。随着商业世界的发展，还将出现更多的方法。

Appendix 2   Reference Translation for Texts

　　在任何类型的选拔中，面试都是很常用的方法。关于领导力的确定，行为事件面试在领导力评估实践中很流行。这种面试是由经过专门训练的面试官进行的有目的的面试，通过提出行为基础问题，以加深理解一个人与将来可能的工作要求有关的行为。因而，面试官会努力地去了解，面试者在过去是否已经展示出了足够多的、与所要求的领导形象有关的能力。

　　因为比面试更加客观，心理测验也被广泛地应用，作为一个有说服力的补充。很多测验要求被试者在一定时间内回答一些关于数字、算术、逻辑推理和语言推理的问题，以了解这个人能够多快多好地解决问题。瑞文推理测验就是其中之一。因为认识到了批判性思维的重要性，华格二氏批判性思考评估测验也在很多组织里被采用。

　　除了智力测验，性格分类在领导力评估中也很热门。普遍认为，诸如自我印象、态度、价值观、秉性和动机等决定了人的行为，而且它们相当稳定。因此，人们热衷于寻找一位典型的成功领导应该具有的性格特质。卡特尔16项人格因素测验、明尼苏达多项人格测验、职业性格问卷都是有名的性格评估工具。

　　在大多数情况下，由于当前商业的复杂性，以及合适领导形象的不断变化，仅靠测验或评估，不足以展示一位候选人相对于预先确定的标准所具有的整体特质。评估中心方法，通过一系列个人参与的工作模拟练习，同时由经过专业训练的评估者进行观察，能够确定大多数有效且可靠的未来成功的预测指标。在评估中心方法过程中，个人可能会经历类似专家面试、多来源反馈、认知或性格测试、案例研究，以及与工作有关的模拟练习。评估中心方法通常被认为是客观的，因为其评估方法是由外部评估者设计的，是现实且具有挑战性的，因为它反映了实际工作情况。而且，有效且客观的行为基础反馈不仅可以用于领导力评估，也可以用于未来的发展。

　　与评估中心相比，工作场所评估是由经过培训的评估者在真实的工作场所，对个人的工作能力、所展示的技术知识和技能，以及工作绩效进行观察。通常，会培训一组人在一定时间内、在一个人进行工作活动时对其进行观察。例如，可能是在2周内，进行2次观察，每次1～2个小时。

　　那么，我们应该在什么时候选择什么评估工具呢？

　　这实际上取决于你想要评估什么，你能够接受的有效水平是什么，你能够付出的时间或精力有多少。还有，要了解每种评估方法的利与弊。

　　例如，技术熟练程度一般不能通过评估中心方法来确定，但可以由一个专家小组来评判。工作场所评估既可以评估技术能力，也可以评估核心能力，但是很难区分领导能力。

　　行为事件面试法可以为所有这3种能力（核心能力、领导能力和技术能力）寻找证据。但是，它不太客观，因为其结果很大程度上取决于面试官的个人能力。

　　工作场所评估和评估中心比其他评估工具客观得多，但它们同时也是最难以进行的。对评估过程的设计、对评估者的培训，以及个人的参与，都是很耗费时间的。外部顾问的牵制也是企业不太愿意采用这种方法的一个原因。

总的来说，行为事件面试对目标岗位人选的选拔比较有用。它在揭示关键行为的内在动因方面非常有效。其客观程度取决于经过培训的面试官的能力。面试官通常能够获得面试者在工作中实际行为的范例。另一方面，面试只能揭示面试者恰巧，或者选择呈现的信息。可能会有一些有经验的，或者机智的面试者，可以把自己刻意表现得像是一个完美的候选人。而且，面试很难揭示有关动机、秉性或自我印象的信息。

前面提到过，因为其效度，有关智力和性格的心理测验在很多组织很受欢迎。它们相对容易进行，因为大多数测验都是采用纸和笔的形式。智力和认知测验是有效的工具，尤其对于评估管理职位的候选人来说，因为它们能够洞察批判性思维、数字推理、阅读理解、分析推理、空间关系，以及有效和准确地处理信息的能力。性格测验是洞察性格、潜在性格偏差和共同行为的有效工具。但是，它们无法对工作知识或经验进行更深入的洞察。另外，如果人们对适合某个职位的性格特质还心存担忧，那么只使用这种测验作为筛选工具是危险的。

关于评估中心，很多人认为它是有效且可靠的工具，能够提供有效且客观的行为基础反馈信息，暴露潜在的性格偏差，反映实际工作情况。然而，进行评估中心方法的前提条件是已经有了目标职位的能力框架。除了耗费时间和金钱之外，其本身的复杂性也让参与者觉得紧张。因此，尽管是模拟的情况，但有些参加者的行为表现可能也跟真实工作中不一样。

工作场所评估的优点和缺点跟评估中心方法类似。但是，如果没有评估中心作为一个执行所有评估步骤的实验室，企业在真实的工作场所准备评估设施并维持一段较长的时间，就更为困难了。

第6部分　组织发展

第16单元　组织发展基础知识

如今，很多大型跨国公司都在人力资源部门之内或之外建立了组织发展职能，就像若干年前建立培训职能一样。越来越多的学习型职业人士都转向组织发展，以进一步开发他们自己的兴趣和职业发展。

什么是组织发展？托马斯·卡明斯在他的著作《组织发展与变革》中写道：组织发展是在整个系统范围内，将行为科学知识应用到发展计划，增强组织战略、结构和程序，以提高组织的效率。琳达·霍尔比契将其定义为："人们和组织如何发挥职能，以及如何使他们在清晰的价值基础上更好地发挥职能。组织发展无疑是人本主义的，具有

Appendix 2　Reference Translation for Texts

强烈的价值驱动力。"当然，我们可以从各种书籍和文章中找到更多的定义。总的来说，这些定义都倾向于认为组织发展具有下列6个方面。
- 它通常是有计划的努力。
- 它由组织范围内的多种活动组成。
- 它应该自上而下地来执行，也就是说，得到高层的支持。
- 它的目标是增进组织的效率和健康。
- 其方法通过组织过程中的干预得以实施。
- 这种改变建立在行为科学知识的基础上。

尽管在很多组织里，组织发展职能有时会与培训职能整合在一起，培训课程往往会与组织发展活动结合在一起，但组织发展与培训明显是不同的。培训是短期努力，而组织发展是长期的。培训的目的是让个人掌握更好地进行工作所需的知识、技能和态度，而组织发展旨在让群体掌握他们之间更有效地进行互动所需的知识、技能和态度。培训方案通常是组织发展架构的一个部分，或者我们可以说培训是组织发展的干预活动之一。除了培训，加强绩效管理、重新设计业务流程、训练、委派任务、指导、小组促进会议、团队建设等，也是典型的组织发展方法。

当我们考虑下列问题时，组织发展的需要就出现了。
- 什么合适的技能能够推动公司获得更高的利润水平？
- 当公司规模扩张一倍的时候，我们如何确定团队经理们的标准？
- 在合并之后，我们应该如何把两种企业文化整合起来？
- 我们如何简化组织结构，以更快地对客户作出反应？
- 我们应该如何在所有职员之中推广公司的价值观，让他们知道公司需要的行为和态度是什么？

在组织发展顾问（无论是来自内部还是外部）开始进行某项组织发展工作时，她需要遵从几个步骤。

首先，她应该跟项目发起人和利益相关方会面，了解清楚谁需要什么类型的改变。然后要签订合同，合同条款要清楚地说明项目目标，并明确界定顾问和客户各自的作用。结构性的客户调查问卷有助于获取项目合同所需的所有信息。问卷上的问题包括：组织的总体运营环境、公司价值观和战略、公司各层级的业绩图表、对经理和员工的能力要求及目前存在的能力差距、主要制度及程序（比如生产管理制度、信息平台、薪酬与奖励方案等）。

然后，顾问要确定需要什么数据、多少数据，以及通过什么样的程序去搜集数据。另外，她还要开发一套合适的组合方法，以确保数据搜集阶段的效率、目标和效力。匿名调查问卷和报告一般是搜集数据的好方法，尤其当我们必须在时间紧迫的情况下搜集足够的数据，而且被调查者希望信息不被泄露的时候。顾问必须很下工夫地设计问卷，确保问题的回答更加准确以用于日后的分析,并使被调查者有兴趣完成所有的问题。像"尖顶"表这样的一个简单表格,就可以提供一个结构框架,用来搜集那些影响组织优势和弱势的内、外部信息。

如果顾问想要充分了解某人的想法或经历,或者对他们的问卷回答了解更多,可以考虑进行面谈。面谈能够提供更多、更深入的信息,但是更加耗费时间,顾问也更难以进行数据的分析和比较。

顾问能够通过查阅文件和单据获得信息,就像财务专业人士进行财务审计一样。这种方法使得顾问可以了解到一些综合性的历史记录,而并不需要打断资源提供者的日常工作。这对于想在客户最忙碌的时候了解到优质信息的顾问很有帮助。当然,文件信息有时候太多了,很难充分地检索,现实中会出现不完整信息,这就意味着还是需要打断(客户工作),进行澄清。

焦点小组讨论也是就某些问题获取深度信息和共同理解的常用方法。这些问题可以是诸如某个重要职位的能力要求、对组织变革的反应、改进团队绩效的方法这样的问题。在讨论中,一位经验丰富的促进者是非常必要的,他或她将确保讨论继续下去,或者在合适的时候停止讨论,并让人们都毫无顾忌地自由表达或激烈争论。这样可以保证时间被充分利用,并能够得到有意义的反馈。这种方法面临的另一个挑战是,它通常耗费时间,而且需要对反馈信息进行睿智的分析。

除了上述方法,还有案例研究、观察等,都可以帮助顾问搜集足够的信息,然后进行组织发展项目的第二个步骤,对组织进行评估。

下一个步骤是根据项目范围(规模、复杂性、改变的类型、在组织内的层次等)、时间安排、预算和资源确定干预方法。不同的顾问可能会对最合适的干预措施有不同的看法。一个可能的原因就是看待组织的视角。顾问从不同的视角看到的是组织的不同重点,因而作出不同的判断。这种影响通常被低估。作为一个经验丰富的顾问,应该始终清楚这种个人偏好,并且确保她也了解别人的视角。

在每一个层次都有可供选择的一些干预方法。组织评估、继任规划、组织重构、重新设计工作流程,是典型的组织层面的干预。团队建设、自我领导工作的团队、改进部门运营及绩效、人际沟通等,是用于管理层面或团队层面的方法。通过培训和教育加强自我认知和个人发展,通过训练以实现更好的业绩,是常见的用于个人的干预方法。这些干预方法中,有些是传统工具,而有些相对比较新颖。再次强调,不同的顾问有不同的选择。

在干预方法的执行阶段(第四步),顾问应该弄清楚各个利益相关方受关联的程度。大多数情况下,一方面应该采用分享最佳经验和加强训练(的方法)激励参与者;另一方面,还应该让他们掌握必要的技能和知识,以适应变化过程。

组织发展项目流程的最后一步是评估一项组织发展干预措施。这通常包括:证实事情是如何按照项目计划发展的，如何适应管理层对程序和实现目标的观点，如何提供数据或证实结果以用来作为基准，或用于比较，或用于公共关系、改进绩效等。

这个 5 步骤的方法并不能保证所有的组织发展项目都得到成功的实施。组织干预并非魔术。

如果只有顾问认为有必要进行组织变革，而其他利益相关方都愿意保持现状，那么，这样的项目无法获得满意的结果。这很容易理解，因为人们在一开始的时候，内心深处对结果就有不同的想法。

由于大多数组织干预都是长期的，在那些想要寻求快速调整的经理们看来，这样的过程太耗费时间和金钱。因此，顾问们也不太容易得到管理层的持久支持。这可能导致组织发展项目后来被搁置。

有时候，尽管经理们表达了他们想从组织发展项目中得到反馈的渴望，但是他们却拒绝听取所提供的数据。相反，他们认为，这些出乎意料的数据显示了顾问们的工作是多么的糟糕！这种不信任不可能带来任何有意义的结果。

第 17 单元　员工敬业度

在当代世界，员工敬业度吸引了经理和企业股东越来越多的注意力。它与员工满意度、组织绩效及利润结果直接相关。

关于员工敬业度的研究，最早的目标是确认员工是否对他们的工作及工作环境感到满意。后来，研究者发现，对于工作满意的员工会向他们的朋友和客户宣传公司；如果公司里有空缺职位，他们会愿意介绍其他人到公司工作。

但是，他们并不一定从未想过另找一份更好的工作。因此，研究者们开始研究如何使忠诚的员工真正地被公司吸引，从而使公司减少人才流失的风险。

今天，员工忠诚度逐渐被员工敬业度这个概念所替代。一个忠诚的员工为他在公司的工作而感到高兴，但是一个敬业的员工会多付出一些，为公司作出与众不同的重要贡献。

为了简化，埃森哲公司将其总结为："说，留，做"。说公司的好话，满意地留下来，为优秀业绩而努力地做工作。

在现在这个竞争的动态商业世界里，员工敬业度的情况如何呢？ASTD 的报告显示员工敬业度是当今最关键的工作问题之一，它们的调查数据来源于大约 800 名高层次的人力资源及培训专业人士。但是，只有三分之一的被调查员工具有高度敬业的特点。大多数人都只是中等程度敬业，这个比率是 40%；而四分之一的人只是最低限度敬业，或者不敬业。

盖洛普咨询公司的 Q12 研究报告显示了类似的数据，在一般公司，大约 30% 的员工是敬业的。它还估计，不敬业的员工每年给美国经济造成的损失大约是 3 500 亿美元；在英国和日本，分别是 648 亿美元和 2 320 亿美元。

除了上面提到的由专业顾问公司提供的报告，如果报告的质量能够得到的保证，而且公司很清楚其具体的重点是什么，那么组织也可以采用由内部培训职员设计的简单问卷。

客户对服务水平的满意度通常也是员工敬业度的一个良好指标。没有多少热情或士气去改进甚至维持业绩标准的员工，不太可能为客户提供满意的服务，从而会对企业利润带来负面影响。这些信息也可以通过客户满意度调查来获得。

人员流失率及从离职面谈获得的反馈，也是反映员工敬业度水平的指标。对流失率和离职面谈反馈信息的分析通常显示，对于不同年龄、资历、职位和业绩的人，其激励因素是不同的。这提醒了人力资源职员和直接上级，（不同员工的）敬业驱动因素是不同的，不存在普遍适用的方法可以提高所有员工的敬业度水平。

翰威特咨询公司提出的敬业度模型被许多公司广泛接受，它将敬业驱动因素分成了下列 6 个类别。

- 人的因素，包括高层领导、上司、同事和客户。
- 竞争性的报酬，包括薪酬与福利，以及其他奖励。
- 公司实际情况，指公司政策、公司声誉、多样性和包容性、绩效评估等。
- 生活质量，指工作与生活的平衡、实际工作、执行情况、安全等。
- 工作本身，包括工作活动、程序、资源和内部激励。
- 机会，主要指职业发展、在组织内学习。

正如之前提到的，敬业是一个非常个人化的问题，它对不同的人有不同的含义。这使得加强经理和员工之间的有效沟通很自然地成为很多组织提高员工敬业水平的最重要的方法。翰威特咨询公司的敬业度模型可以为经理和员工提供一个很好的谈话框架，使得他们符合逻辑地讨论什么是最重要的驱动因素，什么是最不重要的，个人对各个方面的满意度如何，各方可以作出哪些努力以提高满意度，从而提高员工整体的敬业度。

当团队成员只是说他们想要更高工资的时候，一些经理就不知道该如何继续谈话了。

这里的建议是，经理就告诉员工，这个已经超出了他的控制范围。让员工知道，作为直接上级，他可以把这种想法向适当级别的管理者转达。同时，他还可以花些时间向员工解释公司的薪酬政策——让员工意识到目前的薪酬是公平的。

然后，告诉员工，除了工资，还有更多值得挖掘的东西，这些东西是员工期望的，也是经理可以控制并提供的。比如，给员工分配他喜欢的挑战性的工作，让喜欢冒险的人承担更多的责任，让愿意把自己的学习心得跟别人分享的人担任内部培训员，为需要接孩子的年轻母亲安排更加弹性的工作时间表，给那些能够独立且高质量地完成工作的

Appendix 2 Reference Translation for Texts

下属更多的自由,让两个想要互相学习的同事调换工作,给那些想要在组织里取得更大发展的人更多的训练时间,在团队取得良好业绩的时候进行庆祝……

绩效应该是经理和员工之间谈话的重要主题之一。事实上,绩效反馈本身就是提高员工敬业度的一个方法。放到一个更大的背景之下去考虑,绩效谈话是绩效管理流程的一个常规环节。重视推动绩效的企业文化能够极大地提高绩效管理的效率,从而提高员工的敬业度。不及时进行绩效反馈、绩效优劣不同的员工没有受到差别对待、没有个人发展计划、员工实现绩效目标的过程中感觉不到支持,这些都是使员工敬业度降低的、与绩效有关的因素。

很多员工感受不到薪资待遇上的差别对待,部分原因是因为在大多数公司里,个人的具体薪酬信息是保密的,真实的差别无法作为证据公之于众。同时,福利项目通常是大家一样的,或者有时是基于职位级别或在公司的服务年限,比如补充商业保险。如果奖金也不是根据绩效来发放,那么,当然没有几个人会认为公司是在按照绩效支付薪资,这实际上与公司希望在员工中提倡的(按绩效支付薪资的)观念是背道而驰的。

对于很多组织来说,另外一个可以改进的地方是对年轻经理和员工的培训方案。这里的年轻不仅仅指生理年龄,更多的是指缺乏足够的成熟度。

新升任的经理容易在压力和各个任务的最后期限之下乱了方寸,从而忽视团队成员的士气。当问题的迹象明显到被他们发现的时候,他们往往不得不投入巨大的精力去解决问题。因此,由专业培训人员及时组织培训、由经验丰富的经理(最好是他们的直接上级)对其加强指导,将是防止年轻经理偏离正轨太远的好方法。这些培训和指导应该包括从个人工作者向领导的角色转换、时间和资源的分配技能、给出和得到反馈的心态和能力、进行沟通与指导的重要性及必要提示……

员工也应该接受培训,以了解他们的责任。尽管经理们对员工的敬业度负有责任,但是这并不意味着员工没有责任采取任何行动以实现更高的敬业水平。员工也应该及时地公开表达他们的担忧与建议。经理们不会读心术,如果他们无法从下属那里获得有意义的反馈,不应该只是责怪他们。

员工还应该被鼓励去创造性地思考并解决绩效问题,或者积极主动地思考其他问题。对公司的主人翁精神有助于提高员工敬业度,反之亦然。

来自不同文化的员工有时对特定的问题有截然不同的看法。有些文化倾向于更加积极的态度,而有些则更加愤世嫉俗。想要改变员工的文化差异是不明智的,但是应该培训他们或影响他们建立逻辑思维过程和欣赏的态度。

这就是员工敬业度。它对企业的影响如此之深,没有任何一项任务能够脱离其影响。在一个坚持付出努力的学习型组织里,绩效驱动的文化、开放的沟通方式会使得越来越多的员工变得高度敬业,并且对其他人产生表率作用,使组织绩效提高到一个新的水平。

第 18 单元　继任规划

在各种报告中,继任规划总是高层管理者心里考虑或者担忧的五大问题之一。

建立合适的继任规划程序对公司的成功是至关重要的,因为该计划中确定的人选将最终为确保企业未来的可持续发展负责。

如果成功地完成了,继任规划将使得公司能够:
- 建立领导补给线或人才库,以确保领导力的持续性;
- 培养最适合公司优势的潜在继任者;
- 为各个职位确定最佳候选人;
- 根据公司战略清楚地确定公司要求,并使现任领导或新的领导候选人符合这些要求;
- 确认并传承那些可能会丢失的关键知识或信息;
- 确保组织目前的使命和愿景会被未来的领导者继续执行。

这个系统必须是前瞻性的,应该包括常规性继任(现任领导退休、有计划地升职)和偶然性继任(现任领导突发疾病、突然死亡或辞职)。

而且,继任规划不应与接替计划相混淆。接替计划是指关键职位出现意料之外的空缺时,临时安排人接替。继任规划更多的是培养继任候选人,而不是确认谁恰巧准备充分(足以成为候选人)。在组织内部培养人才,可以造就这样的领导者——他们通过自己既有的知识和经验,赢得了组织的信任,并且更容易被看做是有能力的领导。

有些公司在继任规划方面有非常系统性的方法,也有些公司认为正式的程序是没有必要的。无论公司采用何种方式,继任规划都应该比需要先行一步。如果做得正确,公司将拥有一批合格的骨干人员,他们更加敬业,也更加理解公司的核心使命、愿景和目标;他们随时准备承担更广泛的领导责任。

但是,我们在进行继任规划时,总会面临一些陷阱。

1. 缺乏管理层的支持

企业生产力研究机构的《继任规划重点报告》显示,在员工超过1万人的组织中,34%没有为将来的领导职位人选做好准备。该报告的结论还显示,继任规划将是执行官们未来面临的五大挑战之一。

在那些进行了继任规划的公司里,也还有一些公司只是停留在计划阶段,几乎没有后续行动。在经济危机中,由于培训预算大幅度减少,继任规划更多的时候只是某些报告里的名单列表。

有些公司有培养潜在继任者的具体计划。但是,经理们不准备对此进行深入的工作，因为手头的日常工作已经让他们不堪重负。是为将来作准备，还是先应付当前，这始终是个问题。

2. 无效的选拔

挑选那些你认为有能力在将来担任领导职务的人，当然是一项非常艰巨的任务。生活在这样一个快速变化的世界，我们有时候无法准确地预测：在不久的将来，领导者的标准是什么。也没有哪个选拔工具可以保证面试官、高层管理者及工具本身不出现偏差。

在他的著作《了解怎样去做》中，拉姆·查安谈到了"不能讨价还价的标准"，这可以为我们在制定选拔标准的时候提供一些提示。

3. 缺少灵活性

很多继任规划或人才培养计划最终都没有取得令人满意的结果。

有些失败是因为在培养活动结束之前，候选人就离开了组织。这项长期投资的人力资源投入产出比率非常低。

组织经常会发生改变。当今的商业世界，并购经常出现，但是所需要的能力确定标准却没有更新。开始的时候就没有朝着正确的目标前进，那么当然会带来错误的结果。

一个继任规划项目通常会包括很多培养活动。一些公司倾向于设计非常复杂的框架，以引导所有参与活动的人。而事实却是，参与者需要遵从适用所有人的统一原则，但必须有适合特定个人的个性化的培养计划。

References
参考文献

［1］ 张德. 人力资源开发与管理. 北京：清华大学出版社，2007.
［2］ 杨波. 如何成为金牌人力资源管理师. 武汉：武汉大学出版社，2009.
［3］ SCHULER R S. Strategic human resource management. Malder：Blackwell Publishing Ltd.，2007.
［4］ DOWLING P J. International human resource management. Hampshire：Cengage Learning Ltd.，2008.
［5］ DESSLER G. Human resource management. 北京：清华大学出版社，2008.